9/00

EVELYN WAUGH

Literary Lives
General Editor: Richard Dutton, Professor of English,
Lancaster University

This series offers stimulating accounts of the literary careers of the
most admired and influential English-language authors. Volumes
follow the outline of the writers' working lives, not
in the spirit of traditional biography, but aiming to trace
the professional, publishing and social contexts which
shaped their writing.

A list of the published titles in the series follows overleaf.

Published titles

Cedric C. Brown
JOHN MILTON

Peter Davison
GEORGE ORWELL

Richard Dutton
WILLIAM SHAKESPEARE

Jan Fergus
JANE AUSTEN

James Gibson
THOMAS HARDY

Kenneth Graham
HENRY JAMES

Paul Hammond
JOHN DRYDEN

W. David Kay
BEN JONSON

Mary Lago
E. M. FORSTER

Clinton Machann
MATTHEW ARNOLD

Alasdair D. F. Macrae
W. B. YEATS

Joseph McMinn
JONATHAN SWIFT

Kerry McSweeney
GEORGE ELIOT

John Mepham
VIRGINIA WOOLF

Michael O'Neill
PERCY BYSSHE SHELLEY

Leonée Ormond
ALFRED TENNYSON

Harold Pagliaro
HENRY FIELDING

George Parfitt
JOHN DONNE

Literary Lives
Series Standing Order ISBN 0–333–71486–5
(*outside North America only*)

You can receive future titles in this series as they are published by placing a standing order. Please contact your bookseller or, in case of difficulty, write to us at the address below with your name and address, the title of the series and the ISBN quoted above.

Customer Services Department, Macmillan Distribution Ltd
Houndmills, Basingstoke, Hampshire RG21 6XS, England

Evelyn Waugh

A Literary Life

David Wykes
Professor of English
Dartmouth College
Hanover, New Hampshire

First published in Great Britain 1999 by
MACMILLAN PRESS LTD
Houndmills, Basingstoke, Hampshire RG21 6XS and London
Companies and representatives throughout the world

A catalogue record for this book is available from the British Library.

ISBN 0–333–61137–3 hardcover
ISBN 0–333–61138–1 paperback

First published in the United States of America 1999 by
ST. MARTIN'S PRESS, INC.,
Scholarly and Reference Division,
175 Fifth Avenue, New York, N.Y. 10010

ISBN 0–312–22508–3

Library of Congress Cataloging-in-Publication Data
Wykes, David, 1941–
Evelyn Waugh : a literary life / David Wykes.
p. cm. — (Literary lives)
Includes bibliographical references and index.
ISBN 0–312–22508–3
1. Waugh, Evelyn, 1903–1966.   2. Authors, English—20th century
Biography.   I. Title.   II. Series: Literary lives (New York, N.Y.)
PR6045.A97Z89   1999
823'.912—dc21
[B]   99–22583
                                                              CIP

This book is printed on paper suitable for recycling and made from fully managed and sustained forest sources.

10   9   8   7   6   5   4   3   2
08   07   06   05   04   03   02   01   00

Printed and bound in Great Britain by
Antony Rowe Ltd, Chippenham, Wiltshire

for
V. L. C. W.
finally

Contents

Acknowledgements

Since 1966 Evelyn Waugh has been the subject of three full-dress biographies. This fact is owed in small part to the plenitude of documents available to biographers and in large part to the quality of his writing and the fascination of his personality. To these biographers – Christopher Sykes, Selina Hastings, and most of all Martin Stannard – this short life of Waugh is greatly indebted. They have provided the facts, anecdotes, many of the documents and some of the opinions I have drawn upon to shape my account of Waugh's literary life.

The general editor of this series, Richard Dutton, has been a model of patience and helpful guidance. I am astonished and grateful that he found so much time for my manuscript in his busy life.

DAVID WYKES

Extracts from Evelyn Waugh's works are reprinted by permission of The Peters Fraser & Dunlop Group Limited: © as printed in the original volumes.

Key to References

1S   Martin Stannard, *Evelyn Waugh: The Early Years, 1903–1939* (New York, Norton, 1987).

2S   Martin Stannard, *Evelyn Waugh: The Later Years, 1939–1966* (New York, Norton, 1992).

BM   Evelyn Waugh, *Black Mischief* (Penguin Modern Classics, 1968).

BR   Evelyn Waugh, *Brideshead Revisited*, intr. Frank Kermode (New York: Everyman's Library/Knopf, 1993).

BV   Antony Beevor, *Crete: The Battle and the Resistance* (London: John Murray, 1991).

C   Evelyn Waugh, *Edmund Campion* (London: Longmans, Green, 1935).

CH   *Evelyn Waugh: The Critical Heritage*, ed. Martin Stannard (London: Routledge & Kegan Paul, 1984).

CRS   Evelyn Waugh, *Charles Ryder's Schooldays and Other Stories* (Boston: Little, Brown, 1982).

D   *The Diaries of Evelyn Waugh*, ed. Michael Davie (London: Weidenfeld & Nicolson, 1976).

DF   Evelyn Waugh, *Decline and Fall*, revd edn (London: Chapman & Hall, 1962).

DG   Donat Gallagher, 'Evelyn Waugh and Vatican Divorce', in *Evelyn Waugh: New Directions*, ed. Alain Blayac (New York: St Martin's Press, 1992).

EAR   *The Essays, Articles and Reviews of Evelyn Waugh*, ed. Donat Gallagher (London: Methuen, 1983).

EWA   *Evelyn Waugh, Apprentice: The Early Writings, 1910–1927*, ed. Robert Murray Davis (Norman, OK: Pilgrim, 1985).

EY   *The Early Years of Alec Waugh* (New York: Farrar, Straus, 1962).

GP   Evelyn Waugh, *The Ordeal of Gilbert Pinfold and Other Stories* (London: Chapman & Hall, 1973).

H   Selina Hastings, *Evelyn Waugh: A Biography* (London: Sinclair-Stevenson, 1994).

HD   Evelyn Waugh, *A Handful of Dust* (Harmondsworth: Penguin, 1951).

HL   Evelyn Waugh, *Helena* (Harmondsworth: Penguin, 1963).

JB   Julian Jebb, interview with Evelyn Waugh in *Writers At Work. The Paris Review Interviews. Third Series* (London: Secker & Warburg, 1968).

L   *The Letters of Evelyn Waugh*, ed. Mark Amory (New York: Ticknor & Fields, 1980).

LA   Evelyn Waugh, *Labels: A Mediterranean Journal* (London: Duckworth, 1930).

LL   Evelyn Waugh, *A Little Learning: The First Volume of an Autobiography* (London: Chapman & Hall, 1964).

LO   Evelyn Waugh, *The Loved One* (Harmondsworth: Penguin, 1951).

LWC   *The Letters of Evelyn Waugh and Diana Cooper*, ed. Artemis Cooper (New York: Ticknor & Fields, 1992).

MBE   Alec Waugh, *My Brother Evelyn and Other Portraits* (New York: Farrar, Straus & Giroux, 1967).

MX   Sir Nicholas Cheetham, *A History of Mexico* (London: Hart-Davis, 1970).

R   Evelyn Waugh, *Rossetti: His Life and Works* (New York: Dodd, Mead, 1928).

RG   Robert R. Garnett, *From Grimes to Brideshead: The Early Novels of Evelyn Waugh* (Associated University Presses/Bucknell University Press, 1990).

RMD   Robert Murray Davis, *Evelyn Waugh, Writer* (Norman, OK: Pilgrim, 1981).

RP   Evelyn Waugh, *Remote People* (New York: Ecco Press, 1990).

RUL   Evelyn Waugh, *Robbery Under Law: The Mexican Object Lesson* (London: Chapman & Hall, 1939).

SH   Evelyn Waugh, *The Sword of Honour Trilogy* (New York: Everyman's Library/Knopf, 1994).

SY   Christopher Sykes, *Evelyn Waugh: A Biography* (London: Collins, 1975).

WIA   Evelyn Waugh, *Waugh in Abyssinia* (London: Penguin, 1984).

WS   Evelyn Waugh, *Work Suspended and Other Stories* (Harmondsworth: Penguin, 1967).

WTD   Auberon Waugh, *Will This Do? An Autobiography* (London: Century, 1991).

Three Annotated Epigraphs

He was the funniest man of his generation.

(Auberon Waugh)

These words were written soon after Evelyn Waugh died in 1966 by his eldest son. They call attention to his greatest power as a writer, exuberant comedy. He possessed the comic intelligence that has persisted in the English novel, through Fielding and Jane Austen and Dickens, into the twentieth century and into the six comic novels that came before *Brideshead Revisited* in 1945. Waugh's comic intelligence matches Jane Austen's and his exuberance in those six books is Dickensian. No account, biographical or otherwise, can explain how he came by this power, but no account should fail to stress it, for it is the comedy of Waugh's earlier novels that supports the entirety of his reputation and gives him his permanent place in the history of the English novel.

He liked things to go wrong.

(Ann Fleming)

Mrs Fleming, wife of James Bond's creator, was a longstanding friend of Waugh's, who pleased especially by being unintimidated by him. She wrote these words about Waugh after recounting the upsetting of a raft on a Jamaican river. Others have attributed *Schadenfreude* to him, but Mrs Fleming is closer to the truth, since it was by no means simply pleasure in the misfortunes *of others* that he felt (he was on the raft when it overturned). The going wrong of things was reiterated proof that the earthly order was inherently vitiated – by Original Sin, if we go back to basics – and that life as it is lived proclaims, everywhere and always, the need for the divine offer of redemption. Things going wrong – Gilbert Pinfold's bad bottle of wine, impertinent stranger, or fault in syntax – usually brought from him the wrath and incredulity of Pinfold, so often attested to in the

1

memoirs and memories of those who knew or met Waugh, but underneath the rage – as he admits on Pinfold's behalf – was the art of the actor, the wrath half-facetious, the incredulity half-simulated. Things going wrong showed that Waugh was right, particularly to have become a Roman Catholic, since the Church was the only means to acceptance of the offer of redemption, the only way out. In his earlier, greater novels, he felt no need to do more than describe things going wrong, and it was a very profitable *literary* decision.

The reason why humans behave as they do is that they are not living in their true home.

(St Augustine)

These words obviously relate to and expand on 'He liked things to go wrong'. The human behaviour that Waugh depicted in his books is that of exiles, outcasts, people with no valid landmarks or guideposts. For about half his career he was content to depict, with exuberant, comic enjoyment, their unguided and misguided lives. With the exception of the caricature Father Rothschild in *Vile Bodies*, no Catholic character appears in Waugh's fiction until *Brideshead*. When Catholics do appear, they are the sign that he is no longer content to display only the behaviour of those who are aliens and exiles and who do not know it. Catholics accepted Augustine's account of human exile. The 'Catholic novels' are the effect of Waugh's decision to bring into his works the provision of grace, God's offer of a way out of exile through his Church. This was a spiritually and morally progressive development, and almost certainly inevitable, but in the event it proved artistically limiting.

Introduction
Fiction, Autobiography, History

I am not I; thou art not he or she; they are not they.

(Author's note, *Brideshead Revisited*)

In July 1957 Evelyn Waugh was reluctantly present at a Foyle's Literary Luncheon to open the publicity campaign for his new novel, *The Ordeal of Gilbert Pinfold*. The book was so evidently autobiographical that it would have been impossible for him to have gone through the charade of warning his audience not to associate Pinfold with Waugh. He declared the book to be based on his own experience of going 'off my head' three years earlier. The dust jacket said the same thing less bluntly. Pinfold was Waugh. As Martin Stannard remarks, the novel 'has always been read as autobiography rather than fiction' (2S 396) and its author did nothing to discourage that reading. In his diary, he referred to the book as his 'novel', his quotation marks indicating the dubious applicability of the term (D 770). What is really remarkable in this open admission is the implication that fictionalized autobiography was a novelty in his writing. Nothing previously, it is true, had been autobiographical in the manner of *Pinfold*. There Waugh claimed to be transcribing reality, putting a thin coat of fiction – perhaps so that he could call it 'a novel' – over an exact account of what had happened to him. But there was nothing new about autobiographical experience as the foundation of his fiction. *The Ordeal of Gilbert Pinfold* is fascinating for the manner in which it both admits and denies this truth.

'Portrait of the Artist in Middle Age', the opening chapter, defends Mr Pinfold's objectivity and impersonality as an author quite as vigorously as Waugh generally defended his personal privacy. 'He regarded his books as objects which he had made, things quite external to himself to be used and judged by others' (GP 121). Pinfold envies painters to whom are permitted forms of repetition forbidden to novelists: 'painters...are allowed to return to the same theme time and time again, clarifying and enriching until they have done all they can with it. A novelist is condemned to produce a succession of novelties'. Pinfold as a novelist, however, seems to differ markedly in some respects from his creator. Waugh himself did return again and again to certain themes (the unfaithful wife and betrayal in all its forms are conspicuous examples), but there is one way in which he seems an exact counterpart. Like Waugh, Pinfold takes his personal experience as matter for his fiction. This is a large subjectivity, and one that Waugh usually did his best to conceal or deny. In *Pinfold* he owns up. In the last chapter of the novel, Pinfold is shown seated at his desk, looking at the manuscript of the novel he left unfinished at the beginning of his lunacy. 'The story was still clear in his mind. He knew what had to be done. But there was more urgent business first, a hamper to be unpacked of fresh, rich experiences – perishable goods' (GP 269). And he writes the title of *The Ordeal of Gilbert Pinfold*. The drug-induced episode of schizophrenia that was the foundation of *Pinfold* was welcomed by the novelist as a 'gift', an extension of personal experience suitable for use in fiction. (The discovery of the Forest Lawn burial ground on his trip to Hollywood had been an earlier 'gift' of this type, resulting in *The Loved One*.) Unlike, say, Henry James, Waugh could not build a novel on an anecdote told him about someone else. His dependence on his own history was nearly total.

Waugh was not very good at invention, but he was unsurpassed at embroidery. His experience reappears transformed, imaginatively made over and artistically perfected in his fiction, but he denied his genius for embroidery. He claimed – absurdly but irrefutably – to be a fundamentalist of empiricism, an objective recorder of his own experience. Indeed, he went to the extreme of claiming that his transcriptions of reality had to be toned down to make them 'probable' in the literary sense.

> My problem has been to distil comedy and sometimes tragedy from the knockabout farce of people's outward behaviour. Men and women as I see them would not be credible if they were literally transcribed.... People sometimes say to me, 'I met someone exactly like a character out of one of your books'. I meet them everywhere, not by choice but luck. (EAR 303)

His claim to be simply the recorder of human behaviour is so logically unassailable as to undermine the logic of empiricism. He says he put down what he saw; how can that claim be refuted? It is one of his most artful teases, and one of its concealed effects is to emphasize the importance of what happened to him. If we wish to do more than enjoy his novels, to understand something of his process of creation and measure his skill, then one very valid approach is through his life story. All his writing has an autobiographical source, sometimes more, sometimes less, yet none of it is simply autobiography. And that goes for his autobiography too.

Waugh died in 1966, but his reputation has never slumped. His books are kept in print and there is every sign that he will become a classic of our prose. The academic and institutional signs are particularly plentiful: his books are 'set' for examinations; a scholarly journal (the *Evelyn Waugh Newsletter*) is devoted to his life and works; no general history of the twentieth-century English novel can omit him; academic careers are advanced by dissertations and monographs on him. Yet this academic Waugh industry has a paradoxical element in that its subject was the least academic of novelists. It is true that his novels are elaborately allusive; quotations, references and parodies abound, and annotators do good business with them. His fierce cultural conservatism has meant that his biographers have been able to work almost exclusively with documents in the traditional academic form. (His hatred of the telephone has added many pages to the three full-length biographies of him.) But in the great fundamental of academic procedure, in the writer's study and awareness of his predecessors in the English novel, Waugh was willfully and creatively uneducated. Certain writers were acknowledged by him as 'influences', but their effect and stature were limited. (Ronald Firbank and Hilaire Belloc are good examples.) In Waugh's imaginative ancestry – that is, in the form of influence that Harold Bloom has invented and investigated – there were two great figures, Dickens and Gibbon, and Waugh perhaps proved himself a Bloomian 'strong' novelist by publicly denigrating both. Without these two English writers, he would have been a novelist of different formation, but he implied as firmly as he could that it was otherwise, that he was not in their debt.

Dickens stood in a paternal role to Waugh the novelist, but then fatherhood always had elements of antagonism in his life. Waugh adopted Dickens's style of autobiographical fiction, developed in *David Copperfield* and perfected in *Great Expectations*. Gibbon, denounced obliquely but unmistakably in Chapter 6 of *Helena*, supplied Waugh with a model of literary behaviour. In the *Helena* denunciation, and in his later career in general, Waugh tried to limit Gibbon to the role of stylist, but this was in fact a late development. In the earlier novels, it is of course Gibbon's irony and especially his relationship to his narrative that Waugh found valuable and often adopted.

Style and irony are the obvious borrowings for a novelist who surreptitiously follows Gibbon, but there was in Waugh's case a more intangible and even less-acknowledged debt. Gibbon's greatest value in Waugh's eyes was that he was a model historian, a model adoptable by a novelist. And that is the role – the novelist as historian – that comes closest to describing his imaginative conception of himself. Pretending to look forward to books that his brother Alec was to write, Evelyn in 1930 gave a definition of historical writing: '[Alec's] narrative poems, his story-teller's instinct for significant detail, his ability to sort out tangled chains of motive, to assess probabilities, to render incidents dramatic and memorable, seem to me all to fit him for the role of historian' (EAR 75). Evelyn introduces this list of what could assuredly be the abilities of a novelist by saying that Alec 'is growing out of novel-writing'. But amid tease and bewilderment, one thing is clear: history and the novel share family features, and the historian is a novelist as the novelist is a historian.

Gibbon described the decline and fall of a great civilization, and did it with a style and attitude that embodied what was lost. He had no heroes. For much of his career, Waugh's appreciation of those qualities in Gibbon far outweighed the splashier idea that Gibbon 'blamed' Christianity for the decline and fall. When Waugh came to feel that he had to denounce Gibbon for his irreligion, it was because Waugh had modified his definition of the novelist as historian and was no longer the writer he had been.

Satire and Roman Catholicism are the bookends of much that is written about Evelyn Waugh. His own attitudes towards these twin supports of his academic reputation differed. He declined to agree that he was a satirist, and insisted on his Catholicism to a degree that sometimes brought him close to denigration of his earlier, non-Catholic novels. He never did repudiate his younger literary self, but a compliment paid to one of his later books, particularly to *Helena*, would receive a warmth of welcome quite different from the tight-lipped acknowledgement of an enthusiasm for an earlier one.

It is the belief of the book you are reading that Waugh was right about satire – not that it matters much – and most understandably wrong about Catholicism as far as it concerns his literary reputation.

Satire first. 'Fan-Fare' includes Waugh's most direct rejection of 'satire' as a description of his fiction, and since this was 1946 he means what are here called his 'earlier' books, pre-*Brideshead*.

> Satire is a matter of period. It flourishes in a stable society and presupposes homogeneous moral standards – the early Roman Empire and eighteenth-century Europe. It is aimed at inconstancy and hypocrisy. It exposes polite cruelty and folly by exaggerating them. It seeks to produce shame. All this has no place in the Century of the Common Man where vice no longer pays lip service to virtue. (EAR 304)

By basing his definition on forms of society and ideology that no longer exist, Waugh asserts the *historical* impossibility of his being a satirist, and then he goes on to suggest for himself and any like him another historical role. 'The artist's only service in the disintegrated society of today is to create little independent systems of order of his own'. The next sentence shows that he does not mean by this art for art's sake. 'I foresee in the dark age opening that the scribes may play the part of the monks after the first barbarian victories. They were not satirists'. They were, however, primitive historians. If what they recorded seems excessive, it is because they chronicled the deeds of barbarians, persons of habitual excess, but their accounts share the perspective of a religious affiliation. The little systems of order will not therefore be independent of each other. Waugh is defining the role of the novelist as (Catholic) historian, although in 1946 he had modified and would continue to modify the role as he had played it up until the war. He is misleading only if his fans infer that the role he describes is new for him. He had played it from the start of his career.

The debate among Waugh's students and devotees as to whether he was a satirist has not been a triumph for academic criticism. The outcome seems to be that one accepts or rejects his refusal of the role according to the thesis one is pushing. My emphases, therefore, fall on the self-evident delight Waugh takes – in the earlier novels – in the misdeeds and character deformities that he chronicles. Satire is notoriously paradoxical in that writing that is supposedly trying to exterminate something has to be in love with that something if it is to succeed as art. How barren Pope's world would have been without his dunces! Waugh, however, goes beyond the satirists in his evident gusto. He *liked* things to go wrong. There is in his work not a trace of sincere Utopianism. Human life can never be anything but exile, and the fantasy of an earthly paradise or El Dorado – or even of life on a slightly improved model – is the product of a grave misunderstanding of human nature. (The later Waugh would make it clear that this misunderstanding can be explained only by theology.) The behaviour that Waugh's novels depict is to him the assurance that he was religiously right, and so that behaviour gets the support of his artistic intelligence.

It would indeed be possible to argue – and to flirt with paradox – that true satire entered Waugh's fiction for the first time only with the appearance of Atwater/Hooper/Trimmer, the embodiment of the Age of the Common Man, the inheritor of the future. Waugh evidently hates this figure and fears him, and real fear, however deeply buried, seems to be the one indispensable quality of real satire. It is usual to say that Waugh's later novels are diminished in comedy; it is as much to say that they have increased in fear. Any biography of him must try to relate this development of his thought to his art and life, to show how Waugh learned fear.

He became converted to Roman Catholicism in 1930. There is no doubt that in his own eyes this was the single most important fact in his life, but if one confines oneself to matters of literary importance a fact may rank for the biographer more or less highly than it does or did for the subject of the biography. In Waugh's case, Catholicism has far more importance in his writing in 1945 and afterwards than it ever had before. Yet the later novels, most of which can fairly be called 'Catholic', are – in the unashamedly evaluative judgement of this book – of lesser value than those written before *Brideshead*.

Waugh became a Catholic soon after *Vile Bodies* (1930); *Black Mischief* (1932) was his next novel. Catholicism thus stands at least in the background of his fiction in 1932, but the judgements and attitudes detectable in the two earlier novels, *Decline and Fall* and *Vile Bodies*, seem to be quite in conformity with those that are present after the conversion. What really happened is that Waugh found a church and a doctrine that provided a sustaining framework for ideas about human life and society that had been forming in him for quite some time. Becoming a Catholic meant dropping some ideas and attitudes that he had toyed with experimentally, but mostly it meant he could underline, emphasize and expand a group of beliefs that carried over fundamentally unchanged from before to after. The Catholic Church was a new spiritual home for Waugh, but his social, political and historical address did not have to be changed; he could continue to live where he had lived for years already.

This is almost, but not quite, to say that given the elements of the secular ideology that underpins the earlier novels, Waugh could have written his pre-*Brideshead* novels without religious faith. It is possible that had he not found Catholicism, he would have lost the will to continue as a novelist, so in that sense religion may have been essential for fiction. I think it is also true that the alternative implied to the life depicted in *A Handful of Dust* can only be religion, but undifferentiated religion, not necessarily Catholicism. These exceptions apart, Waugh's religion becomes of literary importance only when his work enters its lesser phase, and a short biography must reflect that judgement.

Waugh's tombstone bears the one-word description 'Writer', for novels are only part of his work. Once he had a reputation as a novelist, he used it to build and expand a market for several kinds of journalism. He wrote three biographies and an autobiography, and half a dozen travel books. His diaries and collections of his letters have been published. He declared that 'I wanted to be a man of the world and I took to writing as I might have taken to archaeology or diplomacy or any other profession as a means of coming to terms with the world' (EAR 302). This would suggest that it did not much matter what he wrote, and the list of his works superficially bears that out; a book on wine, commissioned by a firm of wine merchants and paid for in kind, stands next to *The Loved One*. But any notion of mere professional facility, of a hand that could be turned indifferently to anything, is mistaken. Waugh was a novelist who used his lesser literary talents to help him live entirely by his pen, as Robert Graves wrote fiction and much else to support his poetry habit. Waugh's novels were good sellers but there were only so many novels that his life story offered him to sustain the life-style he demanded. Hence his large non-fiction output. Much of his pot-boiling was in fact distinguished writing; it could be tedious, though rarely, for it was very hard for Waugh not to be entertaining. Everything he wrote sounds like him and makes a good fit, in ideas and attitudes, with the rest of his work, even (or perhaps especially) *Robbery Under Law*, the 1939 book that is the least-known large item in his list (least known since he wanted it that way). The travel books, for further instance, could be discussed advantageously from the angle of Waugh's metaphor of history – the traveller as historian. The situation, however, demands selectivity. The novels must have precedence and the other writings have to agree to let themselves be used as evidence in the enquiry that is the only real justification for a biography of Evelyn Waugh: How did this life support this fiction?

1

Second Son:
1903–24

Evelyn Waugh was born in Hampstead in 1903, second son of the late Arthur Waugh, publisher and literary critic, and brother of Alec Waugh, the popular novelist.[1]

His full name was Arthur Evelyn St John Waugh. Since Arthur was his father's name and St John he thought comically pretentious, Evelyn – 'a whim of my mother's' – he was called. He disliked the name and it repeatedly involved him in mistakes of gender identity, but it was characteristic of him to play the hand he had been dealt, to make the world accept that Evelyn was *his* name. His birth in Hampstead occurred at number 11, Hillfield Road, West Hampstead, a Victorian terraced house now divided into flats and awaiting its blue plaque. When he was four, his parents had built for them a villa, 'Underhill', in the then village of North End, Hampstead, 'a very ordinary little suburban villa', his father accurately called it, though he much annoyed his younger son by his sentimental pride in the house. Evelyn thought it hideous and disadvantageously located, since the Post Office changed its address from Hampstead to the far less chic Golders Green, a change that apparently caused Evelyn sometimes to take long walks to get the superior Hampstead postmark on his letters.

Throughout his entire life, people who knew Evelyn Waugh remarked on his courage, for in those parts of his life open to observation he was quite fearless. Since he was a writer, however, and since his own experience was the basis for almost everything he wrote, he revealed to his readers in sundry ways that fears played their part in his life as they do in all lives. His fear of ridicule helped him become the master of ridicule. Another great fear was that his individual identity might somehow be impaired – parodied, stolen, or prevented from achieving its fullest realization. He perceived that he and his father had much in common and that almost everything that they shared was repudiated by Evelyn. He feared coming to

11

resemble his father, and so in the main Arthur became his model to be avoided. His brother Alec saw this clearly:

> In later life Evelyn may have given the impression of being heartless; he was often snubbing, he could be cruel. But basically he was gentle, warm and tender. He was very like his father, and his father's own emotionalism put him on his guard. He must often have thought, 'I could become like this. I mustn't let myself become like this'. (MBE 166)

Arthur Waugh was notably sentimental; Evelyn found the tendency in himself and fought fiercely against it, in life and in art. Arthur, like his sons, was physically brave but had a hatred of antagonism and confrontation; he terminated anything that seemed likely to become a domestic dispute by imposing a hasty decision of his own. He hated discussing things. As Evelyn later realized, 'His primary, overriding, instinctive aim was to make a home', but this compulsion, expressed through the idiosyncrasies of Arthur's character, led to a form of non-violent domination over his family that sat comfortably upon his wife and older son but that galled and from time to time infuriated Evelyn. When he in turn found himself the head of a family, he too became emphatically dominant, but he adopted, as a parody that was often indistinguishable from the real thing, the role of the Victorian domestic tyrant that his own father had consciously rejected, and in a house, moreover, Piers Court, that was utterly unlike Underhill and was conscientiously adorned with Victorian furnishings and bric-à-brac.

For most of his working life, Arthur Waugh was a literary businessman, journeying by tube each day to his job as managing director of the publishers Chapman & Hall, a company founded on the success of its greatest author, Charles Dickens. After Oxford, where he won the Newdigate Prize for poetry and got an undistinguished degree in Greats, Arthur had begun a career as that now diminished thing, a 'man of letters'. One of his largely unfulfilled ambitions was to become a dramatist and librettist, but he could not afford to specialize. He worked first for the Lovell Company, publishers, and was commissioned in 1891 to write a life of Tennyson. When the Poet Laureate died in October 1892, Arthur swiftly finished his book and it was published by Heinemann eight days later, going through six impressions. This seemed to be the success Arthur needed to marry Catherine Raban, whom he had been courting for eight years, but it was a delusive triumph. Lovells went bankrupt in 1893, and although he had no obligation to do so, Arthur distributed everything he earned from the Tennyson biography to their unpaid former employees, and consequently had to postpone his marriage. He worked as a freelance critic and journalist, and was able to marry in the autumn of 1893. After two years of freelancing, he settled for stability and effectively renounced his authorial ambitions by joining Kegan Paul, publishers. Alec was born in 1898. In 1901, when Arthur was thirty-five, he took over as managing director of Chapman & Hall.

It has been said that the heroes of modern life are the fathers of families, and in his self-denial and responsibility Arthur Waugh could certainly be called a hero. His younger son, however, sought heroic models of a very different kind. His boyhood and indeed lifetime hero was the man of action, not one of 'sedentary and cerebral occupations. . . . I should have better respected a soldier or a sailor . . . or a man with some constructive hobby such as carpentry . . . a man, even, who shaved with a cut-throat razor' (LL 27). Arthur's life, moreover, was undoubtedly a literary life, and so it was virtually inevitable that Evelyn, whom both nature and nurture meant for a writer, should for a considerable time have rejected a literary life for himself even while he was almost continuously engaged in writing of his own. In the same paradoxical way, for all his life he never had a good word to say for Dickens, the tutelar of his family. The Dickens copyright did not expire until 1930, and it is not unlikely that it paid for Evelyn Waugh's upbringing and education. (He was never averse to taking a nip at hands that fed him.) Dickens, moreover, was particularly and peculiarly identified with Arthur Waugh in ways that went beyond business. People often described Arthur as 'Pickwickian' and Evelyn resolved that, however rubicund and rotund he might become, he should not be patronized in such terms. It became his art to make people laugh, but they should not laugh *at* him. This said, however, it must be added that no writer taught Evelyn Waugh more about the writing of comedy than Dickens; the comic novels are steeped in his influence, and Waugh was always ready to resort to Dickens. For example, one of Arthur's literary mentors was Edmund Gosse, a more eminent specimen of the man of letters and also a kinsman. Evelyn detested him and turned to *Bleak House* for aid.

To me [Gosse] epitomised all that I found ignoble in the profession of letters. . . . he had little natural amiability or generosity. And

his appearance was drab. I was early drawn to panache. I saw
Gosse as a Mr Tulkinghorn, the soft-footed, inconspicuous, ill-
natured habitué of the great world, and I longed for a demented
lady's-maid to make an end of him. (LL 66)

Selina Hastings' biography includes a photograph of Arthur Waugh
congratulating Evelyn after the presentation of the Hawthornden
Prize in 1936. It might be called 'The twentieth century says goodbye
to the nineteenth'. Arthur is rotund, white-haired, balding and
affably Pickwickian. He wears a rumpled, dark, three-piece business
suit and a wing collar and tie. Evelyn, dark-haired and slender,
smiles but seems embarrassed. He wears a natty, tight-fitting, light-
coloured, double-breasted suit, and a spotted bow tie that can only
be yellow.

Marking his difference from Arthur like this was vital to Evelyn in
the earlier part of his life. Later, especially in his autobiography, he
could relax somewhat and express gratitude. There he thanks
Arthur for his regular readings aloud to him and his brother and so
for opening up to him the English literature – 'most of Shakespeare,
most of Dickens, most of Tennyson, much of Browning, Trollope,
Swinburne, Matthew Arnold' – that the British public schools had
not yet really admitted to their curriculum.

In these recitations of English prose and verse the incomparable
variety of English vocabulary, the cadences and rhythms of the
language, saturated my young mind, so that I never thought of
English Literature as a school subject, as a matter for analysis and
historical arrangement, but as a source of natural joy. (LL 72)

The effect of this 'legacy that has not depreciated' on Evelyn
Waugh's literary career is twofold. It gave him a stylistic base on
which to establish his own prose style (in the comic novels this generally involves elements of parody and stylistic irony playing over
the ground bass of the fundamentally 'classic', nineteenth-century
prose style), and it established in his mind a standard of literary taste
that he held to for much of his life.

A Little Learning modifies considerably Evelyn's earlier view of
Arthur's innate theatricality: 'he was, by amateur standards, genuinely gifted, but it was in the daily routine of his private life that he
acted with the greatest virtuosity', a habit that in Evelyn's teens was
acutely painful to him (in his 1921 diary, for instance, he writes of his

father being 'incorrigibly theatrical as usual'). In the autobiography, forty-three years later, he sees Arthur's incessant acting as amusing, even endearing: 'In greeting visitors he was Mr Hardcastle; in deploring the ingratitude of his sons, Lear. Between these two extremes all the more likable of Dickens's characters provided him with roles which ... he undesignedly assumed'. Evelyn's change of attitude is owed to self-knowledge: 'Everyone ... agreed that he too was acting all the time' (1S 59). But the adult Evelyn Waugh was the quite conscious exploiter of his own histrionic tendency. Arthur's was undesigned, Evelyn's a developed strategy of dealing with the world from behind a rapidly shiftable sequence of masks, the construction and employment of which was a talent cognate with his literary powers. In *A Little Learning* he is undisturbed and unthreatened by Arthur's long-running performance because he has successfully adopted it as his own way of keeping the world at a safe distance.

A literary businessman cum man of letters combined with the personality of Arthur Waugh was a powerful dissuasion from the literary life presented for Evelyn's inspection. An older brother who was a best-selling novelist in his late teens was an even more powerful deterrent and threat.

Born in 1898, Alec was the openly acknowledged favourite of his father, and he in turn adored Arthur Waugh. There were thus two 'sets' within the family. Evelyn claimed to have had a 'paradisal' childhood but his account shows that this was so because his father and brother were for the most part excluded from it. He adored his mother and a second 'deity', his nurse Lucy. His father and brother stood together across an emotional gulf that was not frequently and never permanently bridged. The closeness of Arthur and Alec centred on Arthur's old school, Sherborne, and cricket. Arthur loved the game but at school asthma and poor eyesight had prevented him from playing it. Alec loved cricket too, and he excelled at it. At Sherborne he played in the First XI, and his progress was reported in telegrams to his father. Evelyn detested the game.

Alec was quintessential Public School Material and it is therefore all the stranger that he and Sherborne should have fallen out so dramatically. He himself found it hard to explain what went wrong. His position in his family had given him, as he acknowledged, a 'superiority complex', and his early and clouded departure from the school was caused by a combination of 'Bolshie' attitudes and an episode of homosexual emotion – more emotion than activity, it seems. Alec described the homosexual episodes he was involved in at school as really 'crushes', protective and patronizing attitudes extended by older boys to younger ones, idealistically unphysical. Instead of being expelled, he was asked to leave at the end of summer term 1915, his first year in the sixth form. Having to leave early in wartime, when almost everyone who was old enough had left to join up, was not much of a punishment. Alec left school under a cloud, but it was a high, thin cloud and had he not drawn the world's attention to it, it would have passed unnoticed.

But Alec Waugh at seventeen wrote, and just over a year later published, a novel about Sherborne ('Fernhurst') designed 'to show the public school system in its true colours' (EY 81). The British public school in 1917 was an inviting target for a writer of the type Alec then was, a non-conformist, loathing pomposity, with a predilection for the minority view, eager to expose misconceptions. Stuck in a murderous and drawn-out war, the public was ready to hear how the public school's effects and products had made their negative contribution. *The Loom of Youth* was rather a *succès de scandale* since it included in its general rebelliousness an account – restrained but at that time not easily mistakable – of the protagonist's romantic affection for another boy. It made Alec into a professional writer, after a lengthy intermission while he served as an officer in the Kaiser's War. He read his reviews – very encouraging – while on duty with the Machine Gun Corps on the Western Front. Captured in March 1918, Alec spent the rest of the war in a POW camp at Mainz, his father terrified that the Germans might massacre their prisoners as the war came to its end.

The Loom of Youth was the foundation of Alec's literary life, but for Evelyn it had an obstacular role. Arthur had read the book as it was composed and had helped get it to publishers; it was dedicated in highly emotional terms to him. When Alec was thrown out of the Shirburnian Society, Arthur resigned from it. It not only cemented even more strongly the closeness of Arthur and Alec, but it closed Sherborne to Evelyn, which he saw as an injustice and a handicap. He was an ambitious boy, expecting (though vaguely) to be someone in the world. Alec, however, was occupying and rendering untenable positions that Evelyn might otherwise have taken for himself. Alec was authenticated – for manhood and for government, in the widest sense of the term – by having fought in the war, and after the war he and his generation, having been delayed in their entry into society and the professions, would be there to impede and block Evelyn's own generation. One of the variety of things that Evelyn Waugh's novels are 'about' is consistently the conflict of generations, the clashing of the divergent mentalities of the old and the young. Evelyn's escape (as one instinctively thinks of it) from fighting in the First World War was no simple blessing for him, as his eagerness for active service in 1939 shows. Twenty years later, he was still getting even with Alec.

Evelyn Waugh had been a writing child; he wrote stories and 'magazines', and as he grew older he kept a diary (for most of his time at Lancing – which survives – and at Oxford – which does not) and wrote verse, winning prizes at school. His writing during his adolescent years displays something like an obsession with Alec and *The Loom of Youth*. There were two avenues of approach: he could try to surpass his brother and he could deride him.

While he was at Lancing, immediately after the war, Evelyn was occasionally visited by Alec, who had bypassed the university and was launched on a literary career. After one such visit by Alec and his fiancée, Barbara Jacobs, in October 1920, Evelyn began a novel (untitled) which he had abandoned by January 1921, and for which Alec provided not only the stimulus but the subject. The 'scheme' was to have been 'the study of a man with two characters, by his brother' (D 107). Peter Audley, at school on the Sussex Downs in Easter term 1918, is summoned home for his brother's return on leave from the battlefront. The manuscript ends with Peter's arrival home where he is met by his 'wonderfully fit and hansome [sic]' brother Ralf, recent winner of the DSO, who is apparently keeping company with Moira Gage, daughter of the local vicar.

It is impossible to choose among the many reasons Waugh might have had for dropping the novel. How extensively had he thought out the brother 'with two characters'? Was this dualism or schizophrenia something he thought he saw in Alec? One would like to know if he proposed to go on with the slavish autobiographical procedure. The fact that the fragment stops with the appearance of Ralf may suggest that the character of the brother presented problems that Evelyn had underestimated. As it stands, the most interesting part of the fragment is its dedication: 'To myself'. Here he is ironically open about the problems of belonging to a family of writers.

Much has been written and spoken about the lot of the boy with literary aspirations in a philistine family; little can adequately convey his difficulties, when the surroundings, which he has known from childhood, have been entirely literary. It is [as] a sign of victory over these difficulties that this book is chiefly, if at all, worthy of attention.

The next paragraph describes life in his father's literary household. Then,

> All this will be brought up against you. 'Another of those precocious Waughs', they will say, 'one more nursery novel'. So be it. . . . You have still high hopes and big ambitions and have not yet been crushed in the mill of professionalism. Soon perhaps you will join the 'wordsmiths' jostling one another for royalties and contracts, meanwhile you are still very young. (EWA 101)

The manifest confusions of this statement are characteristic of Waugh's youthful attitude towards the family trade. Writing had an inevitability about it that made his insincere resistance seem futile. The contempt for professionalism was to become thoroughgoing professionalism. And he never seems to have contemplated the most obvious way to avoid sinking into authorship: he never stopped writing, and he tried to get his work published (D 108).

The second approach, derision, is found in the second act of a play Evelyn wrote at Lancing: *Conversion*. The three acts are separately titled. Act I is 'School, as maiden Aunts think it is'. Act II is 'School, as modern authors say it is'. Act III is 'School, as we all know it is'. The only 'modern author' recognizable in Act II is Alec Waugh, whose novel is extensively parodied, and indeed provides all the material for the Act (six pages). The stage directions give an indication of the attitude. 'The scene is laid in Fernhurst, one of the largest and wickedest of our Public Schools'. Parody is sometimes termed 'affectionate', but the purpose of Evelyn's parody of *The Loom of Youth* is to place Alec's view of public school life on a comic level of ignorance and misprision with that of maiden aunts. Alec's good nature might have found it affectionate, but Evelyn had a score to settle with his family's 'nursery novel'.

There is one necessary and surprising footnote to Evelyn Waugh's adolescent engagement with his brother's famous first novel. Evelyn seems to have quite missed the admittedly unemphatic homosexual element in the novel. In *A Little Learning*, referring to *The Early Years of Alec Waugh* (1962), he says that Alec's getting into 'scrapes at school which culminated in his expulsion' was quite unknown to him until he read the book. His father never mentioned them. 'When from time to time I heard echoes of scandal, I indignantly repudiated them' (LL 95). One wonders whether these repudiations came before or after his own homosexual affairs at Oxford.

While Alec was in training in the army, he had become engaged to Barbara Jacobs, daughter of W. W. Jacobs, the writer, an old friend of the Waughs. Anticipating the marriage, and to escape from her own chaotic family atmosphere, Barbara had come to stay at Underhill, using as occasion the need to be in London while she took a college course. Evelyn returned from Lancing for the Christmas vacation of 1917 to find her in residence, and they became good friends. Barbara Jacobs played an important role in Evelyn's nascent literary career and intellectual development; she was also the first of his 'sisters'.

She was less than three years older than he, but her background was of 'advanced' ideas: feminism, agnosticism, socialism. From her he got the first of his several pushes into modernism: 'in Barbara I met the new age'. For a brief period, though it lasted through his Oxford years, Waugh became 'an apologist for Picasso' and for modernism in art. At fourteen he published 'The Defence of Cubism' in the periodical *Drawing and Design* (November 1917); he called it an article, the editor took it as a letter. Its inspiration was Barbara Jacobs's enthusiasm, and under her influence and tutelage Waugh became, as he said, 'an aesthetic hypocrite', persuading himself that he admired works of art that, when he reverted to his true tastes, he truly abominated. But the fact remains; Evelyn Waugh's first real publication was 'The Defence of Cubism'.

In Barbara's company, Waugh explored London, of which he knew little, seeing what was still a nineteenth-century city from the open top decks of buses. There was nothing romantic or sexual between them, Waugh assures his reader, and his biographers have accepted his account unhesitatingly. The absence of conscious sexual feeling does not, however, mean that this friendship was free of psychological complexities. It is surely a bit odd that Evelyn should have made so close a friend of his brother's fiancée. Much of the time Evelyn and Barbara shared was spent by Alec in the trenches or in the POW camp. And on his return, an even odder thing happened. Alec and Barbara were married in July 1919, but Alec had reservations about the marriage. Barbara seems to have lost her attractiveness for him, and without knowing it he had come to share Evelyn's opinion of that aspect of her: 'I never thought her particularly beautiful or attractive' (LL 123). The marriage went unconsummated, a fact of which Evelyn was ignorant for some years, and eventually, in January 1923, was annulled. When Evelyn's first marriage was annulled in 1936, he was willingly emulating Alec for one of the very few times in his life.

For most of his adult life, Evelyn Waugh had friendships with women, his 'sisters' as I think of them, that conformed to the pattern established by his relationship with Barbara Jacobs. Later 'sisters' included notably Lady Diana Cooper, Nancy Mitford, and Ann Fleming. These friendships were – unlike that with Barbara – chiefly epistolary. Meetings between Waugh and his later sisters tended to eventuate in quarrels, often because Waugh disliked their husbands, though in person he was quite capable of quarreling with the sisters themselves. All the husbands had claims to be men of action. Most of them were writers and Waugh despised their work – tacitly, for the most part, but it was a contempt tacitly acknowledged by the sisters. Barbara was clearly an older sister, though Waugh grew beyond her, so to speak, into an older brother. With the later sisters he was predominantly an older brother, though Ann Fleming firmly refused the role of *younger* sister. The sisters were a significant group of supporters for Waugh, the addressees of many of his best letters with their *obiter dicta* about the writer's craft. But psychologically one aspect of their attractiveness as friends was that they had husbands, husbands in whom could be seen one or more resemblances to Alec, thus permitting Evelyn to re-enact with the wife gratifying aspects of his first relationship with Alec's Barbara.

Evelyn's handling of his largely one-sided rivalry with Alec, once he had achieved professional and psychological independence, is interestingly related to the institution of the sisters. Evelyn could not complain that Alec either envied or denied his literary achievement, for Alec endears himself to an outsider by his complete and unfeigned acceptance of Evelyn's superiority – genius, in fact – an acceptance that Evelyn must have known of and that helped to preserve the cool cordiality of their public relationship. 'If I were not myself and if I were to pick up the autobiography of Alec Waugh, the first name I should look for in the index would be Evelyn Waugh' (EY 217). Evelyn therefore found a focus for his persisting resentment in Alec's personal conduct. He converted Alec into a *younger* brother, similar in some ways to the mythical Earnest who haunts Wilde's play. Evelyn could be loftily censorious of Alec, but most often he turned on him the withering power of his comic eye. His contempt for Alec's lifestyle and taste provides some of the best passages in his letters, as in this to his son Auberon in 1958. (Bron was recovering from wounds and had been visited in hospital by his uncle.)

> The man who calls on you purporting to be my brother Alec is clearly an impostor. Your true uncle does not know your whereabouts & supposes you to be here [at Combe Florey] convalescent – as witness this card which came with a volume of his describing the more obvious & picturesque features of the West Indies. Did your visitor offer any identification other than baldness – not an uncommon phenomenon? Had he a voice like your half great uncle George? Did he wear a little silk scarf round his neck? Was he tipsy? These are the tests. (L 514)

The reference to the travel book is strikingly precise in its patronizing contempt. In the 1951 blurb,[2] Alec is described as 'the popular novelist', a term that is again exactly chosen for the disparity between the general interpretation and that of those in the know. (Evelyn wrote fewer books than Alec and sold more copies, but he ensured that no one could call *him* 'the popular novelist'.) Evelyn never conquered his perhaps subconscious fear that Alec, who preceded him in so many ways, might invade his identity, and therefore many of the references to Alec in his writing serve as differentiation. A late, minor episode, Evelyn's action for libel against Nancy Spain in 1957, turned indeed upon the differentiation of the brothers, with Alec loyally testifying in court to his failure as a writer in comparison with Evelyn.

When brothers turn up in Waugh's fiction, they are often unprepossessing and often the brotherly relationship is in some way blighted. Brenda's brother Reggie in *A Handful of Dust* and Bridey in *Brideshead Revisited* are learned fools. Guy Crouchback has one dead brother and one who went mad. But Waugh dealt directly with the relationship only once, in a short story of 1935, 'Winner Takes All'. It is worth pausing over for what it reveals about his style of autobiographical fiction.

'Winner Takes All' could be subtitled 'The Wickedness of Primogeniture'. Mrs Kent-Cumberland has two sons, Gervase, the elder, and Tom. At every stage of the boys' lives, the mother ruthlessly sacrifices Tom's interests for Gervase's benefit. Gervase goes to Eton, Tom to a nameless, lesser school. Gervase goes to Oxford; Tom is found a job in a motor-works. When Tom becomes engaged

to Gladys Cruttwell, who works for the company, he is packed off to
Australia. When he returns from Australia engaged to an heiress,
Mrs Kent-Cumberland steals the young woman to be Gervase's
bride, marries Tom to Gladys from the motor-works, and packs Tom
and Gladys off to Australia.

It is a relentless little fiction, free of any moral commentary or narrator's indignation. Publicly it is non-autobiographical. It is the elder
brother who has the dynastic name – Gervase Peregrine Mountjoy
St Eustace – and there was no ruthless mother in the Waugh family,
but there are details that come from life. For example, Alec had married in 1932 Joan Chirnside, an Australian heiress. And there is a
literary element. One of Mrs Kent-Cumberland's worse misdeeds is
to steal Tom's sole literary accomplishment and bestow it upon
Gervase, who duly appears as the discoverer and editor of the military memoirs of an ancestral Peninsular veteran. Most of all, the story
is autobiographical in its emotional economy. Waugh has isolated
the feelings of injustice and resentment that were frequently compon-
ents of his attitude as the younger brother and has contrived a
largely fictional narrative structure to present those feelings as justified. The reader is made to lament injustice and nourish resentment
on Tom's behalf, while the author's aloofness allows him to insinu-
ate doubt that Tom should be pitied at all. Is this not another
instance of what must be expected of life in this place of exile?

Were it possible to ask Waugh if he approved of primogeniture as
a social institution, his answer would probably have been yes, even
at the time of writing. Carefully considered, 'Winner Takes All' depicts an anomalous abuse of the system, not a repudiation of it. But
Waugh's resentments over his status as 'second son' were powerful,
though irrational, and the story, insignificant as it is, effectively
releases them. This is the Dickensian style of autobiographical fiction.
The external circumstances are largely, though not entirely, invented,
but the emotional centre is taken from the writer's life.

Until Waugh settled finally into his career as a writer, which was
after the publication of *Vile Bodies* and *Labels* in 1930, he continually
suggested that his professional path might lie in another direction
than literature. His non-literary avocation was drawing – draughts-
manship in a variety of forms: calligraphy, woodcuts, graphic design
– he did a number of dustjackets for publishers – and illustration,
most notably of his own earlier novels. He undoubtedly had real talent as a draughtsman, but it was talent and not genius, an ability of
which something good might have been made but only by extended

study and training. As things turned out, he never had to stake much on his drawing, and its importance in his life is chiefly psychological. It was an alternative career, a never-followed road where the possibilities of success were easier to imagine than the potential for failure. Drawing involved very little peril to the psyche, and practising it was a holiday to him once his profession was set.

This talent of Waugh's served his psychological needs in one further way. His practice of drawing, calligraphy, and other variants of this skill led him to study painting and the graphic arts and to achieve, certainly in his own opinion, the rank of connoisseur. We hear the note of this authority when Guy Crouchback, at the very beginning of *Officers and Gentlemen*, calls the night sky of London in the blitz 'Pure Turner'.

> 'John Martin, surely'? said Ian Kilbannock.
> 'No', said Guy firmly. He would not accept correction on matters of art from this former sporting-journalist. (SH 237)

To be able to make such statements was very important to Waugh, so important that in Mexico in 1938 he felt the pressure of his connoisseurship on his religious faith – and the connoisseurship was not defeated. Contemplating the miraculous painting of the Virgin of Guadalupe, Waugh accepts it as a miraculous artifact. 'And yet, it must be admitted, [it] is very like a human composition'. Waugh's knowledge of painting and of styles forces him away from an uncomplicated acceptance of the miraculous towards a highly un-Wavian compromise. 'Looking at it, I wondered if some human agency had not intervened to preserve and ornament the true image which Diego and Zumarraga saw' (RUL 231). The impulse to find voices of authority for himself was hugely powerful in Waugh, more so than in most people. Some of his notorious rudeness in later life is owed to it, for it increased its pressure as he grew older and felt the effects of inevitable decline.

Waugh went to school for the first time in September 1910, when he was seven years old. He was supposed to follow Alec to a preparatory school in Surrey and to spend the interval until he was of age at Heath Mount School in Hampstead, as a day boy. 'Preparatory' meant that the school prepared boys to enter the public school system in their early teens. (The definitive hostile account of such a school is George Orwell's 'Such, Such Were the Joys'.) Alec's cheerful reports of the hardships of his prep school made Evelyn apprehensive and may have influenced his parents' decision to let him continue at Heath Mount as a day boy. Both Evelyn and his mother were very happy with this arrangement for the shelter it afforded to a sensitive child, but later, in his autobiography, Waugh wondered if he had not been too sheltered. Heath Mount in its preparatory role did not 'cram' its pupils to win scholarships to the great public schools, and the system that whipped and spurred Eric Blair into winning a scholarship to Eton was not applied to Waugh – to his (much later) regret.

Because Heath Mount had turned out to be an alternative to the rigours of preparatory school, it stood in Waugh's memory with the sheltering home that he was compelled to leave at the unusually late age of thirteen when he entered Lancing. Consequently, Heath Mount comes off rather well in *A Little Learning*, subjected to only the gentlest of irony. For the adult autobiographer, the most arresting characters are the junior masters, 'drawn from a heterogeneous and undefinable underworld into which – little did I know it – I was myself destined to descend' (LL 84). His darkest hint, however, remains unfolded: 'Some liked little boys too little and some too much'. Of himself, Waugh finds only one article of indictment at Heath Mount. He and cronies tormented the child Cecil Beaton, later the photographer and theatrical designer, 'and we were soundly beaten for doing so'.

When the time came to select a public school for Evelyn – the truly *public* schools, those of the state, were of course out of the question – Arthur Waugh, with Sherborne closed to him, chose Lancing, on the Sussex Downs. Lancing was a High Anglican establishment, and it was in part because of his second son's religious interests that Arthur picked it.

Before he went away to school, Evelyn went through a phase of religious enthusiasm that seems to have been largely aesthetic. He had a collection of religious artifacts arranged as a shrine by his bed. 'I burned little cones of incense on a brass ashtray before these images. . . . I began to recite long devotions from a pious book' (LL 93). He talked of becoming a clergyman, but his mother was unsympathetic to 'this phase of churchiness'. She refused to share, says Waugh, in this 'hobby'. He then ponders the word, and concludes that by means of this fanciful religiosity, and even more so by his service as an altarboy to an Anglo-Catholic curate at his grandparents' home at Midsomer Norton, Somerset, he had attained glimpses of the religious truth he was to see more clearly later. But that his religious phase should have helped his father settle on Lancing was an unintended consequence that he deplored.

Evelyn believed that the choice of Lancing was one of his father's hasty decisions, made swiftly to avoid debate, and that on the whole it was deleterious. It was made worse by another decision, that Evelyn should not wait until September, the customary beginning date for new entrants, but should start as soon after his admission was secured as possible. Evelyn thus travelled with his father to Sussex on 9 May 1917, to begin his public school career, and to experience for the first time loneliness, hunger – wartime rations were short – home sickness, and social regimentation. Evelyn was a belated novice, an anomaly, an outsider who had to spend two full years being different until he could be accepted. And that is what he eventually managed to do, conforming, becoming enough accepted, even achieving some standing of leadership, yet remaining himself while struggling like all adolescents to find out what that self was. His start at Lancing had been blighted, and he never lost the conviction that the school was not first-rate and was wrong for him, but he took what he could get from it without total submission to its ethos. Again he played the hand he was dealt.

Though Evelyn's school was figuratively a long way from Sherborne, still Alec's presence as symbolic predecessor can be detected in his brother's career at Lancing. Alec's attitude and his style of achievement had to be avoided; Evelyn wanted to have success but not in ways that brought his brother to mind. At sport, avoidance was easy. Cricket he was known to loathe. He could play soccer because Sherborne was a rugby-playing school, and so a born front-row forward (as Alec was) became an indifferent soccer player and (at 5' 5") occasionally a goalkeeper. In the classroom, there was much territory where Alec had never set foot, so Evelyn had such academic achievement as he could attain all to himself. A great problem was that Alec had been a rebel of sorts, so Evelyn's rebellious instincts had to pick their way to avoid Alec's style of rebellion. He did enough to establish his credentials as a rebel while attaining success in conventional modes: house captain, editor of the magazine, president of the debating society. His careful balancing of rebelliousness and orthodoxy became visible when he requested to be allowed to resign from the Officers Training Corps. (Ragging the OTC was almost standard practice at public schools in the later years of the war. Orwell was doing it at Eton at about the same time.) It was pointed out that house captains were not found among resigners from the OTC. If he wanted to make a rebellious gesture, he must pay the freight. He gave up this particular rebellion.

To his adult mind, Evelyn's major act of rebellion at Lancing was the renunciation of religious faith. This was a private act (he did not refuse to go to chapel), witnessed by one friend, Tom Driberg, who was later deliberately chosen to announce Waugh's conversion to Catholicism. Alec had no interest in religion at all, so this was another area that Evelyn had to himself; he made quite conventional use of the opportunity. Though he made a spectacular return to religion in early manhood, he never returned to the aesthetic side of religion or religiosity that had a strong hold upon him in earlier years. As a Catholic, he took a careful uninterest in the aesthetic aspects of his chosen faith. Music meant nothing to him, so there was no temptation there, but visual and literary beauty, so important in his secular life, were denied any place in his acceptance of Catholicism or in his continued practice of the faith. (And in any case, all the handsome churches had been appropriated by the Protestants at the Reformation.) Waugh was a Catholic for whom important aspects of the Counter-Reformation were unnecessary, since he denied for himself the need for any aesthetic aids to devotion.

When Evelyn Waugh began to write his first novel, he found that Alec had imparted to him one further change of direction. He instinctively believed that the natural starting place for his style of autobiographical fiction was school, the school story told from the schoolboy's point of view. *The Loom of Youth* had occupied that territory, and Evelyn was forced into brilliant originality. The first thirteen chapters of *Decline and Fall* are the school story from the point of view of one of those junior masters in the 'underworld' of the prep school common room, and Llanabba Castle School is the tombstone of the school story that had developed with the public school system. But Evelyn still felt he had been thwarted in his natural beginnings as a novelist by his predecessor brother, and in 1945 he began a school story, posthumously published as 'Charles Ryder's Schooldays', set in 1919 and based on his Lancing diaries (CRS 241–92). But the blight remained. They are the most tedious pages of fiction he ever wrote, and he could not finish the story. (When he read his Lancing diaries again in 1956, he was appalled by the 'odious prig' he had been. Yet the diary is the largest literary achievement of the school years, if for no other reason than that it was sustained for over two years and so indicates both the strength

of the autobiographical impulse and the power of literary application that even then he could command.)

The 'two mentors' at Lancing to whom he devotes the seventh
chapter of his autobiography, J. F. Roxburgh, a master at the school,
and Francis Crease, a mildly eccentric aesthete living nearby who
taught Waugh calligraphy, are chosen for prominence in the school
story because each in his very different way offered a model of conformity while displaying qualities of dissent; moreover, each offered
an alternative to the dominant Lancing ideology. Roxburgh left in
Waugh's last year to become the founding headmaster of Stowe
School, an appointment that suggests qualities of commitment to the
system and visionary alternatives to some of its established practices.
His selection of Waugh for individual attention was of great psychological importance, since it gave him confidence to know that this
obviously superior person found him interesting and expected to see
him succeed. Roxburgh excelled and yet differed from the pattern of
the other masters; he proved that independence – perhaps even
stretched to eccentricity – could co-exist with superiority inside the
system. One could be independent and diverge from the common
ways of doing things without having to become an outsider or a
revolutionary. He was a model of conservative dissent, and in this
respect his influence over Waugh was perhaps strongest later in life.

Crease offered a different model of divergence. His achievements
were not great and he did not live by his art, but he lived as an independent artist without belonging to a sub-culture or avant-garde.
His tuition and example taught Waugh that devotion to an art was
lifelong hard work, and that artistic devotion carried with it an
authority that might be a desirable alternative to the kinds of authority
acknowledged by the school and the world it represented. (Again,
this influence is perhaps most apparent in Waugh's later life.) The
adult autobiographer could see that 'At Lancing, though it was a
specifically religious foundation, it was never seriously questioned
that power of one sort or another was the proper aim of life. Success
meant riches or reputation or authority' (LL 155). Crease demurred:
'I always feel that those passing through Lancing have had all I
never had – but it seems sad that somehow or other it so often leads
to the Hotel Metropole at Brighton as an Ideal and not to the Truth
which makes you free'. Crease's criticism of the Lancing ethos did
not originate in a religious attitude, but the older Waugh recognized
its harmony with religion. 'I have often wondered whether my subsequent life would have been very different if at this age I had come

into touch with a real, disciplined, religious contemplative' (LL 155). Thank God he did not, since such a different young manhood must have meant the non-existence of his comic novels.

Waugh left Lancing College on 16 December 1921. He had toughed out the misery and isolation of his early days at the school and had emerged with a respectable list of achievements, though significantly no lifelong friends. In December 1921, he went to Oxford, wrote examinations and was interviewed by dons, and received news a little later that he had been elected a scholar of Hertford College. A person admitted to the university in December would customarily leave school and spend the interval until October working, or perhaps abroad, studying. It was decided, however, that Waugh should go to Oxford at the beginning of Hilary term 1922, the second term of the year. He represented this as another of his father's hasty decisions, again getting Evelyn off on the wrong foot, but there is evidence that he himself was eager to get started and at least concurred in the decision.

Waugh fell in love with Oxford and it is commonly said that he 'mythologized' both the place and his time there, predominantly, of course, in *Brideshead Revisited*. What in fact happened was that he bought into an existing myth and retailed it to perhaps the largest audience it has ever had. 'From the first I regarded Oxford as a place to be inhabited and enjoyed for itself, not as the preparation for anywhere else. . . . At least half the undergraduates were sent to Oxford simply as a place to grow up in' (LL 171). This view of the university as the apotheosis of finishing schools, where scholarly pursuits are really distractions from the real purpose of the place and where the students are the principal educators of each other, is a vulgar distortion of Newman's idea of a university, mingled with other myths, such as that of effortless superiority. Some of its concomitants are the value of excess (drunkenness, noise, fairly extensive financial debt, and occasional violence played their parts in Waugh's story), the value of any unconventional experience, and the elevation of style to a virtue – virtually the only virtue. This is largely the account of his own attitude that Waugh gives in his fiction and in autobiography, and his biographers have found that much of their work, in depicting Waugh's time at Oxford, has to be that of the demythologizer. For his first two terms at least, Waugh was more of an ordinary undergraduate than what might once have been called a 'raver'. He spoke at the Union, smoked a pipe, bought (and at a surprisingly late age learned to ride) a bicycle, tried to write a poem to enter for the Newdigate Prize, was elected secretary of the Hertford Debating Society, and passed History Previous, the preliminary examination, allowing him to proceed towards his Finals in the Modern History School ('Modern' History at Oxford is not-ancient-history, that is, not Classical). 'But all the time', he wrote, 'it seemed to me there was a quintessential Oxford which I knew and loved from afar and intended to find'. The quintessential Oxford that Waugh found in his second year was inimical to any real engagement with Modern History, and so an urgent concern of his autobiographical account is to explain and vindicate his *de facto* withdrawal from scholarship. To see the university as 'a place to grow up in' and 'not as the preparation for anywhere else' is really enough to explain his decision, but Waugh's imagination presented him with a living allegory of All-That-Is-Wrong-With-Modern-History in the now notorious form of his tutor, C. R. M. F. Cruttwell, Dean (later Principal) and senior Fellow in Modern History of Hertford College.

'Hate at first sight' is the explanation usually given for Waugh's attitude towards Cruttwell, but in fact the hatred grew slowly and then burst. As a freshman, Waugh expressed no antagonism in his letters towards Cruttwell, and he did get through History Previous without trouble. But he saw little of Cruttwell during his first two terms, and Cruttwell's assumption of the role of his tutor (in Michaelmas – autumn – term 1923) for his final schools coincided with his discovery of 'quintessential Oxford', with results familiar to most students and tutors, at Oxford and elsewhere. Waugh tried to do the minimum of work to be able to stay at the university, while his tutor with mounting exasperation found himself overseeing the scholarly progress of a determined shirker. Personal antagonisms added the upper storeys to this solid foundation for dislike.

In the development of his literary life, the Cruttwell imbroglio was far more significant than he wanted the world to know, or perhaps wanted to believe himself. The most obvious sign of its importance is that Waugh pursued a vendetta with Cruttwell through four novels and four short stories. In each of them a minor character of dubious morals and/or base employment is given the name 'Cruttwell', and apparently this caused C. R. M. F. Cruttwell to wince at the announcement of a new book by his former pupil. This onomastic torment was far more effective than the other teases dreamed up by Waugh and his friend Terence Greenidge, who imputed bestiality to the Dean, canine specifically, leading them to bark outside his rooms and once to leave a stuffed dog in his way in hopes that he would

ravish it. It is not certain that this fine specimen of undergraduate
humour was ever explained to Cruttwell, but he was fully aware in
later years of Waugh's abiding vindictiveness towards him.

'Hate at first sight' really resorts to mystery to explain the antagonism, and to find the explanation in a tutor's attempts to control a
wayward pupil is only a beginning. The generational sensitivity that
Waugh felt did play a large part, however. Cruttwell was still in his
thirties when Waugh knew him, and had served in the First World
War. 'He was, I now recognize, a wreck of the war in which he had
served gallantly' (LL 174). He was therefore of the generation that
Waugh suspected would not step aside for his own, and that had
the unimpeachable and therefore impotently resented authority of
having been under fire. And Cruttwell was not, like most of that
obstacular generation, blithely unaware of the barrier he presented
to the young. He was actively trying to get the young to read their
books and write their essays, supported always by the implied threat
of rustication, expulsion from what Waugh had found 'a Kingdom of
Cokayne'.

Waugh the autobiographer saw Cruttwell as permanently stained
or polluted by his wartime experience. 'It was as though he had
never cleaned himself of the muck of the trenches' (LL 174). And
there was a corresponding effect on his attitude as an historian. 'His
conspectus of history was narrowed to the few miles of the Low
Countries where he had fought...' (LL 174). In other words, as is
true of most modern historians, he was a specialist, and to Waugh
that meant he was incapable of large views, probably uninterested
in the subject that came first for historians, in Waugh's opinion: the
nature and development of civilization. He gives an account of Cruttwell returning 'grossly drunk' from dining out that also functions as
a symbolical statement of the man's incapacity as an historian: he
'was sometimes to be seen as St Mary's struck midnight, feeling his
way blindly round the railings of the Radcliffe Camera believing
them to be those of the college' (LL 174). The Radcliffe Camera contains the principal undergraduate reading room for history.

Cruttwell's antithesis was Edward Gibbon. Gibbon's *History* was a
'set book' for the School of Modern History in Waugh's day and for
long after,[3] and Gibbon was perhaps the only part of the syllabus
that he read with pleasure and profit. He read the autobiography,
too, as he reveals in *Rossetti*, when writing of William Morris's education: 'Like many wise people before and after him, he found the
life there pitiably disappointing....it was still very much like the

Oxford of Gibbon's time ... the dons, idlier [sic] than those of today and more widely ignorant, were no less tedious ...' (R 79). To find his own Oxford years similar, particularly as regards dons, to those of Gibbon was a great comfort, and Gibbon persisted in Waugh's memory as the true historian, the positive alternative to Cruttwell and his ilk. In 1951, Waugh commissioned Martin Battersby to paint for him a *trompe l'oeil* picture to show emblematically his 'life's work' (LWC 118). The picture is filled with objects and documents alluding to Waugh's writing, prominent among them something that looks like a beer-pull and is in fact a reliquary containing a piece of the rope that hanged Edmund Campion (alluding to Waugh's biography of 1935). Just to the right of this is an oval framed picture of 'The Radcliffe Library, Oxford', behind which is tucked a smaller oval picture of 'Edward Gibbon'. In the emblematic scheme of the picture, this is obviously a reference to *Decline and Fall*, but there is considerable 'redundancy' in using this combination of images simply to refer to Waugh's first novel. He said that the picture was to be 'works not life and habit', so the allusion is not simply to his undergraduate years. Long before he put it into words in his autobiography, he summarizes emblematically his attitude towards history and claims as his forebear the greatest English *writer* of history.

Waugh's account of his Oxford career is mainly devoted to the friends and acquaintances he made there, and of one of them, Douglas Woodruff, he wrote in a manner relevant to the present concerns: history and historians. Calling Woodruff 'ageless', Waugh could imagine him at home in any period of European history, 'the Wandering Christian'.

> With heavy head and hooded eyes, he drew in Johnsonian diction on a treasury of curious historical lore which gave the impression of personal reminiscence rather than research; I have since observed him abroad gazing at some famous historical site, a space overbuilt, or a monument reconstructed and totally unrecognizable to the modern eye, with a peculiar air of familiarity as though he had known it well centuries before. ... a sober man who found no one and nothing beneath his notice and very little indeed to command his respect. ... If Cruttwell had been cast in his image I might have made a scholar. (LL 186)

Woodruff had what Cruttwell not only lacked but could have seen no need for: the power of the true writer to enter the past imaginatively, the power of literary art. All his writing life, Waugh maintained a sense of identification with the greatest literary artist among the English historians, and if he himself did not make a scholar he at least made novels in a Gibbonian spirit, 'Nothing beneath his notice and very little indeed to command his respect'.

All of the friends commemorated in *A Little Learning* are men, for Oxford in the early 1920s was 'a male community'.[4] What is not admitted in the autobiography, however, is that in his last two years at Oxford Waugh's sexual interests became homosexual. This is of small importance in his literary life until we come to *Brideshead Revisited*, where is given the only sympathetic account of homoeroticism. Elsewhere in the writings, unambiguous homosexuality is treated uniformly as a negative or at least highly dubious characteristic in men, and in Waugh's letters and recorded conversation there is a definite strain of homophobia. Autobiography for Waugh was no place for confession. In his later spiritual life, it is likely that he saw homosexuality as a grave sin, and therefore as conduct to be reprobated. He no doubt reached a spiritual accommodation about his homosexual past, but chose not to uncover that past in his writing. (He did refer to his homosexual loves in, for instance, letters to Nancy Mitford.)

The only relationship of any length or standing that was part of Waugh's homosexual phase was with Alistair Graham, who is referred to in the autobiography as 'Hamish Lennox'. Waugh's great 'stamping ground' at Oxford was a club called The Hypocrites (club rooms above a bicycle shop in St Aldate's), and Tom Driberg, Waugh's schoolfriend (who wrote posthumously published memoirs describing his careers as socialist politician and promiscuous homosexual; Waugh is silent about both) remembered The Hypocrites as fundamentally a gay hangout. It does not seem to have been so for Waugh. His homosexual phase seems to have been a mechanism of accommodation and qualification to fit the conditions he found to predominate in the Oxford world to which he wished to belong. In fact at Oxford he seems rather like one of those men who is undeviatingly heterosexual before and after a term of imprisonment, but who becomes homosexual in jail.

Waugh was introduced to The Hypocrites by his eccentric Hertford friend Terence Greenidge, and his membership was sustained through his allegiance in bohemian-aesthetic matters to the famous Etonian generation of the early 1920s that had a considerable effect on Oxford undergraduate life during his last two years at the university.

Heavy drinking, as an easily attained rebellious and bohemian activity, played a large part in Waugh's Hypocrite goings-on, though this was not so for Harold Acton, the most important of the Etonian group in his effect on Waugh.

Acton became a lifelong friend, albeit somewhat distant since he lived mainly in Italy. Much older in experience and self-possession than his coevals, he went from Eton (where he had been a leading figure in the Society of the Arts) to Oxford with the intention of promoting aesthetic modernism (T. S. Eliot, the Sitwells, Chekhov, Diagilev, Gertrude Stein). The title of the magazine he founded, *Oxford Broom* – it ran for four numbers – indicates his ambition for a clean sweep. Waugh quickly became a major supporter, and for a fairly brief period was in the modernist camp. Acton was perfectly positioned to supplant Crease's influence over Waugh, just as he was displacing the Georgian literary tastes that Waugh associated with his father, but somehow the sweeping away of Crease never quite happened. In fact, by providing much opportunity for Waugh to publish his drawings and engravings, Acton simultaneously undercut his own efforts to divert him from the path of Crease.

Having in effect given up the study of Modern History, Waugh did not become idle at Oxford. He did a lot of journalism, writing, and editing while devoting his most serious efforts to drawing and engraving. Acton's effect on him thus fulfilled only part of the intention. If he got Waugh away from Georgian influences and introduced him to the novels of Ronald Firbank (a marked though limited influence), he was nevertheless unable to bring him to devote his main energies to writing. Acton's main effect on the non-literary Waugh was in the matter of Victorian art, of which he was a devotee. The earliest credit for Waugh's first book, on Rossetti, may go to Acton; he was pro-Victorian when it was quite unfashionable, but *Rossetti* is pretty much a dead end. Waugh willed it so. Harold Acton is the person in Waugh's literary life who influenced him most, but 'most' is not 'a lot'.

Two interesting stories that Waugh published in undergraduate magazines are included in *Evelyn Waugh, Apprentice*. The titles suggest similarity, but they are very different: 'Edward of Unique Achievement' and 'Antony, Who Sought Things That Were Lost'. Edward's achievement is to get away with the murder of his history tutor, a man remarkably unlike C. R. M. F. Cruttwell. A large and rather 'redundant' element in his story is female infidelity: the wife of the Warden of the college has been having an affair with the

murdered don. 'Antony' makes woman's instability the fulcrum of
the tale, and it is the rather eerie predictive element in the story that
is impressive, not the stylistic influence of James Branch Cabell that
Waugh points out (LL 189).

Published in *Oxford Broom* (June 1923), 'Antony' takes place in the
Italian dukedom of St Romeiro in a revolutionary period following
the death of Napoleon and the post-Napoleonic reaction. The young
count, very beautiful and of proud family, is called 'Antony who
sought things that were lost' because 'he always seemed to be seeking in the future for what had gone before'. He is a romantic, a nostalgic, hoping for things that once existed and have now vanished
from the world. He seems to have found one such thing in the Lady
Elizabeth, his betrothed who reciprocates his intense love for her.
During a revolt against the Duke, Cazarin, leader of the uprising,
remembers that ten years before Antony was imprisoned for liberal
sentiments and that Lady Elizabeth chose and was permitted to share
his imprisonment. Seeking out the turnkey of their jail, Cazarin
learns what happened to them.

They pass an idyllic honeymoon in their cell, sleeping on straw
and eating bread and water. Many weeks pass and Elizabeth's love
turns to weariness while Antony remains in love and sorrows, seeking for what is no more. Elizabeth's weariness now turns to hatred.
More time passes, the hatred increases, but there also comes 'desire
for the love of that man that was lost to her'. She asks the turnkey,
who assures her that she is still beautiful, if she may look at her
reflection in his eyes: 'and there was desire in their eyes ... and so the
Lady Elizabeth, who had known the white arms of Antony, loved
this turnkey who was ugly and low born'. The turnkey promises
her, without her asking, that she may share his lodgings, 'And she
cried, "O my love, return to me soon." ' Antony, helplessly weak-
ened, has watched these happenings impotently, but after the turnkey's departure, he finds the strength to strangle Elizabeth with his
own chain. The jailer returns, sees what has happened, and leaves
for ever, throwing the key into the moat: 'he had known love there'
(EWA 128–31).

Elizabeth's idealism has crumbled while Antony's survives. She
hates Antony (perhaps because his idealism rebukes her) but she
loves the memory of his love. The intellectual surprise of this story is
that Elizabeth really does love the 'ugly and low born' turnkey, and
the emotion is not simply a projection onto him, though projection
may be its origin. It does not occur to her to trade her favours for

freedom. Her nostalgia for the love she knew with Antony is a perverse form of idealism, quite separated from his person and apparently independent of the person to whom she turns to recreate it.
This is a startlingly original analysis of what love could be, and when
we think of *A Handful of Dust*, another story of an Anthony who
sought things that were lost, we have to conclude yet again that
the relationship of life and art is a complex one. That novel could
never had existed without Waugh's divorce, but it seems irrefutable
that the analysis of love's possibilities that it presents, and specifically the idea that a woman could cease to love a completely lovable
husband, and turn to *and sincerely love* an 'ugly and low born' non-
entity, existed in Waugh's mind when he was an undergraduate,
long before he knew he would really need it, so to speak. Part of the
intense pain he felt when his wife abandoned him came from the
realization that a nightmare he had earlier imagined had now come
true.

Waugh took his Finals in Modern History in Trinity term 1924. His
achievement in the examinations disproved for him another myth in
which he had invested: 'there was a prevalent illusion that a man of
parts could idle for eight terms and at the end of it sit up with black
coffee and master the required subjects in a few weeks' (LL 172).
Oxford in those days awarded four classes of Honours degree. A
First was excellence, a Second respectability, a Third mediocrity,
while a Fourth was seen as the mark of native brilliance and a dash
of *chutzpah*, supported by no scholarly effort whatever. Waugh
hoped for a Second, but he was placed in the Third class, and so
regretted the time thrown away in that last spring term. In his case,
moreover, there was a complication. Nine terms of residence were
required for his degree. Having come up a term late, he had completed only eight terms when he did Finals. He expected one more
term of residence, and that to be, since no work at all was required
or contemplated, a term of untrammelled pleasures. The Third
changed all that. Arthur Waugh, himself the recipient of a mediocre
degree, did not consider the extra term's fees a fair exchange, and
Evelyn had to agree. It was the worst of both worlds; he got no
degree, but 'got a Third'.

In the life of a writer of Waugh's formation, as in Dickens's, little
experience goes to waste. His failure to become what the Emperor
Seth was later to call a 'Bachelor of the Arts' of Oxford University
was just as useful to his writing career as a degree would have been.
Seen from one angle, he failed at Modern History, but from another

history and historians became a major strand in his conception of himself as a writer. As his autobiography demonstrates, and as he several times stated, he gained most from Oxford in friendships. Michael Davie puts the Oxford friends into three groups: 'rich, aristocratic friends, among them Lord Elmley and his brother Hugh Lygon [The Duggan brothers, Alfred and Hubert, stepsons of Lord Curzon, should be included here]; intellectual friends, including Peter Quennell, Richard Pares, Robert Byron, David Talbot-Rice, Christopher Hollis, Claud Cockburn, Anthony Powell and Cyril Connolly [Some of these were merely acquaintances at Oxford who became friends later, such as Anthony Powell. Henry Yorke, who became the novelist Henry Green, should be included in this group. Quennell and Connolly were acquaintances who became friends later but whose friendship became for various reasons compromised. Waugh sometimes seemed affable towards them, sometimes not. They were wary of him. Claud Cockburn, a relation of Waugh's, was politically of the Left: 'my communist cousin']; 'and undesirable friends, the "satanic" Basil Murray and the "incorrigibly homosexual" Brian Howard' [Waugh had presumably been corrigibly homosexual]. Above all he met Harold Acton . . . ' (D 158). Peter Rodd, who became Nancy Mitford's husband, should perhaps appear in all of these categories, aristocratic, intellectual, and undesirable, but he deserves inclusion in Waugh's story because, like several of those named above, he was a model, in this case the original of Basil Seal. (The models come predominantly from the undesirables and objects of dislike.) Waugh's female friends were post-Oxford, of course, in conformity with his description of the place as in effect all-male in his time.

When Waugh left Oxford, most of the things that would interest him as a novelist were planted in his mind. Religion is the great exception, but its appearance was reserved for the fairly near future. His joy for most of his life, he said, was in the works of man rather than of nature (LL 154) and the people he found interesting were those of the strata of society just below and just above his own. His downward interest stopped with the middle-middle class but extended upwards into the upper classes as far as he could push it. He therefore incurs charges of snobbery, and it is true that in life, as his army batman recalled, 'he was a bit fond of the Honourables' (2S 27). The picture of the British aristocracy that emerges from his fiction, however, is Thackerayan in its variety of stupidity. His education showed him that the kinds of life he had enjoyed and hated living were the kinds he would write about; with the exception of *Helena* (exceptional in so many ways) his fiction is totally true to the basically empirical cast of his mind. What the biographer finds little advanced notice of, however, and what therefore has to be covered by the mystical term 'genius', is his comic vision. Until the appearance of *Decline and Fall*, nothing he had written indicated its existence, and there is evidence that it surprised, and eventually displeased its owner.

2
Pain as is Seldom Seen in Men: 1924–30

After going down from the University he was for a time a student at Heatherly's Art School and for a short time a master at a private school.

Evelyn Waugh's life from the end of his student days at Oxford to the publication of his first novel will have for many readers a quality of *déjà lu*. The world of *Decline and Fall* is in large part the world that Waugh inhabited in those years, though the book has an economy and speed of action, with lurches from catastrophe to triumph and back, that are art's blissful alternative to the banal ploddings of life. The major unrecognized element of Waugh's life in this period (to which the fiction alerts one only by its mere existence) is writing. He left Oxford without a degree and passed several years in dead-end jobs or attempting unsuitable careers. He continued his avoidance of the literary world of his father and brother; he seemed not to want to be a writer. And yet he wrote, and wrote a lot. He started a novel, *The Temple at Thatch*, in 1924. To his father's pleasure and no doubt surprise, he became suddenly enthusiastic about the nineteenth-century group of English painters calling themselves the Pre-Raphaelite Brotherhood, and wrote a long essay about them, *P.R.B.*, that was privately published, with a spatter of misprints, by Alistair Graham (who was 'trying out' a career as a printer of fine editions) in 1926. Also in 1926, Waugh's short story 'The Balance' was published in an anthology, *Georgian Stories*, edited by Alec Waugh. In 1927, a commissioned short story, 'The Tutor's Tale', was published in a collection called *The New Decameron* and Waugh also wrote the introduction to *Thirty-Four Decorative Designs by Francis Crease*. The publishers Kegan Paul were putting out a series of short books called *Today and Tomorrow*. In 1926 Waugh offered to do one called *Noah; or the Future of Intoxication*. Kegan Paul accepted, though no contract was made. Waugh finished the book in 1927, but it was rejected and never revived. In that same year, Anthony Powell had improved the acquaintanceship begun at Oxford into a close friend-ship in London. Waugh showed Powell *P.R.B.*, and Powell interest-ed Duckworth, the publisher for whom he worked, in the idea of a biography by Waugh of D. G. Rossetti, the Victorian painter and poet, whose centenary fell in 1928. The book was commissioned with an advance of £50, and published in 1928. Later that year came the publication of *Decline and Fall*. In about four years, the would-not-be writer had written three books (none of them very long, admittedly), the beginning of a fourth, and three shorter pieces. And only one of the five items that were published was privately printed. When, after being sacked from his second teaching job, he wrote in his diary, 'It seems to me the time has arrived to set about being a man of letters', he was probably being facetious, but in fact he had already travelled a long way towards becoming a professional writer. He knew, consciously or not, that he had to write his way out of failure and mediocrity, and he had known it ever since Oxford.

In what was in effect the summer vacation after he did his Finals, Waugh took part in the making of a silent film, *The Scarlet Woman*, of which three copies still exist. Terence Greenidge, then a student at RADA, was the prime mover of the project, but Waugh participated extensively and energetically. He wrote the scenario, played two of the parts, recruited Alec to play another (in drag) and got his father's eager permission to shoot scenes at Underhill. The quintessentially undergraduate character of *The Scarlet Woman* is indicated by its plot, 'as simple as it was grotesque' (SY 55). The Pope has decided to bring about the immediate conversion of England to Rome by enfor-cing the conversion of the Prince of Wales by means of a seductress, played before she became famous by Elsa Lanchester. Others of the Pope's agents included the Catholic dean of Balliol, the well-known 'Sligger' Urquhart, one of the roles that Waugh took for himself.

It is easy to overstress the importance of the film in Waugh's development as a writer, but it does offer two reliable indications of future direction. The ambiguously hostile interest in Catholicism accurately reflects one aspect of his own pre-conversion attitude, an attitude that is Gibbonian in its fascination and irony. And cinema can take credit for one of Waugh's narrational techniques that developed from his use of film analogies in 'The Balance'. In *Vile Bodies* he advanced into using sequences of short scenes with rapid 'cutting' from one to another, a technique used again as late as *Sword of Honour* after the Second World War. But it was not *The Scarlet Woman* that was responsible for his adoption of the method. His

interest in silent film is well documented before Greenidge conceived of his production, and 'The Balance' and *Vile Bodies* would
have revealed the influence of movie techniques if the film had
never been made.

Waugh's first thought for his career after Oxford was art. In the
autumn and early winter of 1924 he lived at home, still receiving an
allowance from his father, and made a daily journey across London
to Heatherly's Art School, where he practised mainly drawing. For a
while he persisted and his drawing improved, but what was to be
the demon of his life – boredom – got its hold on him, and his leisure
hours began to supplant his studies in importance. Alistair Graham
had gone abroad, a separation that seems to have ended Waugh's
love affair with him, though the friendship continued for several
years. Waugh found new friends in London, and his diary details a
round of mostly impromptu parties and activities. The life of poverty, chastity and obedience begun on 19 September 1924 (D 179)
hardly lasted beyond his twenty-first birthday on 29 October. His
attendance at Heatherly's became intermittent, and his diary begins
to sound ominous notes. 'In the week following the last entry.... I
learned that it is not possible to lead a gay life and to draw well' (D
183). Oxford was a temptation since many of his friends were still at
the university. A triumphant return on 12 November 1924 led to further weekends and soon he was one of the *revenants*, familiar figures
'who cannot at once sever the cord uniting them to the university
and haunt it for years to come' (LL 213). Heatherly's could hold him
no longer.

His next foray was into fine printing, another defeat handled with
wry irony in the autobiography. He had been impressed by the
work of James Guthrie, who owned the Pear Tree Press in Sussex,
but immediately after Arthur had paid a £25 premium to apprentice
his second son to Guthrie, Evelyn found the whole enterprise to be
quite unsuitable. Guthrie refused to return the money 'with the irrefutable argument that it was already spent' (LL 216).

In the autobriography, Waugh makes this pointless loss serve as a
climacteric in his financial relationship with his father. He claims
that at a settlement conference he proposed, and Arthur evidently
agreed, that his father should pay his debts while he would give up
his allowance and thenceforth earn his own living. In the diary,
however, the agreement with his father is recorded on 1 July 1925,
and so it seems that Evelyn advanced the date to make it appear that
he was quite independent as he set off a-schoolmastering, and that

the despair he was to describe in subsequent pages was the more comprehensible in that he was quite without resources, apart from his salary.

To earn his own living,

There was only one profession open to a man of my qualifications. However incomplete one's education, however dissolute one's habits, however few the respectable guarantors whom one could quote, the private schools [that is the preparatory schools, like Heath Mount] lay open to anyone who spoke without an accent and had been through the conventional routine of public school and university. (LL 215)

On 15 December 1924 he had put himself on the books of Truman and Knightley, scholastic agents, finding jobs for private school-teachers and teachers for schools with vacancies. On 5 January 1925 he went to meet Mr Banks of Arnold House, Denbighshire. 'He is going to pay me £160 to teach little boys for him for a year. I think this will be bloody but most useful to a man as poor as I' (D 195).

He spent the interval before his departure for North Wales in a round of social activities, chiefly dividing his time between old and new friends of his heart, Alistair Graham and Olivia Plunket Greene. Alistair and Waugh went about together in London, visited Alistair's mother near Warwick, and went over to Oxford. When Alistair was away, Waugh pursued his friendship with the family of the Plunket Greenes. He claimed that his affection was for the whole family – the father was estranged and lived apart – and that he focused it 'upon the only appropriate member', Olivia (LL 216). His diary has rather miserable accounts of their relationship; on his part, he says, it was 'doting but unaspiring', on hers 'astringent'. He certainly had sexual aspirations, but Olivia did not find him sexually attractive. It was a hopeless, one-sided love affair that worked better as a friend-ship. It took him some time to realize that Olivia was utterly wrong for him, a depressant where he needed encouragement, but the effect of the whole family on him was long-lasting.

It is important that both Alistair Graham and Olivia Plunket Greene were Catholics. Alistair was a recent convert. At this stage, Waugh kept his emotional and intellectual distance from Catholicism, though he several times went to mass with Alistair. Olivia too was a convert. Not very long before Waugh in 1930 asked her to find a priest to instruct him, Olivia had become a Catholic in the wake of her mother's conversion. She was a highly emotional, even mystical believer, not at all the kind Waugh was to become. He gives no attention to Olivia's religion in the diary, and his appearance at mass with Alistair seems to have been little more than keeping him company. The example of these two beloved people was nonetheless waiting to make its contribution in his eventual progress towards the Catholic Church.

On 23 January 1925 Waugh made the rail journey to North Wales, incompetently and reluctantly herding a group of small boys in red caps back to school. Instead of being 'one of those wholly disreputable institutions in which the country abounded' and which would have suited his mood at the time, he found Arnold House 'depressingly well conducted' (LL 220). It was, as Martin Stannard says of both the prep schools at which Waugh was an 'usher' – to use the term he affected – 'perfectly normal.... The school was quite ordinary. It was Waugh who was so strange' (1S 109).

His approach to ushering was to continue as far as possible to live as he had lived in London after leaving Oxford. He worked on his designs, producing for instance a woodcut bookplate for Olivia. He continued to write, working on *The Temple at Thatch* and later on the short story, 'The Balance'. He kept up his diary and a steady correspondence. The school's Head Boy, Derek Verschoyle, recalled that when Waugh supervised prep, he left the boys to themselves and wrote. If anyone asked, he said that he was writing a History of the Eskimos (SY 61). He deviated as far as possible from the ushering norm. For most of the week he wore plus fours and a turtleneck. He was incompetent and uninterested in supervising games, a point in his favour according to Verschoyle. He records in his diary several academic humiliations, giving the impression that his teaching was utterly incompetent. It was likely not much, if at all, below average; the headmaster apparently complained about his work but Verschoyle found him amiably accomodating.

He took riding lessons, a recreation he was to pursue more keenly later in life. And he caroused. The diaries record about thirty visits to the local pub and to posher establishments in Rhyl and Colwyn Bay ('the Naples of the North') during the two terms of Waugh's career at Arnold House. Waugh was the master of the revels; partygoing and drinking had been his habitual evening activities in London, and in the much reduced world of Llandulas, Denbighshire he followed the pattern, taking one, some or all of the other four ushers along with him to Mrs Roberts' public house or to the Queen's Hotel, Colwyn. Episodes of drunkenness are recorded. Orders for sherry and whisky were despatched to Oxford. And in conformity with another lifelong pattern, Waugh spent money on extravagancies and luxuries to cheer himself up, although – as with drink – the later effects were often depressing, requiring further expenditures. He was not happy though sometimes hilarious. Arnold House was a place of exile, long weeks away from the world of London.

The great power at the school was the head's wife, Mrs Banks; she too was unimpressed by Waugh. The combined disapproval of head and head's wife brought him to contemplate resigning, but he did return after the April vacation and so was there to meet a new usher, W. R. B. Young, destined for immortality as Captain Edgar Grimes.

The vacation was spent partly in London, where money was extravagantly spent and where there were visits to theatres and numerous parties and where, on the evening of 6 April 1925 Waugh and his friend Matthew Ponsonby, son of an MP, a former Under Secretary of State for Foreign Affairs, were arrested in Oxford Street and locked up on charges of being drunk and incapable. Matthew's father came and bailed out his son 'but rather ill-naturedly, I thought, refused to do anything for me'. Happenings like this did nothing to discourage the feelings of persecution that were apt to crop up in Waugh's mind. He was released after several hours in 'an awful little cell just like a urinal' and next day was fined fifteen and sixpence by the magistrate (D 206). It can be confidently assumed that if Mrs Banks heard of this exploit it was only much, much later. Waugh's readers were to come across it, highly embroidered as was his way, in *Brideshead Revisited*.

On his return to servitude in Denbighshire, he wrote in his diary, 'There is a new usher called Young in Watson's place. I think that my finances have never been so desperate or my spirits so depressed' (D 211). One astonishing sentence in the diary reads: 'I debate the simple paradoxes of suicide and achievement, work out the scheme for a new book and negotiate with the man Young to buy a revolver from him'. But there was good news. Evelyn had heard from Alec that the translator of Proust, C. K. Scott-Moncrieff, then living in Pisa, wanted a secretary. Evelyn was apparently in line for the job. At the beginning of June 1925 he heard that the job was his. He gave his resignation to Banks, who accepted it with a disturbing lack of hesitation. But Waugh was happy. In the auto-biography he gives this as the moment when he sent his novel, *The*

Temple at Thatch, to Harold Acton. Then fate showed its true colours. There was no job with Scott-Moncrieff and Acton delivered a report on *The Temple* that caused Waugh to feed it to the flames. He had apparently failed to get hold of Young's revolver so he attempted suicide by swimming out to sea. Maybe. His own account – it forms the superb peroration of *A Little Learning* – deftly sows doubt about his intentions while making them seem perfectly clear.

> I went down alone to the beach with my thoughts full of death. I took off my clothes and began swimming out to sea. Did I really intend to drown myself? That certainly was in my mind and I left a note with my clothes, the quotation from Euripides about the sea which washes away all human ills. I went to the trouble of verifying it, accents and all, from the school text. . . . At my present age I cannot tell how much real despair and act of will, how much play-acting, prompted the excursion. (LL 229)

He swam slowly out 'but before I reached the point of no return, the Shropshire Lad was disturbed by a smart on the shoulder'. He had been stung; the sea was full of jellyfish. He turned back to the beach and tore up his classical quotation, 'Then I climbed the sharp hill that led to all the years ahead'.

It is a wonderful passage, the work of a great comedian, and it makes a superb ending – both ending, or anticlimax, and beginning – for this first volume of autobiography that would have no sequel. Yet Waugh's own doubts about his motivation seem to authorize biographer's doubts.[1] The suicide, thwarted by jellyfish is so right, comically ironic, that one wonders if it might not be *too* right, if the episode has not been beautifully embroidered by a master to be the perfect termination of one volume of autobiography and to lead in to the second that was never written.

An almost forensic study of Waugh's diary and the other documents relevant to this incident has convinced me that there never was a premeditated attempt at suicide (not that Waugh ever quite said there was). Such a thing fits neither the chronology nor the emotional actuality of the time. But since I have neither the space nor the wilfulness to drag the reader through the mass of details needed to make the case, it will have to stand here as my unproven assertion.

The difficulties of fitting a suicide attempt to the diary's account of those days of July 1925 vanish if one rejects the elements of premeditation, such as the quotation from Euripides, that I believe to be superb Wavian embroidery. What did happen was probably far less important at the time it occurred than it is in *A Little Learning*. It became important only as Waugh worked over his memories, looking for an ending for his first autobiographical volume. My guess as to what in fact happened is that he went for a swim one night after his double blow of bad news on 1 July. It came into his mind while he was in the water that he could swim on and not return: the Shropshire Lad solution. He may have been stung by a jellyfish – such a good agent of inglorious retreat – or have remembered (in 1925 or 1963) the possibility of there being jellyfish. Anyway he retreated. And the rest is literature, a great improvement on reality and a fine termination for *A Little Learning*.

Suicide was often in Waugh's thoughts while he was at Arnold House. After he had destroyed *The Temple at Thatch*, he worked on a 'novel' that eventually emerged as the long short-story, 'The Balance'. Its principal subject is an attempted suicide. It is autobiographical, modernist in being formally experimental, and to the reader who can look at it with Waugh's future writings in mind, a fascinating mixture of predictive and dead-end practices. Several events in the story are documented items from Waugh's life. The protagonist, Adam Doure, is a bibliophile who has to sell his beloved collection cheap. (Waugh at Oxford had auctioned his books.) He is in love with the beautiful Imogen Quest, who does not much care for him. He attends an art school but is unhappy with his work. Adam is an Oxford *revenant* and has an extensive acquaintance there of aesthetes, eccentrics, the sober and the stupefied. Most autobiographically of all, he seems to be going nowhere in his life and is profoundly unhappy. Waugh was undoubtedly dramatizing his own miseries, but it is probably not true that a premeditated suicide attempt led him to make an attempted suicide the main event of 'The Balance'. The diary shows that on 5 May Waugh had worked out 'the scheme for a new book'. On 28 May, 'I have quite suddenly received inspiration about my book. I am making the first chapter a cinema film. I honestly think that it is going to be rather good'. This can only refer to 'The Balance', and I submit that with scheme and inspiration achieved, Waugh had more likely than not decided that the story was to include as its main event an attempted suicide before he took his swim one night in (probably) July. After all, the sentence in which he announced that he had his 'scheme' also comprised his debating of 'the simple paradoxes of suicide and achievement' and his attempt to buy a revolver from Young. The likelihood surely must be that 'The Balance' from the first was to involve its protagonist in suicide or a suicide attempt. The diary's references to suicide are not reproduced in the autobiography. Despite references to unhappiness (beneath hilarity) and 'deep self-pity', the suicide possibility is not prepared for the reader in advance of the attempt in *A Little Learning*.

Waugh finished 'The Balance' on 26 August 1925, slightly less than a month after leaving North Wales. The manuscript has not survived, so there is no possibility of knowing which parts were written after his return. The story, entitled in full 'The Balance: A Yarn of the Good Old Days of Broad Trousers and High Necked Jumpers', was published in 1926 in an anthology of *Georgian Stories* edited by Alec Waugh. Thereafter its author studiously avoided it and presumably hoped his readers would too. It was never reprinted in any collection of Waugh's, and he seems never again to have referred to it.

The possible reasons for the implicit distaste Waugh felt for the story are manifold. It is autobiographical, but without the devices of distancing that he would later employ to control the revelatory element in his always fundamentally autobiographical fiction. When he converted to Catholicism, suicide changed its appearance for Waugh. A grave sin not exposed to hostile criticism gave the story an unacceptable moral flavour. The strikingly modernistic narratological experimentalism of the story dated rapidly and soon seemed adolescent. And the story was indebted to Alec and to Chapman and Hall for its appearance in *Georgian Stories*; it was virtually a product of the family trade and there was an inevitable suspicion of nepotism about its publication. Greatest of all, the literary difficulty on which the story founders thematically is that which has plagued tales of youthful suicide ever since *Young Werther*: how to make it seem that the protagonist is not killing himself for childish and risible reasons. Adam Doure's problems are Evelyn Waugh's problems. He believed he was at the end of his tether, but the reader, of the diaries or 'The Balance', might well respond as Waugh imagined Olivia Plunket Greene would have responded to his attempted suicide, with 'a sharp recall to good sense', like the sting of a jellyfish (LL 230). The fine irony of the suicide attempt in the autobiography prompts the suggestion that 'The Balance' could have been a real success if Waugh had been able to write it as comedy. From that perspective, everything in the story that seems adolescently portentous would have disappeared, but Waugh was not yet mature enough to rise to a comic view of his sorrows. He was soon to demonstrate that he did possess that power, and soon thereafter he was to learn what real sorrow was.

Yet the neglect Waugh wished upon 'The Balance' was too harsh a judgement. Some of its elements are truly accomplished and reveal literary skills that he would employ extensively later in his career. For instance, it has quite a lot of 'unsupported' dialogue – pure dialogue, unsupported by narrative, such as might come from a play or a screenplay, but without stage directions – and such dialogue was to be a stylistic hallmark of the earlier Waugh novels. In the first two parts of the 'Conclusion' Adam recalls his suicide attempt of the night before and the childhood accident that first led him to think about 'the struggle for detachment' of which the suicide attempt was, it seems, the latest manifestation. These sections are written in an analytic prose of great subtlety but in this case it is a style that he employed most extensively in the later stages of his career, beginning with *Work Suspended* (written 1939, published 1942). The rapid series of vignettes depicting Adam's progress around Oxford looking for someone to dine with for his 'Farewell Blind' displays the caricature style of social observation that was to become a striking feature of *Vile Bodies*.

The experimental elements of 'The Balance' all derive from Waugh's flash of inspiration to make the story 'a cinema film'. Since films were silent in those days, Waugh was able to add to the rapid 'cutting' (or changes of scene) 'captions' that saved him a lot of time otherwise needed for scene setting. The chief innovation, however, was to incorporate into the narrative the comments of a number of characters in the cinema audience 'watching the film'. Principal among them are Gladys and Ada, 'cook and house-parlormaid from a small house in Earl's Court' (EWA 156). It is a measure of Waugh's rapidly increasing literary sophistication that he realized that Gladys and Ada (and the other voices, one of which seems to be the narrator's) were a distraction from what he meant his reader to focus upon. Gladys and Ada are utter stereotypes, working-class women allowed no vestige of individuality or worth. Waugh cannot see them as having any interest as characters, but their chatter about the 'film' of Adam Doure's life undoubtedly distances his situation, so much that the reader is at risk of never becoming involved in it. Waugh's realization that his device was an impediment to his main purpose is evident in his virtual abandonment of Gladys and Ada (and in effect the whole 'cinema film' experiment) about half-way through. Had he been able to use his audience voices to obtain something more than ignorant commentary on the action (when the Radcliffe Camera is shown, a 'voice' says 'Look, Ada, St Paul's Cathedral'), the multiplicity of viewpoints could have been worth while. As it is, it is experiment for smartness' sake, though the experimental side of the story is surely what caught the eye of those contemporaries who were impressed by it.

Waugh's scholarly students naturally look in 'The Balance' for what might be called 'philosophical' statements that can be used as a basis for generalization about his ideas. The 'balance' of the title appears in section III of the 'Conclusion', a conversation between Adam and his Reflection. The 'balance of life and death' is actually 'the balance of appetite and reason. The reason remains constant – the appetite varies'. The brief debate concludes that 'in the end circumstance decides', which seems equivalent to chance or fortune. Along with this idea goes Adam's yearning for the difficult state of 'detachment', which for both characters and author seems to mean achieving an attitude of indifference towards the subjectivities of life and the pains that life inflicts.

Statements like these serve to make one think about Waugh's ideas. They help to uncover the fact that Waugh throughout his career displayed life as a largely unchanging thing, and that what did change was that he acquired in his religion an explanation to place behind what he steadily saw as life's 'bodiless harlequinade'. For a long while, religion strengthened narrative detachment, but eventually the harlequinade and the meaning of it came together in the fiction. 'The Balance' gives a rather slick and aphoristic account of what was a drawn-out and complicated struggle early in Waugh's career. At the stage of 'The Balance', his attempts to resolved it were by literary means only. Success (and the penalties for success) would come only when he broadened the search.

From North Wales, Waugh carried away with him a lot of history that would go into *Decline and Fall*. There was Young/Grimes, of course, and some details from school life (such as Verschoyle's organ practice). His own sense of helpless isolation (one strand of his complex response to this new situation) was to be developed in the character of Paul Pennyfeather, and there was also the Welsh setting, very important, and so hilariously and mercilessly embroidered as to make Waugh the greatest hammer of the Welsh since Edward I. Arnold House, however, was only in part the origin of the school episodes in *Decline and Fall*. Much of the book came from Waugh's imagination and his reading, and also from his second schoolmastering job at Aston Clinton, Buckinghamshire, from September 1925 to February 1927.

In the summer of 1925, Waugh's first attempt at job-hunting was to write to the directors of art galleries and the editors of art magazines in London. He got some interviews but no offers. His inclination was still for the arts but his qualifications, such as they yet were, kept him at schoolmastering. Richard Plunket Greene, Olivia's brother and a contemporary of Waugh's at Oxford, taught at the school in Aston Clinton, and through his agency Waugh got the job there. In the weeks he spent between his teaching posts, he went out a lot in London, made visits to his friends, and finished 'The Balance', his only literary activity that summer. On one occasion, at a party of Alec's, 'Young of Denbighshire' drank himself insensible. Despite Young's immense value to his novel, and despite the therapeutic value of his 'confession', Waugh in the autobiography gives the impression that he kept Young at more than arm's length, but the diary shows that after Waugh departed from North Wales Young visited him three times, with entirely characteristic behaviour on each occasion ('drunk all the time. He seduced a garage boy in the hedge' [D 250]).

At first, Crawford's school at Aston Clinton was 'this frightful school'. It specialized in teaching what would now be called 'underachievers', whom Waugh at first called 'lunatics'. But in several ways it was a better billet for him than Arnold House and he clearly warmed towards the place, dropped 'lunatics' for 'the boys' and even came to be friendly with some. This aspect of the Aston Clinton school may be its greatest effect on *Decline and Fall*. Waugh claimed that he was universally disliked at Arnold House. Perhaps the sympathetic understanding of boys he needed for a character like Peter Beste-Chetwynde came at Aston Clinton, where he was less depressed and defensive than he had been in North Wales.

Waugh did not have Richard Plunket Greene's support at Aston Clinton for long. No sooner had he got Waugh the job there than he left to teach music at Lancing. He and his fiancée, Elizabeth Russell, had often given Waugh lifts to London, and perhaps to compensate for the loss of their car Richard bought him a motorcycle. Despite many breakdowns, he was thus able to keep up his visits to Oxford and elsewhere, though his frequent trips to London were usually by train. The motorcycle was Waugh's only accomodation in his whole life with that staple of modernity, automotive independence. He never could pass the driving test.

The motorcycle proved useful during the General Strike of 1926. Waugh could ride to London when the trains stopped running, and when he went to do his bit he was first signed up (though never used) as a despatch rider.

The General Strike is one of the litmus test events of British life in the early twentieth century: most people reacted to it by turning either blue or red. Anyone interested in a writer who was in Britain for the strike is likely to learn something by discovering what the writer said and did during it. In Waugh's case – he turned blue – his involvement with this event of public life gives an eerie forecast of his attitudes and experiences during his only other public involvement, the Second World War.

First of all, Alec was enlisted in no time, while Evelyn was some time in getting himself taken on. After false starts and dead ends, he eventually joined the Civil Constabulary Reserve in Camden Town.

> It was comprised of... what I take to be the dregs of civilization – battered little men of middle age, debased and down at heel who grumbled all the time, refused to get up in the mornings, talked on parade, and fought for their food. In the evenings, they got drunk in a canteen upstairs. The officers were solicitors' clerks in military clothes. We spent the morning drawing blankets, tin hats, field dressings and such military necessities. At luncheon the strike was called off. . . . (D 253).

In 1939, against a vaster background, all of the elements of Waugh's General Strike involvement were repeated. An ostensibly dutiful and patriotic enlistment concealed purely private motives, the demon boredom certainly among them. The cause of the conflict and the opponent were ignored. Waugh found himself suffering the frustration of meaningless movement and pointless orders, directing his ample animus at the social inferiority of his fellow enlistees and at authority vested in socially unworthy men. 'Mucking in' he could never aspire to. No one would recognize his own superiority, so no one could treat him fairly. Had he been able to learn the lesson, the 1926 Strike could have taught him that he was a fundamentally unsoldierly man, and that his splendid courage, though indispensable, was not alone enough to make him a serviceable officer in the army of a modern democracy. His experience of discovering these facts, however, gave us the wartime trilogy and in part accounts for the unexuberant tone of those books.

One (minor) benefit of schoolmastering is school holidays, and in his time at Aston Clinton Waugh took full advantage of the several vacations that came his way. Of his various journeys in this period, the most important was to Greece. Alistair Graham had entered the diplomatic service in 1926 and had been posted to Athens. At Christmas, Waugh journeyed out there and saw the sights. The homosexual atmosphere of the flat that Alistair shared was unattractive now to Waugh, but useful; he drew on it for the Moroccan ménage of Sebastian and Kurt in *Brideshead Revisited* (1S 130). The actively homosexual side of his friendship with Alistair had ended sometime earlier, but on leaving Greece he seems to have definitively put away homosexuality as a way of life for himself. On the voyage back to Italy, he stopped for two hours at Corfu, which he liked and which reminded him of Brighton. In *Decline and Fall* he gave Margot a house on Corfu.

Since Waugh was to become a prominent writer of travel books in the 1930's, a confession in his diary of the trip to Greece is fascinating. 'I am afraid I have inherited overmuch of my father's homely sentiments. The truth is that I do not really like being abroad much. I want to see as much as I can this holiday and from February shut myself up for the rest of my life in the British Isles' (D 276). But in this case at least the conclusion of 'The Balance' is valid: 'circumstance decides'. Circumstance was to make him a rootless wanderer for a number of years, and the professional writer he then was worked with the material he had been given.

Despite the fairly hectic social life Waugh was able to live at Aston Clinton, he continued to write. Early in November 1925, he had sprained an ankle at Oxford during the final filming for *The Scarlet Woman*. Lying on the sofa at his parents' house he had discovered his Pre-Raphaelites absorption. 'I want to write a book about them'. He read about them for a couple of weeks in Hampstead and at Aston Clinton. Then references to them cease. In July 1926, Alistair Graham suggested that Waugh write something for him to print. He took up the Pre-Raphaelites again, got out his notes, and in between correcting examinations, wrote a twenty-five page essay in four and a half days. It became his first book. In late October 1926, he proposed *Noah: or The Future of Intoxication* (a subject on which he did lifelong research) to Kegan Paul, who surprised him by accepting. He worked on the book, which he disliked, calling it 'mannered and "literary"' until December, when he sent it to the publishers. They turned it down in late January 1927.

In February 1927, Michael Sadleir commissioned a story from Waugh that became 'The Tutor's Tale: A House of Gentlefolks' (EWA 186), but between the commission and the writing came a small but eventually beneficent catastrophe; he got the sack, apparently because of some indecent remarks addressed while drunk to the school matron, whom he had thought a chum. He was swiftly out of there, but the school had already made a contribution to *Decline and Fall* that is surely large but impossible accurately to gauge. What may be most important is that Waugh was, relatively speaking, happier at Aston Clinton than at Arnold House. It was his practice to use his writing to cope with pains that life brought him, but success in such writing demanded some distance from the experience and an opportunity for the pains to diminish. 'The Balance' was written too close to the experiences it describes, since Waugh was still oppressed by them as he wrote. Aston Clinton was still schoolmastering, but he was not feeling the pull of his tether quite so much, and he was not nearly so isolated. Crawford's school let him get Banks's school into comic perspective.

In late February 1927 he was an unemployed private schoolmaster, living with his parents, writing a bit but not as yet a writer by profession. An agency found him a short-lived job at a state school in Notting Hill. 'The indignity and instability of his position resulted, predictably, in neurotic class-consciousness' (1S 133) but the casual, acid brilliance of the brief description Waugh wrote of the school is perhaps more striking than the insecurities it covered. 'All the masters drop their aitches and spit in the fire and scratch their genitals. The boys have close-cropped heads and steel-rimmed spectacles wound about with worsted. They pick their noses and scream at each other in a cockney accent' (D 282). The only untruth that has to be present here is the word 'all' that is implied throughout. Waugh saw what his fear showed him, and made general truth out of sharp, selected details. It was to be the method of his best writing.

The diary entries after the sacking read for the most part like a description of the social life of a rich and highly gregarious young man. Luncheons, dinners, plays, nightclubs, parties. The Jazz Age of the 1920s was beginning in London, and the night life brought Waugh into occasional contact with African-American musicians. He did not like any music and made no attempt to like the 'niggers' he now encountered, but he took note of their presence among the

Bright Young People, as the newspapers were to call the pack that Waugh ran with for a while and immortalized in *Vile Bodies*. School-mastering was played out; anything more than the Notting Hill job would bring the Aston Clinton débâcle to light, but on 7 April 1927 he made a diary entry that mapped his way forward into new territory.

> The job in Holland Park [Notting Hill] is over but it does not seem at all difficult to earn a living. I am in doubt at the moment whether to go on the *Express* or write a biography that Duckworth show some interest in. I have been to several parties and spent such a lot of money. I have met such a nice girl called Evelyn Gardner.

For a while at £5 a week he worked as a reporter for the *Daily Express*. The next diary entry (9 May 1927) begins, 'I am starting my fifth week on the *Express*'. And the next starts, 'I have got the sack from the *Express* ...' and those sentences are almost the total of our knowledge of Evelyn Waugh, newshound. This is particularly frustrating because the popular newspapers were to be greatly important in his career. Much of his income was to come from the many articles they commissioned from him, and much of what we know of his opinions is found in his journalism. His splendid novel *Scoop* (1938) is subtitled 'A Novel about Journalists', and though much of it deals with the foreign correspondents whom Waugh collected and dissected on his travels, it also deals with the home office in Fleet Street, but next to nothing is known about what Waugh did there in 1927. Young graduates (or near-graduates) were routinely hired by the London dailies 'on space' and given a few weeks to impress as 'discoveries' or be sacked. Waugh was sacked. *Scoop* makes his lack of reverence for the false historians of the press brutally clear, and in *Labels* (1930) he confirms that his attitude derived initially from this brief encounter with the Fleet Street species. Of tales he had been told in Constantinople, he says:

> This may or may not be true. It did not seem to me my business to investigate statements of this kind, but simply to scribble them down in my note-book if they seemed to me amusing. But then, I have had three weeks [at least five] in Fleet Street at one stage in my career. That is what people mean, I expect, when they say that newspaper training is valuable to an author (LA 143).

So it had to be the biography, and on 1 July 1927, after a jaunt to the South of France with his parents and Alec, he wrote: 'I have settled down to work on the Rossetti book'.

In 1927 he published his first work, a life of Dante Gabriel Rossetti, and in 1928 his first novel, Decline and Fall, *which was an immediate success.*

In the diary, the progress of the book and the courtship of Evelyn Gardner are recorded – very tersely – from 1 July to 13 December 1927. He made a couple of research journeys for *Rossetti* and wrote much of it at the *Oxford Union*. On 22 July he had 12 000 words done. On 23 August, 40 000. In September he entered an increment of 20 000 words. While *Rossetti* progressed, however, he was looking elsewhere for career opportunities. Several job opportunities are mentioned; some were teaching jobs, one 'a fantastic job about toothbrushes'. In October 1927 he enrolled for a course in wood-working at the Central School of Arts and Crafts. He studied there until at least December, and when the diary breaks off for six months he was arranging to work with a cabinet-maker in Hamp-shire, perhaps as an apprentice. So while writing *Rossetti* he was simultaneously inclining in William Morris's direction – and in Dick-ens's too, for on 3 September 1927 he recorded in his diary yet another literary event: 'have begun on a comic novel'. *Decline and Fall* had been conceived.

The undemonstrative nature of these diary entries tends to con-ceal Waugh's creative energy at this time. He was getting some-where fast. And in his personal life, the terse notations of meetings with Evelyn Gardner climax surprisingly for the reader on 9 Decem-ber. 'John Sutro asked me to spend Christmas with him. Shall do so unless engaged to be married by then'. On 12 December he records his proposal. Next day Evelyn Gardner accepted, and that is the last entry until 22 June 1927, when, in a manner reminiscent of Dickens's Wemmick, he writes, 'Evelyn and I began to go to Dulwich to see the pictures there but got bored waiting for the right bus so went instead to the vicar-general's office and bought a marriage-licence'. They were married at St Paul's, Portman Square, on 27 June 1928, in the presence of Harold Acton, Robert Byron, Alec Waugh, and Pansy Pakenham.

The gap in the diary from 13 December 1927 to 22 June 1928 seems to have been caused by 'Waugh's subsequent mutilation of the record' (1S 147). Only guesswork can interpret this action, but it should be indulged in because the most likely guess relates the action to an important component of Waugh's evolving aesthetic. I suggest that his motive for deleting the pages that covered the months preceding his marriage was their un-terseness. The entries that refer to Evelyn Gardner before and after the gap have the 'objectivity' that Waugh was to give the third-person narrators in his fiction; there is very little to indicate directly how they feel about the persons or events they describe. Only indirect indicators are present, quite congruent with 'objectivity', and for the sympathetic reader just as directional. With this approach, the author never seems sentimental; there is no 'gush'. The deleted pages probably showed Evelyn Waugh in love, and in light of later events, in life and in art, it was intolerable that they should continue to exist.

When the diary resumes, 'objectivity' is firmly in place. No more is heard of cabinet-making, *Rossetti* has been published (in late April 1928), and Waugh is correcting the proofs of *Decline and Fall*. Writing is now his business, and henceforward he will treat it in an unsentimentally businesslike way. *Rossetti* had been generally well received, and *Decline and Fall*, though no runaway best-seller, did pretty well. Like *Rossetti*, it found an American publisher. It went into a second edition (though editions were kept deliberately small) and its success seemed to show that the gamble the two Evelyns had taken in getting married on the strength of *Rossetti* would pay off. The book had been written as a sort of theoretical accompaniment to Waugh's career in the arts (furniture-making was the latest version) and apparently with no intention that it should inaugurate a career in writing. But the comic novel, begun probably while *Rossetti* was still unfinished, was the true first step on a long road.

Rossetti had had a long gestation but a fairly swift delivery. Biography had from the first been the literary form into which Waugh cast his interest. In the diary, he imagines his biography of Millais, 'a modish Lytton Strachey biography', but the choice of Rossetti for the subject (a very 'professional' choice, determined probably by the closeness of the centenary in 1928 of Rossetti's birth) made him abandon the Strachey mode of ironic undercutting. Millais was a Victorian success; from his schooldays, Waugh had accepted a simplified definition of 'Victorianism' as facile, humanistic faith in progress, and he constantly detested it. Millais would have demanded

an ironic approach, but Rossetti was effectively anti-Victorian, so
Waugh could drop the Strachey mode. Since Rossetti's moral reputation had made him 'the bogey of many Victorian drawing-rooms'
a satiric biography would have been otiose, for Waugh was able to
claim – astonishingly, surely – that 'alone of the fabulous paladins of
the last century' Rossetti 'was never, to any serious extent, a hum-
bug' (R 12). As things turned out, Waugh was to discover that he did
have a fundamental disapproval of Rossetti, but that it applied to his
artistic character, always for Waugh taking precedence over moral
character. The biography as we have it, therefore, has a basic sobri-
ety enlivened by occasional flashes of wit. Its enthusiasm is reserved
for works of art that are manifestations of genius, and Waugh is confident that on several occasions Rossetti did create such works. The
relationship of his life to those works, however, is finally a mystery
to Waugh, but this does not mean the failure of the book as biography.

   In a number of ways, *Rossetti* is an impressive achievement. For
Waugh, it was an effective act of self-realization for his authorial
persona, and authority was the major element he wanted in that
persona. There is nothing to indicate that the author is a youthful
novice: the authorial voice is mature and poised. If the reader has
doubts about some of the judgements, the author has none. He
stands in awe of certain of Rossetti's achievements, but because he
believes that genius is inexplicable and that failure can certainly be
explained, his accounts of what he takes to be the great Rossetti
paintings are rather on the gushy side, whereas the lesser achievements or failures are described with mordant conviction and cutting
phraseology. (Waugh would have been truer to his beliefs had he
done the impossible and refrained altogether from discussion of the
great paintings, but perhaps he discovered his beliefs as he wrote.)
His final judgement on the multiform failure that accompanies
Rossetti's masterpieces is that it is a failure of character, of moral
character.

> It is not so much that as a man he was a bad man – mere lawless
> wickedness has frequently been a concomitant of the highest
> genius – but there was fatally lacking in him that *essential rectitude*
> that underlies the serenity of all really great art. The sort of
> unhappiness that beset him was not the sort of unhappiness that
> does beset a great artist; all his brooding about magic and suicide
> are [sic] symptomatic not so much of genius as of mediocrity.

There is a spiritual inadequacy, a sense of ill-organization about all that he did. (R 226)

To point to the absence of 'essential rectitude' and to 'spiritual inadequacy' indicates the critic's certainty that art has a moral basis; artistic character *is* moral character. Much modernistic aesthetic theory argued otherwise. Waugh is asserting the traditionalist attitude, and one that remained in place when he moved from theory to practice.

His rejection of modernism in *Rossetti* goes even further. In the final pages of the book, he refers back to the epigraphs that stand at the head of Chapter 1. In the first, Rossetti describes how

His first impulse to pictorial expression...came...from an emotional state of mind evoked by firelight and singing. In a significant phrase he describes how in this mood 'shapes rose within him'. That is to say, that in him the state of mind became automatically translated into visible forms.

The other epigraph is from the then-doyen of modern aesthetic theory, Roger Fry: 'I know that real artists generally begin by making an elaborate study of an old pair of boots'. Waugh interprets Fry as meaning that 'the "real" artist fundamentally is someone interested in the form underlying the appearance of things' (R 222). This is an aesthetic theory that can be used to validate abstract art and almost every other variety of modernism. Waugh, by the last chapter of *Rossetti*, has come to reject it. He cannot agree that 'Artistic perception begins with an appreciation of the reality of form, and becomes creative as it begins to associate forms with each other in *necessary*, and therefore agreeable relationships'. Nor is there such a thing as a special 'aesthetic emotion' to respond to works of art so defined. 'The fact that primitive negro sculpture satisfies the aesthetic emotion ought to make the healthy Western critic doubt the formula rather than acclaim the barbarian'. This is the rejection of cultural relativism that will be a stable element in Waugh's personal ideology for the rest of his life. 'Representation and imitation', dismissed in Fry's theory, are embraced in Waugh's rejection of Fry, and for a theory of the nature of the artistic impulse he is left with the Romantic mystery of Rossetti's shapes rising within.

The writing of *Rossetti: His Life and Works* at this early stage of his career was cathartic for Waugh; it purged him of the 'aesthetic hypocrisy' that had developed during his friendship with Barbara

Jacobs years before. By the time he was through the book, he had
declared for traditional aesthetics and methods of representation
and had endorsed moral qualities as the foundation of art. He
defended Rossetti where modernism attacked him, and condemned
him (unemphatically but firmly) where modernism implied that the
critic had no business. Early in the book, Waugh's reference to 'the
pellucid excellencies of Picasso' gives the reader – a reader who
knows something of what Waugh's future opinions were to be – a
moment of wry humour. By the time the end of the book is reached,
it sounds like irony.

The completion of *Rossetti* took place during Waugh's courtship of
Evelyn Gardner. It was published about two months before they got
married. *Decline and Fall* was begun during the later stages of the
writing of *Rossetti* and was published on 18 September 1928, less
than three months after the wedding. The writing had been finished
in mid-April, so when the two Evelyns embarked on matrimony, the
young husband had 'one dim biography' (1S 158) to his credit (it had
been well received but would make very little money) and the
manuscript of a novel that he expected Duckworths to publish. It
was not much as security for an upper-middle-class marriage, but
then such concerns were deliberately flouted by this couple. In February 1928, Waugh says 'there will probably be an elopement quite
soon', for as soon as the idea of marriage occurred the pair could see
that, even if they did not actually run away to get married, they
would be going against the openly declared wishes of Evelyn Gardner's mother, Lady Burghclere, and against the implied principles of
Arthur and Catherine Waugh, who had themselves waited through
a very long engagement.

In its conception, its duration, and its termination, Evelyn Waugh's
first marriage has about it the signs of a modernity that in certain
other areas of experience he had already begun to loathe. It was not
a short-notice elopement, but it was a contract solely between the
parties, depending neither on the sanction of society (as expressed
by parental approval, marriage settlement, and the rituals of a
formal marriage ceremony and a society wedding) nor on that of
religion (though they had a church wedding, religion played no part
in their decision, to Waugh's ultimate advantage). The air of trans-
gression that associates with the word 'elopement' hung about the
marriage throughout its brief duration. The comments of their
friends frequently emphasize its naughtiness. Nancy Mitford said
that the Evelyns married were like two little boys, with the suggestion,

perhaps, that they had pulled off a wonderful prank. The newly-wed Waughs proclaimed themselves rebels, but it was largely a mimic rebellion and the male partner was soon to discover that even mimic rebellion violated some of his deepest instincts.

The form of youth culture that the newspapers of the 1920s publicized so eagerly was largely a consequence of the generational conflict attendant on the First World War, which in itself explains why Evelyn Waugh should have been a participant and in some measure a chronicler of it. It was a 'from the top down' phenomenon, for the young people involved had to come from a social stratum that allowed them considerable financial independence whereby to rebel against the expectations of their elders. The Honourable Evelyn Gardner well exemplifies the characteristics of the 'Bright Young People', though the label implies a manic hedonism that really does not fit the young woman she was in 1927, however much she liked to have fun. She had alarmed her aristocratic family by setting herself up unchaperoned (though with a flat-mate, Lady Pansy Pakenham) in London and by becoming involved with Waugh, a very young and far from established writing fellow. Her attempts to escape her authoritarian mother had already led to several abortive engagements. To the widowed Lady Burghclere, Waugh must have looked like the latest in a series of the unsettled and unsuitable, and gossip – some of it from Cruttwell – had brought her rumours of a libertine lifestyle. They had to marry without her consent, thereby perhaps embracing more rebellion than they had wished.

After the wedding, Waugh had a couple of interviews *tête-à-tête* with his incensed mother-in-law, but could not emerge with even an *ex post facto* blessing. For two months, the couple stayed with the groom's parents at Underhill while they searched for a flat. She-Evelyn[2] seems to have established good relations with *her* mother-in-law by giving warm assurances of her love for He-Evelyn before they were married. They found a five-room flat at 17A Canonbury Square, Islington, an unfashionable address whose unfashionability He-Evelyn's gifts as interior designer and self-publicist rapidly overcame. Publicity, in fact, was soon a large element in the Waughs' life. With his insider's knowledge of the publishing business, and his recent newspaper experience, he evidently decided that getting his name into the papers would be important auxiliary propulsion for his career as a writer, and he went about it with consummate address. He had mentioned the possibility of an elopement in February 1928 to an acquaintance who wrote gossip for

London papers, and once the marriage was launched he saw to it
that the Evelyns (and their flat) were often mentioned in the newspapers. The manipulation of publicity continued throughout his
whole career; the famous fury of the older Waugh at intrusions into
his life by reporters is really the measure of his insistence of being in
control of his publicity. It was essential to his career, but it was
impertinent and barbarous when not instigated by him. The feelings
of those closest to him about his publicity managing seem to have
concerned him very little.

In the early months of his marriage, Waugh's professional and
private lives were uniformly prosperous. *Rossetti* had done as well,
perhaps a little better than could have been expected; *Decline and Fall*
had received good reviews, notably one from Arnold Bennett, and
was selling well if not wildly. He was happily married, working on a
second novel while She-Evelyn was writing herself (a never-finished
novel) and their social life was beginning to include the famous and
the fashionable. *Decline and Fall* despite its quite prominent dark side
and several catastrophes, seems to partake of all this happiness, which
came from the time of writing, rather than from Arnold House,
where Waugh had been mostly miserable.

Decline and Fall is a rather strange *bildungsroman*. It begins with
what seems to be the brutal termination of Paul Pennyfeather's education when he is quite unjustly sent down from Oxford for inde-
cency. His education, however, has only just begun. When, at the
end of the book, Paul starts again at Scone College, Oxford – Paul
has learned to lie in the course of the narrative, and has no trouble
persuading the world that he is a distant relation of the earlier,
expelled Paul Pennyfeather – his education is, in its most important
aspects, complete. He knows what the world is like and he has
decided on his place in it. He reads that the early Christian Ebionites
used to turn towards Jerusalem to pray: 'Quite right to suppress
them'. Decisiveness is the fruit of certainty, and after his experiences
from his expulsion from Scone to his return, Paul can enjoy the certainty of a mind made up.

Yet Paul Pennyfeather is not a surrogate for his creator, and that
helps make this book an unusual *bildungsroman*. Like Waugh, Paul
has discovered that the world is a shocking, arbitrary, and vastly
unjust place – but vastly amusing, too, if one can stay out of its jaws.
Waugh is interested in Paul only so far as he can use him to demonstrate what the world is like, what people are like. He has no idea of
investigating his own character, development or problems via Paul

Pennyfeather. Most readers, I suspect, are a little startled to discover how objective Waugh is about Paul, how unconcerned he finally is about him. Paul is the protagonist but not to Waugh the hero of the book; there is no hero. This is a possibly painful surprise that awaits us as we first read the novel. Paul appears as the innocent victim of injustice; how can Waugh not be his advocate and defender? But so it is. The reader's concern for Paul is allowed to develop as it would in a more conventional *bildungsroman*, and it is one more surprise of a surprising story that the author turns out not to share that concern. The usual label for this unconcern of author for principal character is 'irony', and it is indeed to Gibbon's example that it is owed. Gibbon has no heroes. The title of the novel acknowledges the master of the ironical gaze upon amazing events and astounding characters.

It is, however, to Dickens that Waugh is most indebted in *Decline and Fall*, and in particular to Dickens's second *bildungsroman*, *Great Expectations*. Pip's 'education' begins in the churchyard as he is pounced upon by the convict Magwitch and turned upside-down. It is just barely a probable action; Magwitch wants the contents of Pip's pockets and so takes the swiftest way to get at them. The figurative meaning presses hard upon the literal but becomes apparent only later in the book when the reader, rather earlier than Pip himself, discovers that, by means of those great expectations, Pip's life and character have been turned upside down. The whole book in fact is the story of Pip's upside-down life and his eventual struggle to get back onto his feet, which means learning the true moral worth of those who have brought him up and those who have intruded into his life and distorted his values – for motives both evil and good. Dickens is most concerned to examine through his hero his own moral development, notably his taking of the poisoned fruit of snobbery. Paul Pennyfeather never serves as Waugh's means to examine Waugh, but he had a craftsman's eye for technique and borrowed from *Great Expectations* the astounding opening event that in the long run will be seen to give a summary statement of everything that happens, and serves in miniature as an emblematic enactment of the book's verdict on the world: a place without truth or justice. Paul Pennyfeather is stripped of his clothing by the Bollinger Club because a drunken aristocratic undergraduate cannot appreciate the distinction between Paul's old school tie and the tie of the Club. He is expelled for his virtues. He is quiet, unassuming, unassertive, a sound, steady student. These qualities make him eminently expellable because he will go quietly, as he does, venturing only and 'meekly' 'God damn and blast them all to hell' as he is driven to the station, 'and then he felt ashamed, for he rarely swore'. This muted and nullified soliloquy is the only protest heard in the entire book against the world's injustice and mendacity. It tells us exactly what the author of this novel thinks about the possibility of truth and justice in Paul's world and perhaps his own. Paul's utterance marks the beginning of his own renunciation of this illusion. Later, at Egdon Heath Penal Settlement, when Margot tells Paul she is giving him up and will marry Maltravers, he is 'greatly pained at how little he was pained by the events of the afternoon' (DF 229). He accepts the truth of his world, but can still suffer a little at the loss of the 'enchantment' that has deluded him.

The debagging and sending down are the harbingers of many events to come, beginning, a page or so later, with his guardian's realization that since the young man has been expelled in disgrace, he can legally appropriate Paul's inheritance and throw him out of the house, and can do so while uttering moralistic platitudes about 'fulfilling the trust that your poor father placed in me'. Like Pip's being turned upside down, Paul's debagging and expulsion are an at first unappreciated epitome of the book's theme. And where Dickens is interested in Pip's character, Waugh is determined to force from his reader, by the acquiescence of laughter, the admission that, yes, the world is like this: arbitrary, unjust, mendacious, and hilarious.

The hilarity is owed to the astounding absence in the book: the lack of expectation of truth or justice. Seek another novel whose universe is devoid of truth and justice and Orwell's *Nineteen Eighty-Four* will come to mind. Put Orwell's book down next to Waugh's and see what a hilarious comedy *Nineteen Eighty-Four* could be if Orwell could radically denature himself and lose his insistence that truth and justice ought to exist. In his first novel, Waugh had totally renounced any expectation of a human universe where truth or justice might be found, and therefore how unlike a satire is *Decline and Fall*. There is no indignation at the absence of an ideal because no ideal can seriously be contemplated. The expectation of nothing, however, confers the liberty of comedy. The book is free to be funny and the reader is free to enjoy it because nothing else exists, as ideal or standard, against which these events can be measured or shown to be wicked or deplorable. In theory, *Decline and Fall* should be the portrayal of a nightmare; in fact, it is quite bewilderingly enjoyable, a happy book about a hellish world. Later, when Waugh converted to Catholicism, he put an ideological foundation under the vision of the world that is presented in his early novels. Frank Kermode is right to call *Decline and Fall* 'Catholic *avant la lettre*'.

The publication of *Decline and Fall* was far more of an initiation for Waugh than *Rossetti*'s had been. It introduced him to aspects of asperity in the relationship of author and publisher (and of authorship and the law) and brought him a mark of professional status when A. D. Peters, Ltd. became his literary agent.

Having published *Rossetti*, Duckworths were offered and accepted *Decline and Fall*. When they had the manuscript, however, they made some objections. There would have to be changes. The nature of these illustrates neatly how the definition of obscenity has shifted during this century. No objections concerned the racist remarks that would now certainly be excised. The after effects of the Home Office's prosecution of D. H. Lawrence had made publishers in 1928 hypersensitive about sexual matters, and Duckworths demanded what now seem fatuous changes in the text. For example, the Bollinger Club in Waugh's manuscript throw Mr Partridge's Matisse into his lavatory. In the version published until 1962, it goes into his water-jug. Faced with the demand for such changes, Waugh withdrew the manuscript from Duckworths and took it to his father's firm, Chapman & Hall. Arthur was away and played no part in the decision to publish his second son's novel; the director responsible for technical books was apparently astute enough to cast the decisive vote. So, with an appropriateness that surely no one then understood, Dickens's publishers became Evelyn Waugh's. But only for his novels, at the start. His departure was oddly incomplete. Duckworths continued as the publishers of most of his travel books in the 1930s.

Having made his gesture of authorial independence and principle, Waugh quietly submitted when Chapman & Hall demanded the same and similar changes as they readied the book for the press. It was published with the cuts restored and most of the changes unmade only in 1962.

The Evelyns were married on 27 June 1928. On 3 September 1929, the husband filed a petition for divorce. Apart from his later conversion to Roman Catholicism, the collapse of this marriage was the most important event of his life, though the argument can be made that in his *literary* life it was *the* most important event. Certainly it was a trauma that left a mark on everything of any importance that he wrote thereafter. It may be argued, too, that without the emotional catastrophe of his first wife's infidelity, his conversion to Catholicism might never have occurred. What has become in the later twentieth century an utter banality, marital infidelity and divorce, was for Waugh a never quite healed wound and a symptom of the disease of modernity to which, in his work, he would return again and again. It is hard to over-estimate the effect on him, and on the stratum of twentieth-century literature where his work is found, of She-Evelyn's announcement, in July 1929, that she was in love with, and was the lover of John Heygate.

A quite un-modern reticence by all parties in this situation has meant that Waugh's biographers have been unable to deliver the blow-by-blow accounts that are nowadays expected of such events. In a literary life, the infidelity and divorce are properly the focus because of their marked, immediate, and continuing effect on his fiction. (The most extensive facing-up he did was in *A Handful of Dust*, about five years after the fact.) The events of his one-year marriage have to get some attention too because, after his commitment to writing, which came with *Decline and Fall*'s success, Waugh was never for long diverted from his profession, and his writing activity plays a part in the crack-up.

Inexperience and incompatibility are the major themes in the biographers' accounts. Evelyn Gardner had been unsuitably engaged several times, and she told Nancy Mitford that she had married Waugh to get away from home. One widely quoted letter to his mother, on the other hand, gives a convincing account of the warmth of her affection for He-Evelyn. Several times during the marriage, and particularly during a Mediterranean cruise, She-Evelyn was quite seriously ill, and her husband may have failed, as she saw it, to be properly compassionate. The sexual relations of a probably virgin bride and a husband whose experience had been almost totally homosexual were, at least at the start, predictably uncomfortable. After the return from the cruise, Waugh had large bills to pay and two large writing projects, the travel book he was to mine from the cruise, *Labels*, and his next novel, *Vile Bodies*, on which he worked first. Following what was to be his usual practice, he went off into the country to write his book while his wife stayed behind in London. It seems clear that for her marriage was to mean a social life free of the kind of restrictions her mother had imposed, and accompanying her husband to the country while he worked, even if he had been willing to have her there, seemed far too conventual; she

wanted to have fun. Waugh wanted solitude for work. He went off
leaving his wife to be squired around by 'safe' friends, like Harold
Acton and John Heygate, but she fell for Heygate and the marriage
collapsed.

In 1986, Evelyn Nightingale (as she had become by her third marriage) wrote to Martin Stannard: 'Of course I meant what I said
when I wrote to Mrs Waugh. But my marriage wasn't exactly warm.
Evelyn was not an affectionate person. I was' (1S 185). Waugh was,
perhaps without realizing it, idealistically romantic about his marriage, but he followed (and did so even more later on) a code of
emotional reticence that he saw as aristocratically unsentimental.
His nature, as Alec said, was tender and emotional, but by self-nur-
ture he became reticent and outwardly unaffectionate. The irony is
that his wife, genuinely aristocratic by birth and breeding, craved
the kind of demonstrativeness that Waugh believed to be simply
vulgar. When she left him, his self-esteem was savagely wounded,
but he was confirmed in his own eyes in the rightness of his taste.

> I have decided that I have gone on for too long in that fog of senti-
> mentality & I am going to stop hiding away from everyone. I was
> getting into a sort of Charlie Chaplinish Pagliacci attitude to
> myself as the man with a tragedy in his life and a tender smile for
> children. So all that must stop and one conclusion I am coming to
> is that I do not like Evelyn & that really Heygate is about her cup
> of tea. (L 41)

If he married again, one concludes, it would be to someone whose
taste was as aristocratic in its unsentimentality as he had made his
own.

There is no stronger testimony to Evelyn Waugh's rapidly
developed professionalism than that he finished and published *Vile
Bodies*, his second novel, even though he was thunderbolted by his
wife's defection while he was right in the middle of it, and that he
wrote the travel book, *Labels*, for which he had contracted, despite
the fact that it describes a cruise that he and his wife had taken and
which was dominated by the memory of her illness and a month-
long enforced stay with her at Port Said. When his profession was
involved, sentimentality had even less chance than usual to direct
events.

The break-up meant that Waugh was homeless, and for the next
seven years he remained so, travelling often to foreign parts (and

writing about his travels), using his parents' house for short stays and storage, putting up sometimes at the London club he had joined, the Savile, and sometimes at country hotels to get books written, staying with friends, often in the country and sometimes staying in their houses or flats when they were away. He had many, many friendships. They had come to him with fame (which came with *Vile Bodies*) and he had worked hard to cultivate them, as he did all his life. Two in particular should be described, since they were to be incorporated – transformed – into later fiction.

The first, which eventually made it way into *Work Suspended* (1942), was with Bryan and Diana Guinness. Waugh had known Bryan Guinness, a member of the wealthy brewing family, at Oxford. Diana was one of the (later famous) Mitford sisters; another sister Nancy, had been a friend of She-Evelyn's during the marriage, and later became one of He-Evelyn's 'sisters' and a talented comic novelist. The Guinnesses comforted Waugh with sympathy and esteem, and Diana in particular helped him to start finding the world funny again. Moreover, they had six places where he could stay – in three countries: England, Ireland, and France. With Diana, Waugh had a special friendship that developed deeply – into strong affection on her side, and non-erotic adoration on his – while she was pregnant. But when her baby was born, in March 1930, Diana's intimacy with Waugh came to an end. Thirty-six years later, he explained to her that the friendship had petered out because 'I wanted you to myself as especial confidante and comrade' and what had been an exclusive arrangement during the pregnancy could not survive enlargement of her circle of friends. Diana had refused to become a 'sister' on those terms. Waugh relaxed them for the later 'sisters'. (Another friendship developed as this one ended. Waugh stood godfather to Diana's baby; he met Randolph Churchill, his fellow godfather, for the first time at the christening.)

Waugh's friendship with the Lygons, like earlier and later friendships, was a falling in love with a whole family, or at least with the part that was accessible. The father, Earl Beauchamp, lived in Italy, exiled by the threat of scandal (H 248), and the mother lived separated from him with her youngest son. Of the six remaining children, Waugh had known William, Lord Elmley, President of the Hypocrites Club, and his younger brother Hugh at Oxford, and now in the early 1930s became the close friend of two of the four daughters, Ladies Mary and Dorothy Lygon, 'Blondie' and 'Poll' in his correspondence. They lived at the family's home, Madresfield Court, near

Great Malvern, Worcestershire, and the absence of the older generation, and the playfulness and hilarity of the younger, made it a place
where Waugh stayed often and eagerly, far more of a home to him
than his parents' house – and how far from Golders Green! His correspondence with the Lygon sisters is filled with nicknames, fantasy
and fiction, extravagant characters, and *faux-naif* obscenity. The
Lygons and Madresfield were enormously therapeutic for him in
the years after his divorce, and the affection and gratitude he felt for
them and their house contributed much to *Brideshead Revisited*.

Finishing *Vile Bodies* was a painful effort. Waugh rarely enjoyed
writing, but desertion and divorce piled misery onto the usual
reluctance. He seems to have finished it at a pub in north Devon in
September 1929. The new novel *was* very different from its predecessor, but the difference included blazing popularity. It was a runaway
best-seller (1S 196), a success that transformed Waugh's literary and
social life as much as the marital catastrophe had darkened his outlook and was clarifying his attitudes. Yet though it could be seen as
the good news that followed the bad news of the breakup, the success of *Vile Bodies* never bribed Waugh's judgement. He did not
admire his book, and for reasons that do seem valid. Twice in his career he published best-sellers (*Vile Bodies* and *Brideshead Revisited*)
and in each case – though *Brideshead*'s is much more complicated –
he disagreed with the public that was enriching him. To some extent,
his distaste for *Vile Bodies* was owed to the circumstances in which it
was written. ('It all seems to shrivel up & rot internally and I am
relying on a sort of cumulative futility for any effect it may have' [L
39].) The discovery that the world really was as unjust and mendacious as he had shown it to be in *Decline and Fall*, his actual knowledge of good-and-evil, chopped from the book the gusto that had
gone into his first novel. *Vile Bodies* is often funny, frequently amusing, yet it is steeped in the misery that flooded Waugh's life after his
marriage failed. And sometimes it is just badly written.

Martin Stannard's excellent study of the manuscript of *Vile Bodies*
(1S 204) shows that Waugh began it and carried it through Chapter
VI in a very different mood from that which predominates throughout the finished book. When he took it up at Chapter VII, he also
went back and brought the first six chapters into conformity with
the mood of disillusionment and even revulsion that now gripped
him. Stannard, to take a striking example, shows that originally the
manuscript was prefaced by the 'amiable epigraph: [upper case letters throughout] Bright Young People and others kindly note that

all characters are wholly imaginary (and you get far too much publicity already whoever you are)'. This epigraph, and the attitudes it embodies were deleted from the novel: 'Waugh's pleasure in the anarchic younger set and his quiet pride in being its literary representative are obliterated'. The irony of his situation struck Waugh forcibly. He had been trying – and with success – to earn commissions for newspaper articles as the spokesman of Youth – unorthodox, rebellious, irreverent – but the catastrophe of his private life had drastically changed his attitude. There is a saying in American politics: 'A conservative is a liberal who has been mugged'. It applies not well to Waugh's politics, but very well indeed to his feelings about anarchy and rebelliousness in society. In *Decline and Fall*, he had found positive enthusiasm for the vitality and irrepressibility of Grimes. Margot's rapacity and ruthlessness are there balanced by vulnerability and a palpable attractiveness. But in the middle of the first draft of *Vile Bodies*, anarchy, which Waugh knew and thought he liked, turned around and mugged him. There is no character in *Vile Bodies* at all like Grimes, and although Margot – as Lady Metroland – is several times mentioned, she has lost all her positive attributes. Now she and Lady Circumference can be described as opposed 'poles of savagery'. The simple balanced opposition of these Balzacian carry-overs from *Decline and Fall* defines the shift that has occurred in Waugh's feelings. The drafts and editions of *Vile Bodies* generally show him suppressing 'editorial' comments about his characters. Against his better, later judgement, such comments had forced their way into the book, a testimony to the violence of his feelings; many were excised, but Margot stays as one pole of social savagery.

Irony redoubled as *Vile Bodies* was published on 14 January 1930. The representative of Modern Youth was now before the public as the Savonarola of the Bright Young People, but the mass of the public failed to detect the change of perspective, and the book sold so well, as Waugh said much later, because of his wonderful ear for speech. 'I popularised a fashionable language...and the book caught on'.

This was the paradox of *Vile Bodies*'s success. The 'sick-making', 'unpolicemanlike' vocabulary Waugh had picked up from the Guinness set, in which context it was mildly amusing, but he transformed it in the novel into an example of the 'overdrinking ...underthinking' mind. The public relished it....In attempting to undermine the glamorous image of his young characters he had inadvertently enhanced their image as the object of fashionable imitation. The element of *roman à clef* was supposed to be strong. People bought the book as an adjunct to their romantic absorption in gossip columns. (1S 204)

Waugh's breakthrough into the world of the popular and fashionable novelist was engineered by misunderstanding. And – to adapt the *bon mot* of an avatar of his own, Mr Joyboy – he bitched all the way to the bank.

The reviews were mixed, reviewers from the older generation being notably less enthusiastic than younger ones. Rebecca West, who had become an acquaintance of Waugh's, was an early admirer of his work, and may have drawn on conversations with him in her perceptive review that firmly grasped his objectives. The book was funny but serious, a further stage in the contemporary literature of disillusionment 'that had started with Eliot's *The Waste Land*' (CH 107). Arnold Bennett, who had admired *Decline and Fall* (and who had been dined by the young Waughs after his review appeared [H 180]) had reservations about this one, and his apparently banal comments do get at the root of its unsatisfactory aspects: 'the lack of a well-laid plot has resulted in a large number of pages which demand a certain obstinate and sustained effort of will for their perusal' (CH 199). The truth is that the necessity of following *Decline and Fall* swiftly with a second novel pushed Waugh into writing before he had a story to tell. He never seems to have realized that a 'well-laid plot' was essential for his very best work, and when he had no such scheme in mind he followed, as he does in *Vile Bodies*, his historian's instinct to rely on describing what happened, embroidering the fabric of fact and putting his protagonist through a series of episodes modelled on and adapted from his own life. The central situation of *Vile Bodies* replays the major event of his own life while he was composing the first draft: Adam Fenwick-Symes' efforts to get married to Nina Blount. The ups and downs of Adam's life repeatedly make their marriage 'off' and 'on', and in a consciously 'experimental' narrative style – owing much to Firbank – Waugh depicts many parts of English society, from breakfast at 10 Downing Street to goings on at Shepheard's Hotel (run by Lottie Crump, transparently a portrait of the well-known Rosa Lewis of the Cavendish Hotel), to the dotty Colonel Blount's country house, Doubting Hall, which at one stage serves as the location for an absurd film, to newspaper offices and the frenzies of gossip columnists, to a motor race, and to parties of all kinds and for all sorts of people: 'Oh Nina, *what a lot of parties*'. The last party of all occurs on 'the biggest battlefield in the history of the world' as Adam slumps exhausted while the drunken major, a recurring character now become a general, plies with champagne and seduces Chastity, formerly an 'angel' in Mrs Melrose Ape's troupe of theatrical evangelists (Chastity has latterly been converted to prostitution by the agency of Lady Metroland). After Chapter 7, despite Waugh's attempt to give the manuscript uniformity of tone throughout, events take a sinister but not unexpected turn. Nina deserts the penniless Adam for Ginger Littlejohn but later resumes her affair with Adam. The letter Adam reads from her on the battlefield indicates that she is bearing his child, but that Ginger believes himself to be the father. 'Even the humour tastes of ashes' (1S 203). *Decline and Fall* is, despite everything, exhilarating; *Vile Bodies*, despite everything, is depressing. Barbarism's victory seems imminent, but saving vitality is nowhere found. Certainly the book is 'A manifesto of disillusionment', but beneath that public theme is felt the misery and pain of the novelist, his humour soured by 'the to me sad and radically shocking news' of his wife's desertion.

Since the book had to be finished despite this radical shock, it was perhaps fortunate that it did lack a well-laid plot. The expedient Waugh had fallen back on at the start was to return to the method of 'The Balance', and this was not an unconscious decision. He had borrowed names from 'The Balance', and as with the story, there was no plot in *Vile Bodies* that would have to be reconstructed to fit a different and darker emotional mood. *Vile Bodies* is episodic like 'The Balance', and shares its improvised quality. There is a feeling, notable after Waugh resumed writing at Chapter 7, that things are being included because they are to hand, not because they are needed (Waugh himself instanced the two women in the train discussing the Younger Generation in Chapter 9 [JB 109]). He had allowed himself to be taken to a motor race and it got into the book. His involvement with the making of the film, *The Scarlet Woman*, gets in too. The mood that now governed him as he doggedly finished is openly indicated early in Chapter 7: 'that black misanthropy . . . which waits alike on gossip writer and novelist'. Structurally, he was doing again what he had done in 'The Balance', but with the advance – acquired from *Decline and Fall* – that no one in the book stood for E. Waugh. Humour, however bitter, was possible. The author's distance from the principal character, this second Adam, was even greater, and now all secondary characters were seen as entertaining barbarians, although Waugh's detachment had become so practised that the book could be eagerly bought by those who only wanted to emulate those denounced.

Had Waugh wished to defend the structure and methods of *Vile Bodies*, literary criticism in its mode of justification would have aided him. Form can be said to follow function in the novel. The improvisatory quality is appropriate, for these are improvised lives. The novel goes off to the motor race meeting with as much forethought as the characters themselves give to going there. Death comes as casually into the novel as it comes to end the lives of Lord Balcairn ('Mr Chatterbox') and Miss Runcible. But imitative form was not a concept Waugh needed. He had other successes and he had no need to claim artistic success for *Vile Bodies*, which after all had served his career very well indeed. He could even afford to be more dismissive of it than it deserved. In the Penguin blurb it goes unmentioned; Waugh there implies that *Decline and Fall* was the best-seller that got his career going.

Waugh's insight into the realities of authorship and publishing told him that having a best-seller was a summons to action rather than an invitation to leisure. He had to keep his fame alive beyond the possibly brief day of *Vile Bodies*, and so the travel book for which he had contracted had to be delivered. Waugh had 30 000 words done by 19 February 1930, and it was finished in April. (A. D. Peters had done their best to maximize income from the book; sections had been published as articles in the *Fortnightly Review* and the *Architectural Review*.)

Waugh solved what was now the literary problem of his ex-wife in a surprising way. After the break-up, She-Evelyn swiftly became an unperson; his friends learned not to mention her. In the writing of *Labels*, it would have been easy to omit her in the same way, to make her a literary un-person too. Instead, Waugh handled her, and the innocent husband he now considered himself to have been, by converting self and wife into a young couple, Geoffrey and Juliet, travelling along with the narrator ('Evelyn Waugh') on the same cruise, and presented by him as rather blank figures, Juliet nursed by Geoffrey through a bout of flu that starts on the train to Monaco and becomes pneumonia, requiring a stay at Port Said until she recovers, whereupon she and Geoffrey part from the narrator after Chapter 4.

An explanation for this odd stratagem may lie in the necessity to make *Labels* a cheerful book. *Vile Bodies* could be largely brought into line with Waugh's mood of disillusionment and bitterness after the break-up, but no one would enjoy a travel book with such an atmosphere. To omit his wife altogether might have seemed to be imposing a continuous strain upon himself, her unmentionable presence in memory asserting an influence that could only be harmful to the mood he had to convey. Converting her and his earlier self into a pair of unremarkable, nearly uninteresting fictional characters may have seemed the best way temporarily to quiet the demon of the catastrophe and allow him to write amiably about those aspects of the journey that could be severed from the memories of a relationship that was heading for disaster just over the horizon of the book he was writing.

One result of this decision, of course, was that Waugh had introduced a large element of fiction into a factual genre, the travel book. It was an enabling act, fundamentally necessary if he was to write the book at all, but it seems likely that even without the problem of She-Evelyn he would have early decided not to restrain his novelist's instinct to tell the best story he could, rearranging the facts as artistry demanded. And that was to be his method in all his travel writing, for there he stayed true to the basic premise of his fiction, that these narratives were moral entertainments. Moral issues were fundamental to his writing, but he never forgot that unless his books were entertainments they were nothing. Fiction should therefore properly be brought into the travel writing to maintain the high entertainment quota, which in its turn underpinned the moral viewpoint.[3]

Labels was a hard assignment merely as a travel book, leaving aside the problems presented by the divorce. The Mediterranean cruise had been arranged by Peters, who had got the Waughs free passage in exchange for publicity. So there was a dutiful element, and Waugh dutifully gushed about the excellence of accommodations and arrangements. The voyage was exotic only in the literal sense of being foreign, so there was little assistance to the writer from really remote or unvisited places. These limitations, however, suited what was to become Waugh's manner of travel writing. He had little interest in landscape or exotica; he travelled for people, for culture, and for history (and he liked to have someone else to pay the bills). After *Labels*, his repeated travels in Africa nourished his fascination with the conflict between civilization and barbarism, but that fascination really took shape only with and after his conversion to Rome. In *Labels* he had to discover an ad hoc thematic interest, and so asserted that 'all the places I visited on this trip are already fully labelled' (hence the title). His point in writing about them is to investigate 'with a mind as open as the English system of pseudo-education allows, the basis for the reputations these famous places have acquired' (LA 16).

This project figures very little in the book; it is a purposive justi-fication that can be neglected once the author has his reader's atten-tion and once the reader is happy in the author's company. Where we are going and why are far less important than that we should find the description and commentary amusing. Waugh as a travel writer wanted (mainly) to meet odd people and (less importantly) to see things that were unexpected. Travel writing for him was taking his sensibility for a walk, and he trusted, usually rightly, in his power to amuse. And *Labels* is continually if mildly amusing, a some-times absorbing book plucked from the jaws of boredom and the expected.

The book was published in September 1930. It was thus being pre-pared for publication when, on Wednesday 2 July 1930, he wrote in his diary, 'To tea ... with Olivia [Plunket Greene]. I said would she please find a Jesuit to instruct me'. The major event of his literary life, his divorce, was about to be followed by the major event of his life, his conversion to Roman Catholicism.

3

Something of the Crusader's Zeal: 1930–39

He spent the next nine years without fixed abode travelling in most parts of Europe and the Near East and tropical America; he has been three times in Abyssinia, once as war correspondent for the Daily Mail *in 1935. In 1930 he was received into the Roman Catholic Church.*

English Catholics, Waugh asserted, were 'usually served by simple Irish missionaries', but the priests who were important in his life were rather different. He went for instruction to Father Martin D'Arcy, SJ, who was soon after to become Principal of Campion Hall, the Jesuit establishment at Oxford. Proud of his Norman ancestry, D'Arcy was a great fisher of men among the English *prominenten*, upper-class people and people of talent and achievement.

Waugh presents his conversion as an entirely cerebral matter. Reason alone had brought him to Farm Street and Father D'Arcy, and the reason of D'Arcy's statements and answers would effect Waugh's conversion. Emotion played a very small part and aesthetic feeling even less. When he sat down with D'Arcy he already believed in God and his revelation. All the priest had to do was prove to him that the Christian revelation was 'genuine', by which he mainly meant historically factual. If that could be shown, then any difficulties would be at an end, since he also accepted that 'if the Christian revelation was true, then the [Catholic] Church was the society founded by Christ' (EAR 367). D'Arcy had a straightforward task. Waugh accepted his account of 'the historical and philosophic grounds for supposing the Christian revelation to be genuine', and on 29 September 1930 he was received into the Church. No one was invited to the ceremony but Tom Driberg, Waugh's schoolfellow from Lancing. He was bewildered by his selection, but Waugh had reasons for it. It was to Driberg that he had confessed his loss of religious faith; Driberg should therefore witness its recovery and amendment. And Driberg was now a gossip columnist on the *Daily Express*. He duly included a statement of Waugh's conversion in his column, and so the problem of an announcement was solved.

'On firm intellectual conviction but with little emotion I was admitted into the Church'. Once inside, his faith grew and strengthened and he found the Communion of Saints (RC) made him free of a huge territory that for most of the remainder of his life he explored with delight, both intellectual and emotional. Catholicism was the keystone of the system of beliefs, covering all aspects of life, that he had been assembling for some time; it completed the structure and held it all together.

Conversion at first and for quite some time made little outward difference to Waugh's behaviour. The fragmentary diaries he kept from 1930 to 1936 record the same activities and the same order of sentiments as before. He continued the extensive irregular sexual life he had begun to lead after his divorce; there were prostitutes and married women among his partners, but now the aftermath of a sexual encounter included confession: 'To Farm Street to confess Winnie' (D 387). From before his conversion, he had been in love with Teresa Jungman; she was known as 'Baby' and to Waugh, especially in his letters to the Lygon sisters, as 'the Dutch girl'. He pursued her energetically for some time, never realizing apparently that, like Olivia Plunket Greene, she could not find him physically attractive. Neither, however, did she actively discourage his attentions or agree to continue the relationship only as a friendship, as Olivia had. Baby Jungman combined the role of prominent Bright Young Person with a devout Catholicism; she told Waugh that she regarded him as a married man, and it is possible that it was those remarks and his feelings for her that moved him in 1933 to begin proceedings for annulment of his marriage.

Waugh's conversion to Catholicism concluded a stage of his life and completed the system of ideas that, not greatly modified, was to be his intellectual equipment for the rest of his life. Before going forward with the narrative of that life, we should pause to look at the salient features of the system. Some elements of it did not take their definitive forms until later, but the fundamentals cohered and came into focus with Catholicism, and it will be convenient to set down here a summary of the beliefs that gave Waugh the firm footing for the assaults and the jokes that were concomitants of a nevertheless quite serious attitude.

With Catholicism, the spiritual and supernatural became the true reality for Waugh. They were literally and not just metaphorically the highest order of reality, and much of human life could be seen as frantic aimlessness in comparison with the certainty and stability of the eternal order. Such had been the account of human existence implicit in his earliest writings and in his two published novels. Catholicism added an alternative existence to the one depicted in his work and provided a new assurance to underlie his critique of what now revealed itself as the godless and meaningless modern world. He hardly needed to modify at all his pre-conversion opinions of the hilarious, self-serving and self-defeating machinations of human beings existing without any awareness of that superior order of reality that was his new-found land. Driberg's column in the *Daily Express* announcing Waugh's conversion had described him at a society gathering, 'watching critically from the balcony'. Conversion meant that in one way Waugh had withdrawn from the world of meaninglessness, godlessness, and chaos, yet he remained passionately interested in it, with it if not spiritually or intellectually of it. He could confidently judge and condemn the world he described, but he would not turn away from it. His fiction served his faith at first by keeping the criterion of religion reserved, a dim burning light, hard to see but never extinguished, the token presence of the eternal order. He believed that God had assigned a task to every human soul, and that to live in harmony with God's will meant identifying correctly the task assigned and doing it to the best of one's ability. In his own case, the task was to be a writer. He was fascinated as a writer, however, by the vast number of men and women who had misconceived their tasks and frantically pursued ambitions to which they were not called. His first book, *Rossetti*, dealt with a calling only partly understood; his two later biographies, of Edmund Campion and Father Ronald Knox, described callings fulfilled. In his fiction, vocation is either wildly misconceived or discovered too late; the exceptions – neither an unalloyed triumph – are found in his two novels of vocation, *Brideshead Revisited* and *Helena*.

What must be grasped at the outset is that this is the politics of Original Sin.

The widely accepted hypothesis of the Fall of Man and the Atonement – leaving aside the supernatural credentials on which they are held – did and still do explain the peculiar position of man in the universe.... Man is by nature an exile, haunted, even at the height of his prosperity, by nostalgia for Eden; individually and collectively he is always in search of an oppressor who will take responsibility for his ills. The Treaty of Versailles, Sanctions, Jews, Bolshevists, Bankers, the Colour Bar – anything will do so long as he can focus on it his sense of grievance and convince himself that his own inadequacy is due to some exterior cause. (EAR 246, 161)

From this point of view, the arguments about 'secondary' causes and effects that are the business of politics are shown to be mere instances of a great principle ignored by all but those who hew to this fundamentalism. Most politics is the diagnosis and treatment of symptoms, while the underlying disease is steadfastly and willfully unrecognized.

All of Waugh's opinions are adjusted to the idea of man as a fallen creature, never to be perfected except by God's grace, operative only in the life to come. Individual and collective human effort, without reliance on the redemption offered by God through the Incarnation, was inevitably futile. Those who failed to recognize earth as a place of exile were doomed to lives of meaningless chaos and frustration, and to afterlives of hellfire, in which Waugh quite seriously believed. (His efforts to convert his friends to Catholicism were, in his eyes, his most sincere acts of friendship.)

In the accounts that he published of his conversion, politics of this religious alignment gets pride of place. In a *Daily Express* account (20 October 1933) he described 'the essential issue' as between Christianity and Chaos. (Since Roman Catholicism was the only valid form of Christianity, for 'Christianity' read 'Catholicism'.) 'Civilization – . . . the whole moral and artistic organization of Europe – has not in itself the power of survival. It came into being through Christianity, and without it has no significance or power to command allegiance'. One must assume that his conviction of Catholic truth was the primary reason for his allegiance to Rome, and that his published reasons – mainly the need to uphold civilization – were secondary. Otherwise it looks as if he became a Catholic for reasons of cultural politics. The truth must be that the defence of civilization was a motive he was willing to discuss in public. Other, and perhaps more profound motives were not to be retailed in newspaper articles.

The pessimistic view of unaided human possibility that came to Waugh with his acceptance of the doctrine of Original Sin justified his unremitting opposition to what he called 'humanism', the idea that humans are alone in the universe, since there is no deity or none concerned with their deeds and affairs, and that their happiness depends solely on their own efforts. For Waugh, humans were not perfectible and humanistic projects for the improvement of their condition would inevitably split on the rock of flawed human nature.

At the beginning of his book about Mexico's appropriation of British and American oil companies (*Robbery Under Law*, 1939), he wrote a statement of his conservative principles that conveniently locates him on the spectrum of twentieth-century politics and focuses on his rejection of humanism. He begins by showing that his views are rooted in his religious conception of human nature: 'I believe that man is, by nature, an exile and will never be self-sufficient or complete on this earth'. Next, he declares the general impossibility of humanistic projects to improve humankind's lot, based again on flawed human nature: '[man's] chances of happiness and virtue, here, remain more or less constant through the centuries, and, generally speaking, are not much affected by the political and economic conditions in which he lives'. No project or reform or improvement can mend the flaw that keeps humankind from earthly happiness. Government – a necessary minimum of it – is always needed to restrain humankind's innate capacity for evil. 'Barbarism is never finally defeated...we are all potential recruits for anarchy'. He shows that the anti-Americanism that appears regularly in his writing is not solely a matter of taste; he finds a heresy in the twentieth century's tendency to idolize democracy, which is likely no more than a short-term expedient: 'there is no form of government ordained from God as being better than any other'. Celebrations of the Age of the Common Man enraged him. Communism, as the most 'humanistic' of political philosophies, was anathema to him; its materialism was a gigantic fallacy; he saw atheism as its starting point, its fundamental premise. In contrast, with the Roman Church as the divinely ordained model, he saw hierarchy as a 'natural' principle of human social organization. 'I believe that inequalities of wealth and position are inevitable and that it is therefore meaningless to discuss the advantages of their elimination; that men naturally arrange themselves in a system of classes; that such a system is necessary for any form of co-operative work....' Correspondingly he abominated relativism in just about all its forms. In *Robbery Under Law*, for example, there is a contemptuous evocation of

> the familiar thesis of the professors of 'comparative religion' all
> over the world; that man's disposition to worship comes from his

awe of natural forces and from his own dreams; that there has been no special revelation but a cycle of myths, finding new names in the different stages of man's progress to rational atheism.... (RUL 220)

Cultural relativism was equally bogus. In Mexico City, Waugh is shown the great Calendar Stone in the National Museum, but he brushes aside the established truth about it as self-evidently untrue since 'flattering to its Aztec carvers.... It has been the base of a patriotic claim that before the Spanish conquest, the Indians had advanced beyond Europe in the science of chronology' (RUL 78). For Waugh, the Catholic civilization of Spain (with its flaws, of which he gives terse acknowledgement) was obviously superior to that of the Aztecs, and the future civilization of Mexico depended on its following the traditions of Spain. It was no contradiction to Waugh that Spain had civilized by conquest: 'war and conquest are inevitable; that is how history has been made and that is how it will develop' (RUL 17). The Catholic writer Hilaire Belloc held the view that only countries conquered by Rome were truly civilized. In some respects Waugh was a disciple of Belloc. He notes that there was no memorial in Mexico to Cortés, and adds: 'come to think of it, is there anywhere in England a memorial to Julius Caesar'?

Relativism's equalizing of cultures was particularly repugnant to Waugh because high culture, especially art and architecture, was the essential component in his idea of civilization. A nation's claim to civilized status could be equitably judged by its works of art, and Waugh's Eurocentric standards were quite unwavering. In *Labels*, he records a visit to a museum of Arab art in Cairo. Muslim law, of course, is often taken to restrict visual and plastic art to decorative forms. Waugh makes no allowances.

I was moved by something of the Crusader's zeal for cross against crescent, as I reflected that these skilful, spiritless bits of merchandise were contemporary with the Christian masterpieces of the Musée de Cluny [in Paris].... during those centuries when the Christian artists were carving the stalls of our cathedrals and parish churches, these little jigsaw puzzles were being fitted together beyond the frontiers [of Christendom, which is to say, of civilization], by artificers whose artistic development seemed to have been arrested in the kindergarten stage... (LA 110).

Labels, be it remembered, was written before his conversion, though published after. Waugh claimed, truthfully, that aesthetic elements in Catholicism played no part in his great decision, but it is also true that the civilization that it was Christianity's great task to uphold had art objects at its centre. His devotion to art in this sense did carry over into commitments of politics and values.

The eternal war of civilization against the chaos and anarchy that originate in man's originally corrupt nature is the foundation theme of all of Waugh's fiction. He recognized this as a Gibbonian theme, but with Catholicism a marked contradiction entered into the elective affinity of the novelist as (Gibbonian) historian. Staying concealed, he stated what was for him a personal dilemma as if it were a general issue in which he had only general involvement: 'It is no longer possible, as it was in the time of Gibbon, to accept the benefits of civilization and at the same time deny the supernatural basis upon which it rests'. If civilization stood on the foundation of Christianity, could he somehow bring the atheistical Gibbon over with him in support of a Catholic defence of civilization? This little problem nagged him on and off for years. We shall note his attempts to solve it in his later writings.

The politics of Original Sin is perfectly suitable and adequate equipment for a writer; Waugh's novels validate his beliefs as the foundations of a fictional universe. But as the politics of day-to-day existence it seems bizarre. In day-to-day terms, in fact, Waugh was an eccentric conservative. On the great issues of the 1930s he took stands that are simultaneously expected and odd. He was, as one would expect, pro-Franco in the Spanish Civil War debate, but he characterized the opposing sides as 'two evils', with the Nationalists the lesser of the two. 'I am not a Fascist nor shall I become one unless it were the only alternative to Marxism' (EAR 187). He did not see the choice as imminent in 1937. Nazism he always opposed. He saw its evil, but was alerted to it, I believe, because of its paganism and atheism. Mussolini for a long time had Waugh fooled. Donat Gallagher, the editor of Waugh's collected journalism, points out that in the 1930s there was a reasonable, conservative case to be made for Mussolini as a rival who might check Hitler's ambitions, notably towards Catholic Austria (EAR 158). And Mussolini came to a Concordat with the Church that seemed to many Catholics a benevolent arrangement. In January 1936, on his way back from inspecting the Italians at war in Abyssinia, Waugh had a meeting in Rome with Mussolini, though on condition that he did not write about it.

Unexpectedly, he was genuinely impressed, though there is debate among his biographers as to how long he retained his favourable impression of Il Duce. (Christopher Sykes doubts that he ever gave it up [SY 168].)

Day-to-day politics is essentially compromise, and Waugh's refusal to compromise meant that he was effectively disenfranchised. The great necessary compromises of the Second World War provided him with the thematic framework of his novels about the conflict, but despite his military service his attitude towards the war was that of an outsider. He made the hero of the war novels, Guy Crouchback, an exile. Politically he was himself an 'internal' self-exile. His own later politics – in their absurdity – are summarized in an article he wrote before the 1959 election, 'Aspirations of a Mugwump' (that is, one who holds aloof from party politics). His detestation of the post-war Labour governments made him hope for a Conservative victory, but he would not vote: 'Great Britain is not a democracy'. His literalism encouraged him to insist that, since the monarchy existed still, its power was unmodified by the Revolution (of 1688) and nineteenth-century reform: 'In the last 300 years, particularly in the last hundred, the Crown has adopted what seems to me a very hazardous process of choosing advisers: popular election'. It is a quintessentially Wavian stroke to define voting in a parliamentary election as a presumptuous aspiration to 'advise my sovereign in her choice of servants' (EAR 537).

By making high culture his determinant of civilization, Waugh allowed himself selective blindness to the barbarism that can co-exist with high culture. At the least, as with the Spanish war, he should have acknowledged that the struggle of the Abyssinians and Italians was between two evils. But he did not, at least in *Waugh in Abyssinia*. In his novels dealing with Africa, *Black Mischief* and *Scoop*, there is a balance of barbarisms, British and African; his British characters can make no claims upon him because of their national high culture, but in *Waugh in Abyssinia* the Italians wear boots, build roads, and are the modern representatives of *Romanitas*; the Abyssinians go barefoot and their buildings make extensive use of corrugated iron. In *Remote People*, Waugh mentions that he bought modern Abyssinian paintings: 'mostly either hunting-scenes or intensely savage battle-pictures'. His estimate of their cultural value is perhaps indicated by the fact that they were installed in the downstairs gentlemen's lavatory at Piers Court. Barbarism was mainly on the Abyssinian side. The European and American journalists covering the war are barbaric, but not the Italians. His investigation of civilization's struggle with barbarism was the thematic energy of much of his work, but its power over him did not derive from rational analysis, nor was it rationally developed. It could be argued, in fact, that it was a prejudice trained up into an analytic obsession and thereby made respectable – in the 1930s if not in the last three decades of the twentieth century.

Evelyn Waugh's prejudices, unlike his famous rudeness, are more apparent in his novels than in reminiscences of him. And even then his most persistently noticeable nastiness, his anti-Semitism, is less visible in his novels than are the other racisms that are given prominence by the setting of two novels in 'Azania' and 'Ishmaelia', mythical but recognizable African countries. The anti-Semitism was usually though not always of the jocular variety. It existed before he became a Catholic, but Catholicism seems if anything to have strengthened it. The events of the Second World War effected a belated change in Waugh's attitude towards Jews, even though the change may never have worked through to his social behaviour. *Unconditional Surrender* is in part an apology for a lifetime's sneers about 'jewboys' and 'four-by-twos'.

His assumptions concerning the superiority of whites over blacks are an illogical extension of his views on the naturalness and rightness of hierarchy as the principle of social organization. A hierarchy of the races was as 'natural' as the class organization of society. And if the matter is to be decided by vocabulary, then Waugh is unredeemable. Like many writers of the early twentieth century, he makes liberal use of the late twentieth century's great obscenity, 'nigger'. In *Black Mischief* and *Scoop*, African characters are objects of ridicule, a fact perhaps unmitigated by the fact that European characters are treated even more severely, since generalized judgements tend to apply to blacks and not to whites. Waugh was an eccentric conservative of his time. Attitudes from sixty years ago that are now unacceptable confront his modern readers because his work survives, as it must if it is to survive at all, 'uncorrected'. The shift of expectations and assumptions has forced new activities upon Waugh's reader; one must make choices and discriminations where none were demanded of most readers decades ago, but that new awareness is no bad thing.

Between his conversion to Rome in 1930 and his second marriage in 1937, Evelyn Waugh's life had little stability but a pattern. He made three major journeys in those years, and on his return from each he wrote a travel book about the trip, followed by a novel that similarly and differently depended on the journey. In October 1931 he travelled to Ethiopia (usually in his writing called 'Abyssinia', though he uses 'Ethiopia' interchangeably) to cover as a journalist the coronation of Ras Tafari as Emperor Haile Selassie. From this came *Remote People* (1931) and the novel *Black Mischief* (1932). In December 1932 he voyaged to British Guiana (now Guyana), producing from this expedition *Ninety-Two Days* (1934) and the novel *A Handful of Dust* (1934). He went back to Abyssinia in August 1935 to cover the Italian–Abyssinian crisis and returned to London in January 1936. He started what was to be *Waugh in Abyssinia*, but interrupted its writing to return to Abyssinia (from 8 August to 9 September 1936) and update his information to include the Italian victory. So, strictly speaking, two journeys were needed for *Waugh in Abyssinia* (1936) and *Scoop* (1938), the novel that followed. He spent the winter of 1933–4 in Morocco, writing, and put the experience to literary use in *Work Suspended* (written in 1939), and in the summer of 1934 he went on an expedition to Spitzbergen, of which he made some use in journalism but none at all in fiction. His attitude towards travel had changed radically from that which he had described on returning from his visit to Alistair Graham in Greece. He now indicated that he had to get away or go mad, and there is truth in Selina Hastings' opinion that the 'hostility and chaos of the external world' in Africa or South America provided 'a welcome distraction from the hostility and chaos of the world within' (H 270). Religious conversion had not brought calm and placidity to Waugh. It had given him eagerly embraced certainties, but nothing, not even a happy marriage, could calm for long his restless spirit. Religion and writing – the oases of eternal order and created order – were brief stopping places for Waugh in a life journey that was internally far more demanding than any journey to Spitzbergen or Boa Vista could have been.

Ras Tafari was planning to be crowned Emperor of Abyssinia in December 1930. Waugh was seized by a desire to go there that was quite obsessive, so much so that he was willing to pay for the trip himself should Peters be unable to find a newspaper willing to send him as its correspondent. (At this time, and up until his marriage, he spent the considerable income from his books as fast as it came in, and relied on journalism, mostly for large-circulation London newspapers, to keep his head above the water of his heavy spending.) In the event, he went to Abyssinia as the correspondent of *The Times*, so commencing the experience of journalism in Africa that was to bear later literary fruit in *Scoop* (1938).

The coronation of Haile Selassie ('Power of the Trinity', as Ras Tafari became) obviously had much to attract Waugh. It was, for example, a social occasion with many European dignitaries in an exotic setting. Yet the urgency of his desire to be there seems to go beyond such attractions. The real clue to his eagerness is found in his account of the rumours he had heard about the country:

> that the Abyssinian Church had canonized Pontius Pilate, and consecrated their bishops by spitting on their heads; that the real heir to the throne was hidden in the mountains, fettered with chains of solid gold; that the people lived on raw meat and mead...that, 'though nominally Christian, the Abyssinians are deplorably lax in their morals, polygamy and drunkenness being common even among the highest classes and in the monasteries'. Everything I heard added to the glamour of this astonishing country. (RP 11)

When he chanced on these rumours, Waugh was under instruction and about to be received into the Catholic Church. He was embracing certainty, acquiring a standard against which all important things could be measured. Like Paul Pennyfeather, only on more certain grounds, he was now in a position to make authoritative dismissal of unorthodoxy. The pleasure, the sheer fun, of looking at the heretical Abyssinian church from his now Catholic viewpoint would be augmented by everything that the coronation promised of barbarism meeting and trying to ape civilization, to say nothing of the barbarisms of the ought-to-be civilized Europeans and Americans. He *had* to go to Abyssinia. The situation was made for him.

Remote People, the book that includes the account of this first visit to Abyssinia, is the best of Waugh's travel books (stretching the term to include *Waugh in Abyssinia* and *Robbery Under Law*). All the others were written with metaphorically and perhaps literally clenched teeth. He did not like writing *Remote People* any more than the others – he did not like writing – but he enjoyed the experiences that went into this book and the enjoyment communicates itself very clearly. The book is divided between accounts of 'Ethiopian Empire' and 'British Empire' and there is a clear intent to contrast the two. The contrast, however, is of differing pleasures. 'British Empire' describes visits Waugh made to Aden, Zanzibar, and Kenya after he had completed his reporting from Abyssinia. He had not expected to enjoy visiting these British territories but he did. Aden, often abominated as an armpit of empire, introduced him to Antonin Besse ('Mr Leblanc' in the book), an amazing character who became part-model for the mysterious and omnicompetent Mr Baldwin in *Scoop*, and in real life the founder of St Antony's College, Oxford. Then there is the meeting of the Adeni Boy Scouts, a hilarious masterpiece of Waugh's deadpan descriptive style. With Kenya, Waugh simply fell in love, with the Kenya of the upland white colonists on their farms, that is to say, which he claimed was 'a community of English squires established on the Equator'. He had discovered a colonialism of nostalgia, an English way of life no longer possible in England, transported to Kenya and flourishing there. With it, he drew a fascinating parallel. 'The Kenya settlers are not cranks of the kind who colonized New England, nor criminals and ne'er-do-wells of the kind who went to Australia, but perfectly normal, respectable Englishmen, out of sympathy with their own age, and for this reason linked to the artist in an unusual but very real way' (RP 138). His conversion had given him the concept of the artist as the creator in the secular sphere of the kind of order and consistency that the Church had established on earth. But these were islands of order in a sea of chaos. The settlers of Kenya had likewise established order and civilization – the embodiment of order – in a world where disorder and the conflict with barbarism were the norm. In *Remote People*, the unexpected discovery of this El Dorado of civilization comes to balance the squalid disorder and chaotic comedy of what the ignorant and opinionated hold to be the civilization of the Abyssinian Empire.

Waugh loved Kenya, but the artist in him loved Abyssinia far more. Things going wrong delighted and comforted him with their confirmations of the general disorder of the world and licensed him to do what as a writer he was best at: to complain, and by complaining to be funny.[1] Things going wrong in Abyssinia were more solid reassurance for the negative than the obviously uncertain existence of the settler El Dorado in the Kenyan highlands was for the positive. What the settlers had achieved was a stay against a chaos that always threatened to engulf them (a chaos voiced and represented in *Remote People* not by Africans but by disaffected immigrant Indians in Kenya). Islands of civilization, like works of art and even the Church on earth, could disappear. Waugh preferred to work on the assumption that barbarism threatened and might eventually be victorious, so Abyssinia signified more than Kenya.

In both *Remote People* and *Waugh in Abyssinia*, he vastly enjoyed
(and stored up for future use) the mendacity and incompetence of
journalists. For their part, the Abyssinians had bought from the con
men of the West the gold bricks of modernity and progress. Their
attempts to present themselves as an up-to-date, progressive modern
state are doomed to farce by their basic barbarism and by the barbar-
ity of what they have taken from the West to use as their facade of
civilization. The Abyssinians, of course, could not win. If they had
managed to make themselves completely and successfully modern
and progressive, they would only have emulated all that was worst
about Western civilization. And they would have remained barbaric
underneath. In *Remote People*, Waugh's attitude towards the Abyssinians' Westernizing is good humoured, but only because of his confidence of superiority. At the beginning of Chapter 2, he describes
his attempts to find a 'historical parallel' for life in Addis Ababa at
that time. *Alice in Wonderland* has the strongest claim – 'historical'? –
but there are others: 'Israel in the time of Saul, the Scotland of Shakespeare's *Macbeth*, the Sublime Porte as one sees it revealed in the dis-
patches of the late eighteenth century'. But in *Alice* only is there 'the
peculiar flavour of galvanized and translated reality, where animals
carry watches in their waistcoat pockets' and so forth. Waugh chooses
the only parallel that is basically comic; the others are listed to
remind us in each case of the savagery that can lie beneath a civilized
surface. In *Waugh in Abyssinia*, several years later, his fundamental
hostility, mainly cultural, to Abyssinia's claims to civilized status are
more openly laid bare. It is a less good-tempered book than *Remote
People*, and antagonisms are correspondingly clearer. In Chapter 4,
he describes 'the Emperor's Maskal', 'a personal religious function of
the emperor's', attended by the court, the foreign legations, and the
press. It was the opportunity for the latter to compose some 'good
colourful stuff. . . . What was more surprising was that many of [the
reporters] seemed genuinely impressed by what they saw'. His own
descriptions of decor and costumes are very careful. 'Petrol cans,
painted pale green, held ragged little palms. At the far end was
a great, gilt, canopied divan-throne, in the style which graced the
old Alhambra Music Hall'. The camera was kind to the priests and
deacons 'for their robes at close quarters were of the shoddiest
material – gaudy Japanese vegetable silks, embroidered with sequins
and tinsel; there were gilt crowns and bright umbrellas' (WIA 97).

The next paragraph is his systematic demolition of what he has
already undermined. 'It was customary for apologists to liken the

coronation of Ethiopia to that of medieval Europe; there were close parallels, of a kind, to be drawn between Ethiopia . . . and our own high and chivalrous origins'. There is no irony at all in this last phrase, and the aspects of Ethiopian culture that he lists – 'its unstable but half-sacred monarchy, the feudal fiefs and the frequent insurrections, the lepers and serfs, the chained and tortured captives, the isolation and ignorance, the slow *tempo*' – are a comparison between what is utterly characteristic of Abyssinia and what was peripheral and, in his view, inessential, in medieval Europe. 'We had seen the highest expression of historic Abyssinian culture; this was the Church's most splendid and solemn occasion . . .'. Then he mentally compares this ceremony with his utterly confident idea of what a similar event would have been like in medieval Europe:

> the avenues of fluted columns, branching high overhead into groined and painted roof, each boss and capital a triumph of delicate sculpture, the sweet, precise music [and him confessedly not knowing a harp from a handsaw!], the embroidered vestments, the stained and leaded windows to which later artists look, hopeless of emulation, the learning and austerity of the monastic orders, the royal dignity of the great Churchmen, of a culture which had created an object of delicate and original beauty for every simple use. . . . It was significant to turn from that to the artificial silk and painted petrol cans of Addis Ababa. (WIA 98)

The fallacies and unfairness of this are staggering, but what most impresses about it is its assurance. In Catholicism Waugh had a place to stand and a confidence that together gave him the authority he had always sought. In both *Waugh in Abyssinia* and *Remote People* he claims the authoritative position of being the sole person – it is Alice's role, of course – able to see what is going on, unaffected by prejudices or wishful thinking or journalistic cliches or any of the mental miasmas that impede the sight of those who surround him. His empirical fundamentalism and his Catholicism combine into a confident authority that exposes as fantasies and delusions the statements and attitudes of those among whom he moves, the clear-eyed observer of the always simple truth. 'Over his shoulder I watched an American journalist typing out a description of the women under their mushroom-like umbrellas. There were no women and no umbrellas . . . ' (WIA 102).

The fantastic rumours that had first attracted him to Abyssinia had intermingled history and religion. Current Abyssinian politics and morality had been mentioned, but the 'glamour' that seized Waugh came from the canonization of Pontius Pilate and episcopal consecration by expectoration. The True Church, of which he was even then being made free, let him see the Abyssinian Church as quintessentially representative of the absurdity of heresy and the farce of 'reformation' and dissent. There was nothing ecumenical about Waugh's religion, and he would never concede that an unorthodox Christian (a non-Catholic) was really preferable to an out-and-out pagan. Abyssinia was not only an independent African country seduced by the lies of modernism and progress; it was also a Christian country of delirious unorthodoxy. A coronation would be the perfect event for an observer of his orientation, since it was essentially a religious ceremony at the heart of secular politics. What he made of it is given in essence in his account of the Emperor's Maskal, described above. But his interest in the Abyssinian Church went beyond the coronation, and Chapter 4 of *Remote People*, the account of his visit to the monastery at Debra Lebanos, became surprisingly the heart of the book and one of the most important things he ever wrote.

He was invited to visit Debra Lebanos by Professor Thomas Whittemore, an American ecclesiologist, presented in the book as a splendid comic foil to the narrator's calm and unyielding record of what he saw. 'Professor W' sees almost everything having to do with Abyssinian religion through a distorting haze of veneration and wishful thinking.

> 'Look', he said, pointing to some columns of smoke that rose from the cliffs above us, 'the cells of the solitary anchorites'.
> 'Are you sure there are solitary anchorites here? I never heard of any'.
> 'It would be a good place for them' he said wistfully. (RP 61)

Waugh's attitude towards Debra Lebanos, 'the centre of Abyssinian spiritual life', is established by his description of the site at the beginning of the chapter.

> It is built round a spring where the waters of the Jordan, conveyed subterraneously down the Red Sea, are believed to well up endowed with curative properties; pilgrims go there from all parts

of the country, and it is a popular burial ground for those who can afford it, since all found there at the Last Trump are assured of unimpeded entry into Paradise. (RP 54)

He could easily have completed the chapter in this fashion, establishing his critical attitude without openly declaring himself, letting the 'facts' and Professor W's foolishness make the case against absurdity and unorthodoxy, but he did not. In the middle of the chapter, they attend mass at the monastery. The liturgy is unintelligible: 'No doubt the canon of the Mass would have been in part familiar, but this was said in the sanctuary behind closed doors'. Unexpectedly, Waugh comments directly and *in propria persona* on this experience. 'For anyone accustomed to the Western rite it was difficult to think of this as a Christian service, for it bore that secret and confused character which I had hitherto associated with the non-Christian sects of the East'. He brings himself forward at this point because mass at Debra Lebanos is to become a moment of revelation and vocation in his literary life. 'I had sometimes thought it an odd thing that Western Christianity, alone of all the religions of the world, exposes its mysteries to every observer, but I was so accustomed to this openness that I had never before questioned whether it was an essential and natural feature of the Christian system'. Observing mass at Debra Lebanos gives him sudden insight, almost a vision, of what distinguishes Catholicism from all others of the world's religions, and these 'other' religions include Eastern Christianity, here represented by the Abyssinian Church. His revelatory meditation then moves to the evolution of Christianity. The primitive church, often presented as simple, unelaborated, and therefore pure and unsophisticated, was in fact secretive and tainted, very much like the Abyssinian Church: 'the pure nucleus of the truth lay in the minds of the people, encumbered with superstitions, gross survivals of the paganism in which they had been brought up; hazy and obscene nonsense seeping through from the conquered barbarian'. As the Church grew and evolved, it moved away from this obscurity and syncretism.

At Debra Lebanos I suddenly saw the classic basilica and open altar as a great positive achievement, a triumph of light over darkness consciously accomplished, and I saw theology as the science of simplification by which nebulous and elusive ideas are formalized and made intelligible and exact. . . . these obscure sanctuaries

[of the primitive church] had grown, with the clarity of the Western reason, into the great open altars of Catholic Europe, where
Mass is said in a flood of light, high in the sight of all.... (RP 68)

Waugh is describing and defining a Church that a sage of the En-
lightenment could love – if he could let go of his atheism. The sanctuary they have been shown is littered with junk: 'I noticed a wicker
chair, some heaps of clothes, two or three umbrellas, a suitcase of
imitation leather, some newspapers, and a tea-pot and slop-pail of
enamelled tin'. This litter can exist because the sanctuary is secret,
not open to the worshippers, even to their sight; the mess is the
product of 'Oriental' obscurantism. The well-lit openness of the
'altars of Catholic Europe' is the product of reason, of theology as
'the science of simplification' and the model of consistency (RP 138).
Waugh is here defining the faith he had recently embraced, to the
surprise and admiration of Father D'Arcy, but there is a different
order of surprise in the literary method he chooses for this exercise.
    Waugh looked at the monks of Debra Lebanos – 'All the monks
had mistresses & children & most of them carried rifles & swords.
None of them went to Church' – and saw only the disparity
between them and the ideal he knew had existed when the Church
in the West had replaced its primitive 'Orientalism' with the reason
and openness of the Counter-Reformation. The Abyssinian monks
are stuck at the primitive stage, and Waugh's attitude towards them
is very Gibbonian. His drafting of the whole passage summarized
above was governed by the memory of one famous sentence from
Memoir E of Gibbon's autobiography. Recounting his Italian tour,
Gibbon writes: 'It was at Rome, on the 15th of October 1764, as I sat
musing amid the ruins of the Capitol, while the barefooted friars
were singing vespers in the temple of Jupiter, that the idea of writing the decline and fall of the city first started to my mind'. In this
formulation, it was not just the ruins, but the ruins in the possession
of modern discalceate barbarism and superstition that composed
Gibbon's revelation of his 'mission'. Gibbon 'suddenly saw', and in
his own sudden seeing Waugh is given a vision, not of decline and
fall but of darkness and light, the 'hazy and obscene nonsense' of
'Orientalism' giving way to 'the clarity of the Western reason'. He
has used the Gibbonian sentence as the model for his own vision,
and in so doing has brought the Gibbonian literary virtues into his
own camp. Waugh looked at Abyssinian Christianity and civilization through Gibbon's spectacles, and deftly defined *his* Catholicism

in terms that might have persuaded Gibbon to convert once again to the Church of Rome.

Waugh's diary entry covering the visit to Debra Lebanos (10–11 November 1930) gives no indication at all of the occurrence of this momentous revelation. It is most likely that it came to Waugh as he went over the mass in his memory, perhaps even when he was writing the book. But this too is Gibbonian: Gibbon's journal of his Italian tour records nothing of the vocational revelation of 15 October 1764.

Remote People was Waugh's first book as a Catholic, and he made clear in it that henceforth he would be a Catholic author. His manner of declaration, however, without the Debra Lebanos passage, could have struck some, perhaps many, readers as oblique. The moment of revelation he gave himself at the monastery should have left no one in doubt of the religious commitment of his work, but even then he was not yet willing to put Catholicism front and centre in his fiction. It would stay reserved, and he would – though not without protest – shoulder the burden of misrepresentation that some devout Catholics heaped upon him by reason of his promotion of his artistic judgement above the obligation he had accepted to campaign for his faith.

In Addis Ababa for the coronation, Waugh stored away for future use the hopeless aspirations of the Abyssinians for modernity and progress, the lies and rank incompetence of the press corps, and the 'hysteria' and inefficiency of the British legation, headed, he was pleased to note, by an 'Envoy Extraordinary'. (Those legation people would soon learn what a truly extraordinary Envoy Extraordinary could be!) One encounter was prophetic, though quite wasted on Waugh, as prophetic as his participation in the General Strike of 1926 had been. He met Wilfred Thesiger, who was shortly thereafter to depart on his expedition to the mysterious and fearsome Danakil of Ethiopia and Djibouti. (Thesiger was eventually to be a writer of 'travel books' that are true masterpieces of the genre.) Waugh had been idly hoping to be able to join a real exploratory expedition, and the idea of his accompanying Thesiger surfaced for a moment only to be sunk at once. Thesiger, son of a former legation head, born in Addis Ababa, educated at Eton, detested Waugh at sight. He loved the Abyssinians, and he was a man of action, the genuine article, an aristocrat in all but title, impervious to Waugh's charm and humour, and with an ego quite as large as Waugh's own. Had Waugh gone with him, 'I'd have been tempted to knock him off' (H 236). During his military career, Waugh had a brief but bloody encounter with another genuine article, the fifteenth Baron Lovat, who had all of Thesiger's imperviousness to Waugh and an equal detestation of him. The aristocratic persona Waugh constructed for himself was seen through but was left undisturbed by the real aristocrats who were his friends. But there were holdouts, Thesiger, Lovat, Conrad Russell, and with them Waugh had no chance.

Waugh travelled back from Abyssinia by an ill-chosen route and was in England again in March 1931. He was nearly £500 out of pocket but thought the expense worth while. He had already written several chapters of *Remote People*, and he had told his parents in a letter, 'I have the plot of a first rate novel'. The interval until he left on his next journey, to British Guiana (2 December 1932) was filled with writing, for which he needed near solitude (he found it in friends' houses or country hotels), and smart social life. By the summer of 1931 he was doing well financially (*Vile Bodies* was in its eleventh printing, *Decline and Fall* in its sixth), although prosperity for Waugh always meant large expenditures, too. Duckworth published *Remote People* by early November 1931. He wrote newspaper articles for quick cash, and in November 1931 he started on *Black Mischief* at the Easton Court Hotel, Chagford, on Exmoor in Devon. (This became a favourite hideaway for writing.) The book was published on 1 October 1932, and for the first time there were two 'first editions', that for the public and a special one for Waugh's friends. This became his practice for all his subsequent novels.

The most notable social event of this period was Waugh's acquisition as the most prominent of his 'sisters' of Lady Diana Cooper. There were periods of estrangement between them, and after the Second World War they got on better by corresponding than by meeting, but Diana Cooper became a lifelong friend and has a place of some importance in Waugh's fiction. She was the daughter of the Duke of Rutland, and so 'Lady Diana' in her own right. Her husband, Duff Cooper, was a Conservative politician, minister, and ambassador, and was eventually ennobled as Viscount Norwich, but having achieved celebrity under her own title, she remained 'Lady Diana Cooper' and lived a life that demanded three volumes of memoirs. Duff Cooper fitted the pattern as husband of a Waugh 'sister'. He was an author whose work Waugh despised (his biography of Talleyrand was well received in 1932), and Waugh felt more than the usual hostility towards him ('Duff he considered an amiable but dull man whose superior 'sex-appeal' unfairly secured

him the love of beautiful women' (1S 305). After some missteps at
the beginning of the relationship, there was no overtly sexual element, and although Lady Diana was older than he, and in social
stature towered above him, Waugh took the dominant role and was
able in many ways to be instructive with her, something he was
rarely comfortable without in a relationship. For his fiction, where
she supplied the groundwork for Mrs Stitch in *Scoop* and in *Sword of
Honour*, Waugh used only two aspects of her life: the society hostess
and the politician's wife, hyperefficient and all-encompassing in
both roles. Diana Cooper was happy to acknowledge Mrs Stitch as
herself, but she was a in reality more many-sided and less self-
assured than that superb caricature.

From the first, Waugh's feelings about the novel that was eventually
entitled *Black Mischief* were highly optimistic. He was sure that he
was writing a best-seller. His confidence in his abilities here seems to
have come from the theme he had grasped, the disastrous attempt
to marry European 'progress' to African barbarism, since, despite
what he had written to his parents, the plot of the novel was 'slow to
emerge' (RMD 57). He gained confidence too from his early conception of the characters of Basil Seal and Seth, Emperor of Azania.
Having each aspect of his theme represented by so marked a character was bound to generate a fine comic conflict. A plot to frame these
elements would surely take shape, as indeed it did. His confidence is
also visible in the displacement of the *naïve* character, Seth, from the
position of sole protagonist to that of dual protagonist, sharing the
role with Basil, or perhaps being somewhat subordinated to him in
the economy of the novel as well as in its action. Neither character is
autobiographical, but both are figures in whom Waugh could invest
elements of his own emotional make-up. The depiction of Basil owes
a lot to Peter Rodd, man of action, difficult, overbearing, anarchic
and relentlessly informative. (In 1933 he became Nancy Mitford's
husband, after a pre-engagement negotiation with her father at
which he reduced the original of 'Uncle Matthew' to reeling boredom with a two-hour lecture on the toll-gate system of England and
Wales.) As Waugh indicates in his autobiography, however, the
character of the 'satanic' Basil Murray contributed to Basil, too (LL
204). Waugh clearly had the measure of both Rodd and Murray, yet
he responded with a controlled warmth to their intellectual and

emotional buccaneering. This was a side of the 'man of action' that he could neither approve of nor dislike. By making Basil Seal the unexpected but willing representative of 'modernization', Waugh condemned him, yet Basil's depredations are given with a gusto that reveals the author's subversive endorsement. He later said 'There is an ineradicable element of caddishness in all my heroes' (2S 200), but in fact Basil Seal is the first of the cad-heroes ('hero' presents more of a problem than 'cad') and one with whom Waugh's identification remained close.

In *Black Mischief*, confidence on the author's part asserts itself by moving the naïve figure to the side, to accomodate Basil Seal. But Seth still has a prominent place, and the largely unacknowledged excellence of his portrayal is owed, as in the case of Basil, to a powerful element of identification with his author. The Seth who glories in his modernism – 'We are Progress and the New Age. Nothing can stand in our way' – is grossly deluded and destined to a sticky end, but Waugh's subtlety appears in the realization of the reader that Seth is a victim of British barbarism quite as much as he is in the unbreakable grip of African barbarism. Basil and Seth were at Oxford together: 'Basil had enjoyed a reputation of peculiar brilliance among his contemporaries'. Seth meanwhile had been 'of no account in [the same] College, amiably classed among Bengali babus, Siamese, and grammar school scholars as one of the remote and praiseworthy people who had come a long way to the university' (BM 112). Paul Pennyfeather and Evelyn Waugh in his first year had been such 'remote and praiseworthy people'. Waugh had fought tigerishly to move himself towards 'brilliance', about which he had consequently learned a great deal. If he had remained unenlightened he might perhaps have made Seth's mistake about Basil, 'who still stood for him as the personification of all that glittering, intangible Western culture to which he aspired'. Oxford has permitted this crass misidentification of Western culture with undergraduate social 'brilliance'. In 1945, Waugh claimed that he had travelled before the war 'with the belief that barbarism was a dodo to be stalked with a pinch of salt' in remote places, far from civilization. The truth is, and *Black Mischief* shows it, that he had known for long that barbarism flourished in London and Oxford. Africa brought barbarisms into open conflict, and that is why two of his novels are set there. A large part of the action of *Black Mischief* and *Scoop*, however, takes place in Britain, shown to be quite as deluded as Azania. The criterion of true civilization exists only outside the novel, an implied standard against which to measure all these goings-on. As R. M. Davis puts it, 'the idea of Europe could command [Waugh's] allegiance without his respecting the actuality' (RMD 56).

The manuscript of *Black Mischief* shows Waugh at that stage to have been obsessive and careful in handling details, revising and expanding. The book has many Firbankian features and mannerisms, but they have been given muscle and are used to ends very different from Firbank's. Azania is a small, imaginary nation with a hereditary aristocracy and a variety of church establishments, but this Firbankian arrangement is modified by Waugh to produce effects all his own. From Zanzibar he took the idea of an island nation, with a now powerless and nostalgic Arab community. Almost everything else came from Abyssinia, except that Seth is quite unlike Haile Selassie (although Waugh based his illustration of Seth on native portrayals of the Abyssinian emperor). Most of all, this comic novel is replete with deaths, from Amurath's hangings in Chapter 1 to Prudence's culinary obsequies in Chapter 7. Death in a multitude of forms is there to indicate the cost of barbarism (it is hard to see Prudence as a barbarian, but by Waugh's definitions she undoubtedly is), and the price is paid mundanely, every day, and not just extraordinarily and extravagantly. In the Palace Compound in Debra Dowa stands 'a minor gallows...used for such trivial, domestic executions as now and then became necessary within the royal household' (BM 118). The savagery of *Black Mischief* is sometimes attributed solely to Waugh's temperament, by calling it 'cruelty', but the gravity of his judgment of barbarism, strongly reinforced by his religion, acquits him. His power of being wonderfully funny while deadly serious continues to wrong-foot some of his readers, and the ferocity of elements of *Black Mischief* and the author's insistence on letting things speak for themselves caused a famous uproar over the novel that became one of the major events of Waugh's literary life.

Black Mischief was published on 1 October 1932, and three months later Waugh sailed for British Guiana. Strict chronology requires an account of that journey next, but when Waugh returned from it, in early May, 1933, he found that during his absence his latest novel had come under savage attack from a startling quarter: *The Tablet*, 'an official organ of the Catholic faith', the personal property of Cardinal Bourne, Archbishop of Westminster. Before following Waugh to tropical America, we should take up *The Tablet*'s assault on him and his response.

The editor, Ernest Oldmeadow, 63 years old, had been a Noncon-
formist minister before converting to Catholicism. (He had also been
a wine merchant and was a 'pedestrian *littérateur* who had turned
out some dull novels' [1S 366].) In going for *Black Mischief*, he apparently believed he was acting in support of a recent papal encyclical
against 'immodest' books. He was Waugh's first encounter with
Catholic puritanism, and the experience was nearly traumatic. In the
issue of 7 January 1933 Oldmeadow published a paragraph about
'a recent novel' (he never would use the book's title). The attack was
double-pronged: blasphemy and obscenity. He called the book 'a
disgrace to anyone professing the Catholic name', with the unmis-
takable implication that Waugh was not a good Catholic, and condemned its 'coarseness and foulness'. Twelve Catholic luminaries,
including four priests, D'Arcy among them, with Catholic writers
and artists, most but not all of whom were Waugh's friends, signed a
letter of protest on 10 January 1932, printed two weeks later. Several
items about this matter appeared in *The Tablet*. His outrage was profound. Under attack were the two pillars of his existence: that he
was a devout convert to Catholicism and that his writing stood in
support of Catholic truth.

His reply took the form of 'An Open Letter to His Eminence the
Cardinal Archbishop of Westminster'. He was addressing to Cardinal Bourne a complaint about his employee, Oldmeadow, sustaining the fiction that the Cardinal did not know what his underling
was up to and would not approve of it when informed. The 'open
letter' was in fact a pamphlet that Waugh intended to publish. It got
only as far as the proof stage; half a dozen or so copies were pulled,
but the full impression was never made. Waugh, however, carefully
preserved the manuscript in his collection of his work, and a slightly
abbreviated version appeared in Amory's edition of the *Letters* in
1980 (L 72–8). It was claimed that the letter was withheld because
Bourne was sick, and because more powerful representations were
being made to the Cardinal on the subject. There were other considerations. Oldmeadow was not easily separated from his 'employer',
and in 1933 Waugh's quest for an annulment of his marriage was
afoot. The cost of antagonizing Bourne could have been high.
Waugh decided that public opposition to Oldmeadow by the twelve
apostles of the truth was sufficient vindication and let it go.

Publication, however, albeit in 1980, did occur, and though the
controversy over Waugh's book will never come to life again in its
original form – Oldmeadow was really very stupid and in effect

self-destructive – the open letter is an invaluable document for understanding much about Waugh's writing and career. On a smaller scale, it is comparable in its power of illumination to Malcolm Lowry's letter of 2 January 1946 to Jonathan Cape 'explaining' *Under the Volcano*.

If Oldmeadow had a sense of humour, it does not appear in his dispute with Waugh, who consequently found himself having to spell out his jokes to vindicate himself. The parts of the letter in which he does this display a weird comedy of their own, though they are of slight importance compared to other elements. Oldmeadow had written: 'There is a comic description of a Nestorian monastery with a venerated cross "which had fallen from heaven quite unexpectedly during Good Friday luncheon, some years back". If the twelve signatories of the above protest find nothing wrong with "during Good Friday luncheon" we cannot help them'. Waugh offered two explanations for Oldmeadow's mistaking of this joke: 'Neither is particularly flattering to his intelligence, but I can think of no others'. One is that the editor believed Waugh to be referring to real relics, rather than obviously spurious ones. (Not likely. If Oldmeadow thought that 'David's stone prised out of the forehead of Goliath' could truly have been 'a boulder of astonishing dimensions' he was hopelessly mad.) The second explanation, which does seem likely, is that Oldmeadow did not know that Nestorius was a fifth-century dualist heretic, and, as Waugh suggested, he took the name 'to be a disguise for a Latin order of monks'. Waugh's summary is obviously fair: 'it does not constitute blasphemy to impute superstitious reverence for relics to a notoriously superstitious heretical church'. An orthodox Catholic should find no unjustified disrespect in Waugh's suggestion that the Nestorians lunched on Good Friday when unheretical religious would have been fasting.

The obscenity accusations were similarly disposed of. Oldmeadow had objected to the scene in Chapter 5 where Prudence visits Basil's room and where even so unsophisticated a reader as he can deduce that this is a sexual assignation. Waugh pointed out that everything sexual about the scene was depicted by indirection, and that the sordidness that Oldmeadow objected to – 'the unsavoury room (the soapy water unemptied)' – was designed to imply the unromantic and opportunistic nature of the relationship. 'What a picture this editor draws of himself, as one avid to nose out impurity yet doubly enraged to find it in unattractive guise'! The manuscript of the novel amply validates Waugh's intention of making the cigar disintegrating

in that soapy water an 'objective correlative' of the emotional malaise of the scene (RMD 64).

Mistakings of this kind could be effectively countered by appeal-
ing to readers – normal readers, such as Waugh's hypothetical 'Cardinal Bourne' – of greater literary and theological sophistication
than Oldmeadow. But Waugh was aware that, in the matter of Prudence's gruesome end (he says nothing of Basil's participation in it)
even his most loyal supporters might fail him. In addressing 'the climax of the story, when Prudence is eaten at a cannibal feast', Waugh
had to pick his way carefully yet is at his most informative and
self-revelatory. He makes considerable play of his possible, even
likely, miscalculation in the matter – 'It is not unlikely that I failed in
this' – 'this opinion has been represented to me by many whom I
respect' – but does his best to justify the 'sudden tragedy when barbarism at last emerges and usurps the stage'.

> The story deals with the conflict of civilisation, with all its attend-
> ant and deplorable ills, and barbarism. The plan of my book through-
> out was to keep the darker aspects of barbarism continually and
> unobtrusively present, a black and mischievous background
> against which the civilized and semi-civilized characters per-
> formed their parts: I wished it to be like the continuous, remote
> throbbing of those hand drums, constantly audible, which every
> traveller in Africa will remember as one of his most haunting
> impressions. I introduced the cannibal theme in the first chapter
> and repeated it in another key in the incident of the soldiers eat-
> ing their boots, thus hoping to prepare the reader for the sudden
> tragedy when barbarism at last emerges from the shadows and
> usurps the stage. (L 77)

He appears at first sight to be apologising for the event of Prudence's eating when he admits to a likely mistake here, but in fact
he was merely admitting that he may have failed in preparing the
reader. It may have been that 'the transition was too rapid, the catastrophe too large'. He does not regret the event. People had told
Waugh that this was 'a disagreeable incident'. He replied, 'It was
meant to be'. The only ambiguous aspect of his defence of his book
is his implication that the European characters represent civilization.
Basil Seal? General Connolly? Sir Samson Courtney? Dame Mildred
Porch? It is impossible to believe that Waugh was unaware that
the ideal of 'Western Civilization' that he did adhere to was hardly

represented by these characters. Perhaps in presenting his book as the conflict of civilization, even with 'all its attendant and deplorable ills', and barbarism he was simplifying for the sake of his polemic. It was much easier to present the book in this way than to try to justify it as a conflict of barbarisms against a background ideal of civilization that is nowhere embodied in the story. As to the inherent shock of the incident, Waugh never made any attempt to revise the text, and in *A Handful of Dust*, his next novel, he began with a final catastrophe, in effect the burying alive of Tony Last, that is if anything more shocking, since Tony is a character in whom the reader has invested far more sympathy than in Prudence.

The possible concessions Waugh made in his 'open letter' address only artistic weaknesses in his book. He was more concerned to defend himself against the accusations of obscenity and, even more, of bad faith that Oldmeadow had made. His decision not to go through with publishing the pamphlet indicated that he accepted that the letter of his friends and co-religionists had done enough to re-assert his standing as a Catholic and a Catholic author. The annulment proceedings must not be imperilled by the desire to thrash Oldmeadow; he would let it drop if Oldmeadow would. But Oldmeadow would not. When *A Handful of Dust* was published in 1934, he reviewed Waugh again in similar terms, and this time Waugh replied by passing on to Driberg, for use in his *Daily Express* column, a couple of ripostes drawn from his pamphlet. Stannard says, 'Perhaps this review did more than anything to turn [Waugh] firmly in the direction of writing overtly apologetic books' (1S 376). I would prefer to say that *The Tablet*'s review of *A Handful of Dust* confirmed Waugh in the suspicion that is never expressed openly but that underlies everything he wrote in his open letter about *Black Mischief*: that those who could see that he was a Catholic writer in *Black Mischief* and *A Handful of Dust* were not numerous enough or representative enough to grant him the public acceptance that he needed. His fury at the attack on *Black Mischief* was fuelled by the reluctantly acknowledged truth that there would have to be radical changes in his literary persona if the world was to accept him unhesitatingly as a Catholic writer. More openly polemical works than *Remote People*, such as his biography of Edmund Campion, would be his first attempt, but this course was ultimately unsatisfactory. He was above all a novelist, and if the religious element in *Black Mischief* and *A Handful of Dust* went unperceived by all except an elite or a coterie, then he would have to become an openly Catholic novelist.

That step would be taken first at the approach of the Second World War.

The period between Waugh's return from Abyssinia and his departure for British Guiana was filled with writing – the completion of *Remote People* and the composition of *Black Mischief*, together with much journalism – and with smart social life. In January and February 1932 he did a stint of screenwriting, living high and fast on the expense account (the film was never made). In the summer of 1931 he visited France, and in August and September he was with smart set friends in Venice. During this period he also took riding lessons at an establishment near Madresfield so that he could ride to hounds with his horsey new friends. His unrequited love for Teresa Jungman co-existed with affairs with married women and encounters with prostitutes. He was basically miserable beneath the jokes and hilarity, and when he set out for British Guiana in December 1932, the unhappiness came to the surface and coloured the whole of his journey and the book he wrote about it, *Ninety-Two Days*.

It had been 'a journey of the greatest misery' (L 71), and the book's title, to British ears, sounds like a jail sentence. (He worked out that he had spent exactly 92 days in British Guiana.) The journey he had chosen to make would supply exactly the wrong kind of experience for his writing. It was not really exploration (the country he travelled was sparsely settled) but it had the trappings: travel by horseback and canoe; camping out, sundry injuries, hardships of diet and insect attacks, exhaustion and massive banality. (The wonderful frontispiece photograph of Waugh in 'explorer' gear, including vast shorts, is a clear statement of the poor fit between the author and his project.) But exploration, especially of the scientific kind, was really quite uninteresting to him. And British Guiana had little in the way of culture or history. Interesting people were an absolute requisite, and on this trip he met mostly boring, ordinary, nice people, and found himself again and again in situations of frustration and tedium. The extended stays he had to make, even those with noble Catholic missionaries, are all polluted by boredom. In fact, nearly the most entertaining aspect of Waugh's book, and the diary on which it was based, is supplied by Martin Stannard's analysis of Waugh's distortion of events in the teeth of the facts to produce the most favourable image of himself (1S 327). In *Ninety-Two Days* Waugh took his sensibility on an exhausting and frustrating cross-country slog, and came close at times to making his reader wonder why he ever left home.

As a literary experience, however, the trip was saved by a couple of Wavian eccentrics, both borderline lunatics: Mr Haynes (called Bain in the book), and Mr Christie, described cryptically in the summary of Chapter 3 as 'a mystic', meaning evidently a religious maniac. In his literary incarnation, Christie was first Mr McMaster and later Mr Todd. Haynes/Bain was useful in the amusement he provides for the reader of *Ninety-Two Days*. Waugh reconstructs passages of the man's logorrhoeic monologues, turning what had been agonizing boredom into welcome refreshment for his readers. Christie makes a memorable appearance in the travel book, but his real value to Waugh is owed to his place in the conception of *A Handful of Dust*.

Waugh's diary of the journey gives hints, though hardly more. On Friday 20 January 1933, he and his entourage had arrived at Christie's ranch at four in the afternoon. That night, while getting through a bottle of rum, Waugh had absorbed Christie's highly individual conversation, later reproduced in its nutty splendour in *Ninety-Two Days*. On 4 February 1933, he had arrived at the farthest point of his journey, the Brazilian town of Boa Vista, where he stayed at the Benedictine priory. There he rested, or, in his own words, spent several days in 'degrading boredom'. This was enough to drive him to write. On Sunday 12 February, he recorded, 'Wrote bad article yesterday but thought of plot for short story'. On Tuesday 14 October, 'Finished short story'. Next day, he mailed the story to his agent, A. D. Peters, along with several newspaper articles (RMD 71).

In a 1945 article, 'Fan-Fare', Waugh described the origin of *A Handful of Dust*. It 'began at the end. I had written a short story about a man trapped in the jungle, ending his days reading Dickens aloud' (EAR 303). His visit to Christie had caused him to reflect 'how easily he could hold me prisoner'. But the completed story was not the end of it; neither that narrative nor the whole of his South American experience would leave his mind after the writing of *Ninety-Two Days*. The persistence of these memories led him to his next novel, and so discussion of the story should wait until *A Handful of Dust* comes up for discussion.

He returned from British Guiana in early May 1933. He had first to deal with *The Tablet*'s attack on *Black Mischief* and then he had to write newspaper articles he had contracted for and think up others to offer to editors. He was not writing well at this stage and the thought of the travel book that lay in wait after the journalism was dispiriting. Teresa Jungman was unchanged in her attitude towards him. Hearings on his petition for annulment of his marriage might soon occur, so he would have to face that misery and Evelyn Heygate again. It is understandable that he seized opportunities to cheer up his life and that he was doing little serious writing.[2]

The expansion of his friendships at this time encompassed Nancy Mitford, who was then Mrs Peter Rodd, and Katherine Asquith, a devout Catholic convert, widow of Raymond Asquith, the former prime minister's son. Nancy Mitford had been She-Evelyn's friend first but became a prominent member of Waugh's 'sisterhood'; their correspondence over the years was very extensive. Katherine Asquith was older than Waugh, never a 'sister', and Catholic life was the basis of their friendship. At her home at Mells in Somerset he found a Catholic community that was both socially engaging and a spiritual refuge. At this time Waugh also became acquainted with Gabriel Herbert, who led him into friendship with her family. He went on a Mediterranean cruise in 1933, and one of his shore excursions was a stay with the Herbert family at Portofino. One member was an eighteen-year-old daughter, Laura, whom he described as a 'white mouse'. Less than four years later she became his wife.

His return to London in October 1933 was very much business after pleasure. Sessions of the Westminster Diocesan Court were scheduled in October and November for his nullity hearings. Several who had been friends of the Evelyns were called to testify. She-Evelyn (Mrs Heygate) was the principal witness and Waugh's last meeting with her seems to have gone off in a civilized manner. He had referred to her as his 'poor wife' in a letter to Dorothy Lygon (H 291) and She-Evelyn told Stannard that she had been 'more than anxious that [Waugh] should be able to marry again'. The biographers differ, however, on what Waugh said to Evelyn Heygate at their pre-trial luncheon. Stannard, who was the only one to contact She-Evelyn, reports her allegation that Waugh 'nobbled' his chief witness by telling her to say that she had refused to have children, that they had intended to 'remain childless' and suggesting that she stay silent about his 'earnest desire for a fruitful marriage with her' (1S 353).

Stannard naturally took Mrs Nightingale's letter to be the best evidence available and did not investigate the official report of the case by the Holy Roman Rota at the Vatican (DG 82). This shows that in her testimony Mrs Heygate actually said only that the couple had agreed to a postponement of children until their financial situation permitted. Her memory had failed her and her account misled

Stannard into putting all emphasis on an intention by the couple to remain permanently childless. The Vatican account shows that two arguments were brought forward on behalf of Waugh's petition for nullity. There was the agreement to *defer* having children and there was an agreement that they would divorce if the marriage did not work out. The Church court rejected the former as grounds for annulment but accepted the latter. Evelyn Waugh's first marriage was annulled solely 'because the couple by a positive act of will excluded permanence from their marriage' (DG 77). Waugh did not 'nobble' his witness.

His marriage, however, was not speedily terminated. After the hearings in London, the papers were to go to Rome where the Rota would review the London declaration of nullity and ratify it. But this did not come until July 1936. Waugh blamed the huge delay in forwarding the papers on the incompetence and perhaps malice of Church officials in London. Gallagher, however, argues that Waugh's petition was not, as it has been represented, a simple case, and that the delays were caused by 'official hesitation'. Whatever the cause, from November 1933 until July 1936, Waugh lived in ecclesiastical and legal limbo, hoping and really expecting to marry again, but not yet free to do so.

In the momentary exuberance of setting the annulment proceedings into real (though delusive) motion, Waugh made his proposal of marriage to Baby Jungman, was rejected, and in a deflated and depressed frame of mind went alone to the Coopers' house in Sussex to write *Ninety-Two Days*. He did so in record time for him (12 October to 13 November 1933). Then, with an advance from Chapman & Hall of £100, he sailed to Tangier and went on to Fez. Most of *A Handful of Dust* was to be written during the two months he spent in Morocco.

His routine there was used for that of John Plant in *Work Suspended*: writing steadily in the mornings, with regular visits to brothel (and to mass, in Waugh's case) and to the British consul's for baths (in Plant's case, at least). When he returned to England, he went off to Chagford to finish the book. It was completed in mid-April, just as *Ninety-Two Days* was published (15 April 1934) to rather better reviews than it deserved.

A Handful of Dust is Waugh's greatest single achievement. It was received unenthusiastically by the reviewers, but ever since its reputation, unhampered by the ifs and buts that cling to *Brideshead Revisited*, has advanced. It is Waugh's best novel because it is his most courageous and skilful act of fictional autobiography, and because in finding a form and a fable for what most closely concerned himself he made a definitive statement about the spiritual condition of Western man that commands enduring respect. He himself had no doubts about it: 'it is excellent', 'faultless of its kind', 'better than the others'.

Like *Black Mischief* and *Scoop*, it was the fictional product of his journeying abroad, each novel balancing its travel book. The journey to British Guiana had been largely miserable, even penitential, but the solitude and the periods of enforced idleness had driven him to introspection. The night he spent with Christie had shown him how powerless he could have been, and he had swiftly put his realization into a short story.

> The idea came quite naturally from the experience of visiting a lonely settler ... and reflecting how easily he could hold me prisoner. Then, after the short story was written and published, the idea kept working in my mind. I wanted to discover how the prisoner got there, and eventually the thing grew into a study of other sorts of savage at home and the civilized man's helpless plight among them. (EAR 303)

The explanation for Tony's plight became a critique of humanism: 'It was humanist and contained all I had to say about humanism'. The 'civilized man', helpless among the 'savages' at home, is the *merely* civilized man, his system of values and beliefs unsupported by the truths of religion, leaving him vulnerable to Fortune, that 'least capricious of deities', who 'arranges things on the just and rigid system that no one shall be very happy for very long' (LA 206).

'The Man Who Liked Dickens' (he never allowed it to be republished in its original form) shows that some decisions one might assume to have been made after the story's publication, during the time when the idea 'kept working' in his mind, had been made earlier, suggesting that from the first the story was something Waugh might well return to. Paul Henty, the predecessor of Tony Last, joins the expedition to South America because he has been betrayed by his wife, so from the start Waugh was confronting the great trauma of his life. Waugh's brilliantly successful attempt 'to discover how the prisoner got there' did not involve the mechanism of wifely infidelity and the husband's flight to the jungle; they were already in place. Brenda Last as a literary creation is quite incommensurate with the cipher who is Henty's unnamed wife; the wife's character was reinvented in the transformation of story into novel. But when Waugh sat down to write his story at Boa Vista, the central event of his next novel was decided. Paul Henty's shock would become 'Hard Cheese on Tony'.

A second decision made early was that Mr McMaster (later Mr Todd), the settler who so deftly imprisons Paul/Tony, should not, unlike his original, Christie, be a religious maniac. Waugh greatly enjoyed lunacy of a religious hue, as Prendy's slayer in *Decline and Fall* shows. In *Ninety-Two Days*, he transcribes from his diary and amplifies for the reader's delight the manifestations of Christie's mania, but in the story, as in the novel, Christie/McMaster/Todd is, so to say, a wholly secular lunatic. This subtraction makes him a simpler character, and thereby perhaps more effectively appalling in his role, but if the religious dimension of Tony's impotence in keeping savagery at bay had dawned on Waugh, then Christie's secularism has considerable thematic value. Religion's presence in *A Handful of Dust* is denoted by its absence from Tony's life, and the religion to which he pays humanistic lip service, the farcical formalism of the Revd Tendril, is the only representation of Christianity Waugh would allow into his book. Mr Todd's role is to represent Fortune, the deity who rules the universe of humanism, random, arbitrary, and permitting happiness to none of her subjects for very long.

The great revelation of 'The Man Who Liked Dickens' is that from the moment of conception what Waugh wanted to write about was the protagonist's helplessness and shock when he discovers that his universe is quite different from what he has deemed it to be. Waugh focused first on Henty's and Tony's catastrophe, the fatal consequence of an absurd and impulsive decision, living death in South America and a very marketable short story. But McMaster/Todd, though absolutely right as the non-terminal terminus of the journey, was in a manner a distraction from what really gripped Waugh's imagination; hence his 'continuation' of the subject to find out how the prisoner got there, which is in fact what had really interested him from the first. His own impotence and fury when his wife had made her announcement, seen now from the point of view of one who had discovered what had been missing from his life, allowed him to depict in 'poor Tony' a malaise of the spirit and a consequent moral blindness that translates literature's most persistently banal comic figure, the cuckold, into an emblematic representative of a culture cut off from spiritual nourishment. Tony's shock at the discovery of his blindness entails a further helplessness upon him when all he can find to fill his spiritual void is his vision of Dr Messinger's City as a transfigured Hetton, a Victorian Gothic El Dorado, the delusive termination of a path that leads in absurd reality to another Victorian horror, a tomb with a view that parodies the womb with a view, the idyllic terminus of most Dickens novels. Tony has desired to live in a Victorian fantasy, and as matters conclude he is dying in one.

The element of transformed personal experience in *A Handful of Dust*, its autobiographical element, is thus Tony's inadequate conception of what human behaviour can be ('He had got into a habit of loving and trusting Brenda' HD 125) and his helplessness in the face of 'the all-encompassing chaos that shrieked about his ears' (HD 137–8). In studying his own reactions to the thunderbolt that had hit him, Waugh discovered that by his religious conversion he had given himself the explanation, and he found a narrative that enabled him to focus on what had been the most shocking as well as the most intellectually fertile element of his trauma. The purgatorial journey in South America, for Waugh just as for Tony, was where he again confronted his unfaithful wife. The novelist, however, had a power of self-confrontation that Tony never attains, and the loving depiction of Tony's life and what is missing from Tony's life is the fictional recreation of Waugh's pre-Catholic self, his recognition and proclamation of what he lacked that had made him helpless in the face of 'savagery'.

Tony Last, therefore, in his spiritual and psychological aspects only, is an *alter ego* of the naïve Evelyn Waugh in the blindness of irreligion. The two other corners of the triangle, however, are carefully not reproductions of their equivalents in life. Brenda is not Evelyn Gardner, neither in outward or inward qualities, and John Beaver is a brilliant literary libel on John Heygate.

I think it likely that Waugh could never understand with a novelist's empathy his first wife's motives for leaving him. The unfaithful wife and the cuckolded husband became recurrent figures in his fiction, but the nature of female infidelities is never deeply probed. The consequences of betrayal, rather than betrayal itself, are what Waugh focused on after *A Handful of Dust*, but in that novel itself, his first fictional approach to the topic after the event in life, he had to handle woman's infidelity directly. He did so by returning to one of his pieces of undergraduate fiction, to 'Antony, Who Sought Things That Were Lost' (*Oxford Broom*, June 1923, see Chapter 1 above). The

Lady Elizabeth has committed herself utterly to Antony, but her love turns without cause to hatred. Even more inexplicably, she turns to *and truly loves* the foul turnkey: 'so the Lady Elizabeth, who had known the white arms of Antony, loved the turnkey who was ugly and lowborn' (EWA 131). It is the incomprehensible love of beauty for the beast. But when Waugh placed Brenda Last in this situation, he saw that hatred was a weakness; Brenda never hates Tony, and her love for Beaver is thus the more incomprehensible, to herself as to everyone else. Otherwise Waugh allows this adolescent terror of female mystery do duty for Brenda and Beaver too. It was an 'explanation' that would work because of the character that Waugh had embodied in Beaver.

When one encounters John Heygate in Anthony Powell's memoirs (*Messengers of Day*, 1978) it is almost startling to realize that to someone other than Waugh, Heygate was not John Beaver, that the dreadful nullity of the fictional character was Waugh's invention and revenge, a fiction so fierce that it has obliterated the reality in the minds of readers of literature. John Beaver is to Heygate as Dryden's Achitophel is to the first Earl of Shaftesbury. Beaver is an elaboration of Waugh's view of Heygate after the elopement. She-Evelyn had preferred 'the basement boy' to himself, and by his comments and by his creation of Beaver, Waugh proclaims the absurdity, even lunacy, of that preference. Beaver is the most impressive non-entity in literature, even a little frightening in a Dantean way. To do what he could to protect his self-esteem, Waugh in his conversation and letters emphasized the utter meaninglessness of his wife's choice; in his novel, he refined that self-protective fiction into a minor character of paradoxically Dickensian vitality.

Dickensian, too, is the nature of *A Handful of Dust* in relation to its genre, the comic novel. Readers, especially first-time readers, may find the novel sad: 'the saddest book in the world', one said to me. And so it is, but in form and attitude *A Handful of Dust* is still a comic novel – as are *Little Dorrit* and *Bleak House* and *Great Expectations*. Like them, Waugh's novel has its moments of hilarity – the Revd Tendril's sermons, or the table habits of Brenda's brother, Reggie St Cloud – but generally the mood tends to the sombre. There is an element of *contrafactum* in this, to use a musical term: the form and conventions (the music) are those of the comic novel, but the content (the words) is different and tends to work ironically against the form. Waugh's relationship to Tony Last is basically the same as his relationship to Paul Pennyfeather; it is a critical relationship, more critical, if anything, than that in *Decline and Fall*. Yet the element of personal identification of author and character is much greater than in the earlier novel. Tony is Waugh in ways that Paul is not, and this identification is perceptible in the novel's emotional atmosphere. Yet simultaneously Waugh's attitude towards Tony is critical in the mode of comedy. Tony has had the opportunity not to be naïve and a fool, and though the explanation for his state of unenlightenment is sympathetically delineated and understandable, it is not accept-able to Waugh; Tony's is not invincible ignorance. To understand him is not to forgive him, and it is in respect of this refusal to forgive that the book's ending is to be understood. It is a parody, of course, of the happy ending – hermetic domesticity – of the Dickensian novel, and in form it is a happy ending. Tony likes to read aloud, and he has come to South America in search of an ideal home, the 'City' of his fantasy, the 'transfigured Hetton'. Since this is a human-ist ideal, paradise needs must be an earthly paradise, and since humanism is absurdly fallacious, the earthly paradise is in reality Mr Todd and a diet of Dickens and farine. Tony has got what he sought, and is left to enjoy it. It is a happy ending in *contrafactum*, ironical, like the 'happy ending' of Orwell's *Nineteen Eighty-Four*, where Win-ston Smith weeps in the genuine happiness of his love for Big Brother. The structures of comedy are preserved, though only by irony, so Waugh does not here abandon the comic novel outright. The abandonment had been mooted, however, and the novels he wrote in the next eight years, up through *Work Suspended* (published first in 1942), and his commentary upon them, show him moving hesitantly but decidedly away from the comic novel as the main vehicle of his art.

His best known books before Brideshead Revisited *were* A Handful of Dust *and* Edmund Campion, *the biography of the Jesuit martyr of Elizabethan times, which won the Hawthornden Prize in 1936. In 1937 he married Laura, youngest daughter of the late Honourable Aubrey Her-bert, and he has six children.*

Despite generally unenthusiastic reviews, *A Handful of Dust* went through five impressions by the end of the fourth week after pub-lication and was a Book of the Month Club selection. The blurb is probably right in calling it his best-known novel before *Brideshead*. It was to be four years, however, until he published another. Before *Scoop*, in 1938, he published *Edmund Campion* (1935), *Mr. Loveday's Little Outing and Other Sad Stories* (1936), a lot of newspaper and magazine journalism, and *Waugh in Abyssinia* (1936). Material for the last was gathered on two visits to Ethiopia, and much of the non-writing time between novels was filled with his courtship of Laura Herbert and in painfully awaiting news from the Rota in Rome of the annulment. The only lucrative item in this list was the journalism. He turned over all his royalties from the biography to Campion Hall, and although he got a £950 advance for it, *Waugh in Abyssinia* appeared after the public's interest had turned to Spain. *A Handful of Dust* paid well, but Waugh spent fast, and it is henceforth a permanent feature of his life that he was short of money while being one of the best rewarded of modern British writers. Marriage changed his lifestyle in many ways, but it did not make a spender into a saver, and luxuries and extravagancies were the staff of life to Waugh.

The author's blurb, it will be noted, gives a deal of prominence to *Campion*. It is doubtful that it was one of his 'best-known' books (certainly not one of his most widely read), but that he should have made the claim is very revealing. The only Roman Catholic periodical to review *A Handful of Dust* had been, again, *The Tablet* in the person of the insufferable Oldmeadow. It was not an appreciative review. Martin Stannard suggests that this lack of suitable public acknowledgement by the Catholic establishment made up Waugh's mind for him: he would become a Catholic author who could not be ignored or misrepresented. A biography of a martyr for the Faith, a convert, an Oxford scholar, on the occasion of the opening of the new Campion Hall at Oxford, whose head was Martin D'Arcy, would give Waugh what he wanted. He worked on it from September 1934 until May 1935, and when it was published it did even more for him than he had initially hoped. It brought him a public honour, the Hawthornden Prize. Better still, it gave him respectability in the eyes of Laura's family, chiefly her mother, Mary Herbert, who was reluctant to approve the marriage because she had doubts of various kinds about Waugh as a prospective son-in-law.

Laura was a sprig of nobility; her father was the second son of the fourth Earl of Carnarvon, and she was, to everyone's embarrassment or amusement, a cousin of Evelyn Gardner. (Evelyn Gardner's mother was the half-sister of Laura Herbert's father.) Waugh had to present himself to the Herberts as different from the person who had virtually eloped with cousin Evelyn. Like the Herberts, he was now a Catholic convert, his stature effectively raised to prominence by *Campion*. The annulment proceedings he had brought showed that he claimed not to be to blame for that first marital catastrophe, and as his courtship of Laura advanced, he eventually made it clear that his desire was to abandon the rootless life he had adopted when his first marriage failed. Since Laura loved him and wanted him, since his religion and his profession had become wholly suitable, he was certain to win in the end. His social origins were acceptable, and finally the only real obstacle became the long-delayed approval of the annulment. When that came through, in July 1936, the engagement was accepted, though Mary Herbert delayed its announcement until January 1937.

Waugh proposed to Laura Herbert in a letter of 1936, while he was writing *Waugh in Abyssinia* and several months before his first marriage was finally annulled. Here his instinct served him well. A proposal in writing enabled him to make a fine choice of tone, self-deprecating yet realistic, obliquely revealing the positive aspects of his apparent disadvantages.

> I can't advise you in my favour because I think it would be beastly for you, but think how nice it would be for me. In fact it's a lousy proposition. On the other hand I think I could...reform & become quite strict about not getting drunk [a failed aspiration] and I am pretty sure I should be faithful [which he was]. Also there is always a fair chance that there will be another bigger economic crash in which case if you had married a nobleman with a great house you might find yourself starving, while I am very clever and could probably earn a living of some sort somewhere. (L 103)

He stressed his untrammelled condition, making himself out to be effectively an orphan: 'though you would be taking on an elderly buffer [he was thirteen years older], I am one without fixed habits. You would not find yourself confined to any particular place or group. Also I have practically no living relatives except one brother whom I scarcely know'. But this offer of what may have looked like a gipsy life did not appeal to Laura's family, or, it seems, to Laura herself. The married life that the Waughs actually led was anything but rootless, apart from the universal uprooting of the Second World War. As to his work, Waugh made it pretty plain that, when writing a book, he expected to go off alone 'for several months every year'.

Laura accepted his proposal. Nothing, of course, could be made public until the annulment came through. In early July 1936, he had apparently decided to use one arm of the Church against another, since he went on pilgrimage to Lough Derg in Donegal, and on his return to London found waiting the answer to his prayers, a telegram from Rome: 'Decision favourable'.

Evelyn Waugh and Laura Herbert were married on 17 April 1937 and after an Italian honeymoon (paid for by Alec's wife, Joan) settled down at the house Evelyn had chosen, Piers Court, Stinchcombe ('Stinkers'), near Dursley, south of Gloucester. The house was a wedding present from Laura's grandmother, Lady de Vesci – no mortgage for the Waughs. They lived at Piers Court from 1937 until January 1957, when they moved to a house at Combe Florey in Somerset. Waugh lived in the country for privacy (country pursuits had no attraction for him; he never tried to be the squire) and Stinchcombe was becoming built up. Combe Florey was satisfactorily remote. During the war, Piers Court was let to a convent, and Laura, when not with her husband at various of his postings around Britain, lived with her family at Pixton.

The zeal with which Waugh's biographers rush to assure their readers that Laura was no 'doormat' or model of wifely submissiveness suggests that it would be easy to think so. Those who maintain her independence and self-assertion concede, however, that those qualities were operative only in the private sphere of life. Within her family – eventually there were three daughters and three sons – she was found to possess a cool wit and a satirical eye ('you are a critical girl', he had observed in his proposal letter), and her authentically aristocratic instincts could if necessary deflate her husband's pretensions. Waugh had judged her well, however, for she desired no public life at all. She shared his dislike of literary life, and whereas he required frequent expeditions to London to visit his club (White's from 1941 onwards; the Savile or the St James earlier), to go to the London Library, to get his hair cut, to lunch at the Ritz, and sometimes to put up at the Hyde Park Hotel to entertain his friends, Laura preferred to stay at home, having transformed herself after the war into a farmer, much more interested in her cows than in smart social life. This was exactly as Waugh's wishes evolved; he had a handsome, aristocratic wife with few social and no literary interests, younger than he, like himself a Catholic convert. When he felt the need for a jaunt, or the need to go to Chagford to write, there was no great problem. He saw to it that in times of affluence Laura should

enjoy a shopping expedition, putting up at some grand hotel, pre-
ferably near a casino for a little gambling, but he could rely on such
excursions being rare saturnalia in a life devoted chiefly to small-
holding and rather *distrait* motherhood. His library was ever inviol-
ate. Everything was combined to let him begin construction of the
persona that would shield him from the world's gaze. The life Laura
made possible was the stage and background for the role-playing that
over the last part of his life was his most elaborated work of fiction.

The work that Waugh published after *A Handful of Dust* until the
Second World War includes only one book of real distinction, *Scoop*
(and Waugh seems always to have thought that *Scoop* was an infer-
ior novel). Despite the Hawthornden Prize, *Edmund Campion* is so
rigidly biased that it has no claims to make as history. For those interested primarily in Waugh as a writer, admiration has to be confined to the excellence of its prose (in the rather mandarin style he
was developing for that kind of subject) and for its small revelations
of his opinions at that stage in his life. Chief among these is his idea
that Roman Catholicism is the truly English religion and that the
Protestant Tudors were the first step in the direction of all that was
hateful about modern England, a step that an uninterruptedly Catholic England would never have taken. The great test of any writer on
the penal years of English Catholicism is Pope Pius V's bull of 1570,
Regnans in excelsis. Waugh's solution is startling. The Pope had
excommunicated Queen Elizabeth, declared her illegitimate, and
released her Catholic subjects from their allegiance, an action that
was read by the English government as a declaration of war on England by the Church of Rome, making 'Catholic' and 'traitor' synonym-
ous. Waugh calmly resorts to his habitual stratagem of literalism. 'It
is possible that one of his more worldly predecessors might have acted differently, or at another season, but it was the pride and slight
embarrassment of the Church that...the See of Peter was at this
time occupied by a Saint'. Saint Pius V (canonized 1712) made his
decision, according to Waugh, without political or prudential calcu-
lation. 'His contemporaries and the vast majority of subsequent historians [Protestant *and* Catholic] regarded the Pope's action as
ill-judged'. In that view, Pius V was 'a disastrous figure, provoking
...the bloody ruin of English Catholicism'. Waugh proposes a different conclusion, a doubt and a hope.

had he, perhaps, in those withdrawn, exalted hours before his
crucifix, learned something that was hidden from the statesmen of

his time and the succeeding generations of historians...understood that there was to be no easy way of reconciliation, but that it was only through blood and hatred and derision that the faith was one day to return to England? (C 44)

And could anyone reading this doubt that this writer was truly of the faith?

The other major effort of this period of Waugh's life was *Waugh in Abyssinia*, published in 1936. His second visit to the country came when, as everyone knew, Mussolini's Italy was preparing to invade (August 1935 to January 1936). Waugh's return to Addis Ababa placed him in the kind of situation where he found it relatively easy to plan fiction but difficult to organize a book of current affairs or reportage. Unfortunately for his peace of mind he was there as a reporter, not as a novelist. Nevertheless, he soon conceived of the novel he would get out of the experience, though it was a long time writing. His actual employment was as a reporter for the *Daily Mail* and as a writer under contract to Longmans for a book on the war – or crisis, as it obstinately remained for the duration of this stay. The conditions were conducive to Waugh's kind of fiction because he was the outsider and could also be seen as *naïve*. The British legation had read *Black Mischief* and so he was *persona non grata* with them. The other journalists there to report for the British and American press saw him – he was – as an amateur, for his qualifications were not journalistic know-how but experience of Abyssinia. Moreover, Waugh and his paper were in a minority in being decidedly pro-Italian. This isolation and these enveloping antagonisms were just what Waugh needed to be able to see this society from his comic and critical point of view. His new novel would be about foreign correspondents – with a naïve amateur among them – in a country not unlike Ethiopia.

Waugh had to go back to England before the balloon went up. He was in fact thrown out of the country, but took his time leaving. He had bagged a novel's worth of journalistic howlers and horror, but he had to force himself to grind out the book for Longmans. Then the Italians did invade, and soon had the larger towns and routes under their control. Haile Selassie in exile was whistled at and booed by Italian journalists at the League of Nations. Having missed the fighting, Waugh asked permission of the Italians to go back to the country to update his material. He was there for a month in August and September 1936, flying around in Italian aircraft, briefed by amiable and impressive Italian big shots, and becoming confirmed that the conquest was a Pax Italica – at least that is what he said in print, though he privately admitted to finding the victorious Italians less attractive than before. The result of all this ego-buffing was that *Waugh in Abyssinia* ends with passages of pseudo-Bellocian bombast about the civilizing mission of Italian arms and roads. The earlier parts of the book are much saner and more typical of the Wavian travel book. The passages discussed earlier give its flavour. Waugh was a better journalist than it suited him to admit, and although he was politically most incorrect, the book is readable for those devoted to or merely interested in Waugh. But he was lucky that Peters had negotiated a large advance; the book's moment had passed before it appeared (26 October 1936).

Soon after getting *Waugh in Abyssinia* off his back, he began writing what was to be *Scoop*. But the writing of this fifth novel was, by his standards, unusually prolonged. He began it in October 1936, before his marriage, and it was published in May 1938, more than a year after. Quick cash was needed around the time of the marriage, and Peters was very successful in arranging for Waugh to produce articles and reviews, but they took him away from his novel. Moving to Piers Court, and furnishing the house and embellishing its grounds were another major distraction.

> *On his marriage he purchased Piers Court, near Dursley, Glos., which was his home until the outbreak of war, and to which he has now [in 1951] returned.... His chief interests are wine, architecture and his library, for which he collects among other things 18th-century builders' books and 19th-century chromolithographic books of illuminations.*

Waugh's life at Piers Court was designed not to be the expected life for a writer. He was a gentleman living in the country with the interests of a connoisseur and collector. Servants were necessary, and Waugh's chosen status is indicated by his insistence, which lasted until after the war, that they should include a manservant, functioning as combined butler and valet to himself. He designed embellishments and improvements to the gardens and took great pleasure in finding pictures, furniture and *objets d'art* for the house. Laura commanded the farm and, somewhat distantly, kitchen and nursery. Waugh lived like a gentleman whose income was inherited and came from his estates. But there were no estates, and the income came from the family trade, his writings.

Scoop was finished early in 1938, but another Waugh came into the world before it, a daughter, Maria Teresa, born 9 March 1938. Laura went to London, where Waugh joined, or visited her after the birth. Laura became pregnant seven times in all (one child, Mary, died at birth), and Waugh always managed to be absent when his children were born.

Scoop was published in early May 1938. If one gives most weight to Waugh's own opinion and those of his scholarly critics, then this novel ranks rather low in the list of his fiction. His own reasons for disliking it offer insight and are examined below. For their part, the critics seem to be out of step with unprofessional readers. *Scoop* is one of the most popular of Waugh's novels by the sales figures and seems to get more unsolicited tributes than any other. The difference in reactions is mainly owed to the fact that both Waugh and the professionals see the book in the context of his whole career. After the grand macabre of *Black Mischief* and the objectified anguish of *A Handful of Dust*, *Scoop* seems like a step backwards. One of Waugh's more sensible critics suggests that the 'shallow imaginative roots' of this novel are owed to its 'lack of strong autobiographical impulse' (RG 131). I agree, though I interpret 'strong' to mean 'personally painful'. *Scoop* is autobiographical in the manner I have been defining, but it does not draw on the most painful aspects of Waugh's own experience, as *A Handful of Dust* does. Yet the wonderful comedy of *Scoop* is nearly complete compensation for the reduced emotional intensity of the book. *Decline and Fall* is the novel that *Scoop* most resembles, like a child that is the spitting image of its great-grandparent. But the surprises of genetics are not an acceptable analogy to literary critics committed to models of linear progressive development. Readers at large, however, take the book for itself, and in itself it is a splendid comic novel, with the power to keep its reader laughing even on repeated readings, when the effect of novelty and surprise has gone. It seems ungrateful to complain that a writer is repeating himself when he does it to such effect. It is possible to make progress without much change.

One of Waugh's reasons for disliking his fifth novel was that the book was hard to get finished, absorbing a great deal of time and many drafts and emendations. In literature at least, a difficult birth may sour the parent on the offspring. His major reason for his slighting of *Scoop*, however, somewhat resembles the critics' disappointment that the book seemed less intense than its immediate predecessors. Waugh, too, saw himself making advances from one novel to the next, but he was beginning to feel strongly that he needed to make a major shift of direction in his fiction and that the progress he had made, especially with *A Handful of Dust*, was insufficient for the need he was experiencing. Characterization and style had changed slightly but significantly from book to book, but the 'deep structure' of the comic novel and the unintrospective narrational style were still there. The form of change that he decided upon is best discussed in relation to *Work Suspended* below. Suffice it to say now that, in its author's eyes, *Scoop* did not represent change enough.

In the period of Waugh's marriage and his settling at Piers Court, ideological commitment grew and hardened somewhat in him. *Scoop* can be defended, as Martin Stannard has ably defended it, as a criticism of society in which the positive values are indicated by 'negative suggestion' (1S 472), as had been the case with *Black Mischief* and *A Handful of Dust*. Yet *Scoop* does not really seem to be operating in the same manner as those novels, even though one cannot refuse to call it a satire in view of its all-out attack on modern journalism. The truth is that, painful as it was to write, the book radiates enjoyment and happiness, and that is its closest resemblance, among many resemblances, to *Decline and Fall*. In neither book is there a hint of the satirist's essential and deep-lying fear. *Scoop*, moreover, is a vigorous reminder that the satirist will love what he hates, and how Waugh loves and hates his journalists! The weight of love is clearly felt here as it is not felt (though it is present) when he is writing of the Beavers, mother and son, in *A Handful of Dust*. I think, in fact, that the happiness of *Scoop*, much of which may be owed to its dedicatee, Laura, rather surprised Waugh and possibly annoyed him a little. Intending to be severe and a little fierce, he found that he could not stop smiling. Intending to savage certain aspects of the modern world, he had unintentionally revealed how much pleasure their awfulness gave him.

Scoop competes with *Decline and Fall* to be proclaimed Waugh's funniest book, and it has the wonderful simplicity of the greatest clowning. For example, since before Aesop, writers had been placing the town mouse in the country and vice versa, yet Waugh not only accepts the challenge of this hackneyed situation but makes it entirely fresh and repeatedly funny. Mr Salter's journey to Boot Magna is far more dificult to bring off than William's journey to the heart of the Megalopolitan empire, simply because the newspaper offices are news to the reader. The perils of the pastoral are conventional and fully anticipated, yet Salter's purgatorial odyssey is quite as funny as William's penitential pilgrimage to the shrine of Lord Copper. The beautiful contrivance whereby William Boot gets John Boot's appointment has the delicious symmetry of John Boot eventually getting the knighthood intended for 'Boot of the *Beast*'. Mr Leblanc of Aden (*Remote People*) appears in *Scoop* transmogrified into the ultimate man of the world, the omnicompetent Mr Baldwin, descending to the roof of the Pension Dressler by parachute, a god from the machine, asking for a ladder, courteously, in five or six languages. In *Scoop*, if only momentarily, Waugh has the Shakespearian power of putting words into our mouths. Who has not at least once contemplated the expedient of 'Up to a point, Lord Copper'? And when Corker and Pigge, after their 600-mile *anabasis* to the Sudan frontier, are not barbecued by the natives but 'kindly received by a District Commissioner, vetted and revictualled and sent on their way home', perhaps this is a kinder, gentler Evelyn Waugh, but it seems churlish not to rejoice.

Scoop was published on 24 May 1938. It was generally well received and was selected by the Book Society and by the Catholic Book Club. Not long after, he and Laura were *en route* to New York, their first visit to the USA, although their destination was in fact Mexico; they travelled to Vera Cruz by ship from New York. The Mexican journey (August–October 1938) resulted in *Robbery Under Law: The Mexican Object Lesson*, published in 1939 by Chapman and Hall. This book is the closeted skeleton in Waugh's *oeuvre*. He never allowed it to be republished, and explained its exclusion from the collection of extracts from his travel books, *When the Going Was Good*, by saying 'it dealt little with travel and much with political questions'. Waugh was not one given to apology, but this suppression of *Robbery Under Law* after the initial publication perhaps indicates a touch of shame. Moreover, he was embarrassed by the book, but that he could never admit.

On 18 March 1938, the government of Lázaro Cárdenas had expropriated the foreign oil companies operating in Mexico. Compensation was offered but negotiations did not progress. The oil companies launched a campaign of anti-Mexican propaganda, and one of their recruits was Evelyn Waugh. A British company, Mexican Eagle, was prominent among the companies expropriated. Its director, the Hon. Clive Pearson, offered Waugh 'a blank cheque'

(1S 478) to visit the country and write a book blackguarding Mexico and the expropriation.

When contacted by Pearson, Waugh knew no more of the affairs of Mexico than he had learned from casually reading the papers. His published opinions, however, made it clear that he would share Pearson's view of Mexican affairs, so no betrayal of his principles was involved. He was, as Stannard says, 'selling his skills for propaganda in advance of his findings', but that involved no significant hypocrisy or embarrassment. His own interpretation of his task included a defence of the Catholic Church in Mexico, which had been persecuted by Cárdenas's government, so he was able to balance political propaganda with a labour that was *ad dei gloriam*. Nor was the Church's condition very different from that of the oil companies, in Waugh's eyes. Both Church and companies had been plundered from the same motive, human greed and cupidity. It is no hyperbole to say that for him oil expropriation and the persecution of the Church were both consequences of Original Sin. As such, of course, the crimes did not have to be attributed to social and political causes, and so Waugh could effectively brush aside the Mexican government's case for its actions. What the government had done, in Waugh's view, was simply to remove the restraint on the innate human impulse to do evil, a restraint that was any government's fundamental *raison d'être*.

A corollary of this resort to flawed human nature to explain the crimes of Mexico is Waugh's assumption – truly the foundation of his attitude – that the Mexicans would not pay the compensation to the oil companies that had been announced. Robbers can never mean to repay. The book repeats this assertion, usually by implication, again and again. If Pearson had intended Waugh's work to strengthen Mexican Eagle's hand in the negotiations over compensation, he must have been disappointed. Waugh could only believe that what was gone was gone: '[Mexico] bears debts of the New and Old World which she will never be able to pay. She is feverishly augmenting them by confiscations' (RUL 274). But his faith in the Mexicans as exemplars of human degeneracy was ill-founded. They let him down; they paid.

> As soon as relations between Great Britain and Mexico were resumed in November 1941 [before Pearl Harbor, after Mexico had declared war on that Nazi Germany whose practices Waugh claimed she was zealously emulating], negotiations were opened

through the diplomatic channel, and lasted for just under six years. Mexico eventually agreed to pay eighty-one million dollars, in fifteen annual installments, but the debt was happily acquitted some years before the date envisaged. (MX 279)

This accomplishment contradicted the fundamental assumption Waugh made in writing *Robbery Under Law*, and he resolved that the book should as far as possible disappear from the record.

In July 1939 Waugh was at work on a novel. His diary for 27 July records that he had rewritten the first chapter 'about six times', perhaps an exaggeration but certainly a truthful indication that this novel was something different. It was never finished, but it is nevertheless a landmark in his literary career, for it is the initiation of a great change in his fiction, the end of the 'early Waugh', the exclusively comic novelist, and his development into what might be called the 'post-*Brideshead*' Waugh, a greatly altered literary personality.

The fragment, *Work Suspended*, was published in a limited edition in 1942 and, considerably revised, in editions for the public at large in 1949 and later. Such widespread knowledge of it as occurred, therefore, came after the great success of *Brideshead Revisited*, but it is really as first steps on the road to *Brideshead* that it should be appreciated. *Work Suspended* shows Waugh with some of the 'literary innovations' in place that he would need for *Brideshead*, but not all of them. He knew in 1939 that he was finished as solely the comic novelist, but he was not yet clear in his mind as to what he would fully become when he next returned to fiction.

Work Suspended is about John Plant, a writer of murder mysteries (*Vengeance at the Vatican*, *Murder at Mountrichard Castle*), who returns to England from Morocco, where he has gone to write, on learning of the death of his father, knocked down in the street by a motorist. His father is a mildly eccentric painter, acerbic, an RA, pretty successful in a wilfully outmoded style. The only offer for John's father's house comes from a developer, who tears it down. With his inheritance, John plans to buy himself a house in the country, and he hunts for it with Lucy, the wife of his friend Roger Simmonds, who is also a writer, a 'professional humourist'. (Waugh gave what had been hitherto his own literary specialty to this unloved friend.) Lucy is pregnant and near to term, and so though John falls in love with her – a fact that she seems only to half comprehend – he assumes and accepts that this cannot be a sexual relationship ('deprived of sex, as women are, by its fulfilment'). It is a love thwarted from its inception, and as soon as the baby is born Lucy loses all need for John's friendship – which is where the fragment ends.

The motorist who has run down John Plant's father is one Atwater, and he is the first of a string of similar characters in Waugh's later fiction (Hooper in *Brideshead* and Trimmer in *Sword of Honour* are the others) who are there to embody much that is repulsive and fearsome in the modern age. The pregnant Lucy is based – as regards Plant's feelings, that is – on Diana Guinness as she had been in 1929 and 1930 when pregnant and when Waugh had been something like her *cicisbeo*. The psychological process that had led Waugh back to Diana is elusive. His own wife's recent pregnancy must have had something to do with it (Teresa was born on 9 March 1938; Auberon, the second child, was to follow on 17 November 1939). Perhaps the point is that Laura was never to be a topic for fiction, and that anything for which she was the inspiration could be used only if it was diverted to another person. The recollection of Diana Guinness as the substance of so much of *Work Suspended* indicates that Waugh in 1939 had assumed the retrospective frame of mind that predominates in his fiction henceforth, but the autobiographical roots of the fragment contrast markedly with what John Plant says about his writing. He takes professional pride in his detective stories in part because they contain 'absolutely nothing of myself'. Waugh certainly wished, and occasionally claimed, that so it was in his own case.

Work Suspended is most radically a departure from Waugh's previous fiction in its style and its narrative method. It is told in the first person by John Plant in an introspective and meditative manner quite different from the 'objective' and 'externalized' style that had hitherto reigned in the comic novels. In those books, the narrator is remarkably unobtrusive with no real assertion of 'omniscience'. John Plant's voice is, of course, subjective, but, like that of Charles Ryder in *Brideshead Revisited*, is that of a very well-informed narrator. When the narrative voice in the comic novels becomes expansive and eloquent, it is the sign of parody (as in the account of the milch-goat's triumph in *Scoop*). Here Waugh lets John Plant luxuriate in simile, sometimes teetering on the brink of self-parody:

> her beauty rang through the room like a peal of bells; thus have I stood, stunned, in a Somerset garden, with the close turf wet and glittering underfoot in the dew, when, from beyond the walls of

box, the grey church tower had suddenly scattered the heavens in tumult. (WS 173)

This narrator embodies a drastic rearrangement of Waugh's attitude towards his own romanticism and, a little ominously, towards sentimentality, romanticism's morbid state.

Waugh referred to his writerly condition at this time as at 'a climacteric', and he was indeed going through the change. Atwater, a distant kinsman of Grimes, would once have been welcomed into the fiction as a bearer of anarchic vitality. John Plant is no *naïf*, but neither is he a very engaging character. He is, apparently without conscious intention on Waugh's part, the first of those low-spirited protagonists of the autobiographical fiction who are to culminate in Guy Crouchback, in whom Waugh openly faces and thematizes the 'unsimpatico' atmosphere in which he was compelled to envelope his later heroes. *Work Suspended*, in its relation to *Brideshead Revisited*, is as 'The Balance' had been to *Vile Bodies*, a first attempt of considerable achievement, but failing – failing in this case to be finished – because not all that was needed was as yet present. John Plant is an early version of Charles Ryder. The love of Plant for Lucy Simmonds, thwarted *ab ovo* by her pregnancy, is to flower into the three-sided, equally but differently doomed relationship of Ryder, Sebastian, and Julia. Plant's country house, for which he is willing to pay £3000 (£550 less than Lady de Vesci had paid for Piers Court) burgeons into that baroque symbol, Brideshead Castle, and Plant's free-handed way with a simile is the first shooting of the luxuriant growth of the prose style of the first edition of *Brideshead*. To complete the materials *Brideshead* would need, Waugh had to undergo the savage disillusionments of his military experience that ratcheted up his disgust with the modern world to unprecedented height and brought with it a complementary nostalgia for a world swept away by the Age of Hooper. Most of all, he had to find a religious theme; that absence left a great void in *Work Suspended*. At his climacteric, Waugh knew, perhaps not yet consciously, that man represented without the spiritual element of his being was comically and tragically incomplete. He had been so representing human beings for over ten years. But he thought that comedy was now behind him, and the claim that he had made while writing *A Handful of Dust* – 'for the first time I am trying to deal with normal people instead of eccentrics' (1S 359) – was to be made true in a more profound way than he had originally intended. Christopher Sykes claims to have heard

(from Philip Dunne) how Waugh had planned to continue and conclude *Work Suspended*, but had forgotten what Dunne had told him. I
wonder if Waugh really knew. He gave it up, in my view, chiefly
because of the lack of a religious theme, and it is very hard to imagine that it would have been continued without one. A comic novel
could have been, but clearly *Work Suspended* was not to be a comic
novel. The fragment that exists could have been turned in a religious direction only by a violent wrenching. Waugh could not finish it for he had not yet been granted the experience that he needed.
When it came, it took the unexpectable form of the deathbed of
Hubert Duggan.

On 7 December 1939, Waugh reported to the Royal Marines depot
at Chatham. His military career would be incompatible with novel
writing until he could obtain long periods of leave or effective un-
employment, so the failure with *Work Suspended* was disguised by its
author's receipt of the king's commission. His next novel would be
Put Out More Flags, written on board ship, 12 July to 3 September
1941.

4

A Legitimate Contribution to the War Effort: 1939–51

In 1939 he was commissioned in the Royal Marines and served as a company commander. Later he joined No. 8 Commando and went with them to the Middle East. Later he joined Brigadier (now Major-General) R. E. Laycock's staff and transferred to the Blues. In 1944 he went to Yugoslavia as a member of the British Military Mission to Marshal Tito.

No part of the 1951 author's blurb is more misleading than this account of Waugh's military service. It states some of the facts but sets them out as if they formed a normal and unremarkable sequence. In reality there are great oddities here, particularly in the moves from posting to posting. His military service was very unlike the 'plain regimental soldiering' that proved 'an orderly and not disagreeable way of life' for John Plant (Postscript to 1949 edition of *Work Suspended*).

Waugh pulled many strings in his search for wartime service, and finally he pulled one that worked. He had become slightly acquainted with Brendan Bracken, Winston Churchill's parliamentary private secretary. Churchill was now the First Lord of the Admiralty. He approved strongly of writers who wanted to fight, and so Waugh's application to the Royal Marines had an irresistible backer. With Churchill's thumb on the scales, it mattered not at all that Waugh failed his medical examination. The Marines ignored the doctors' verdict and he was accepted for Marine Infantry, commissioned immediately as a second-lieutenant and reported to Chatham on 7 December 1939. The Marines were forming a brigade in an experimental manner whereby men with no experience were given officer training without serving as officer cadets. Waugh had found a way into the forces that let him bypass the stage where he would most likely have washed out.

Waugh was thirty-six in 1939. He was sedentary, overweight, out of condition and very short-sighted. He was eligible for conscription, but the likelihood of that was small. (By May 1940, no one over the age of twenty-seven had been called up.) He could have avoided military service with no difficulty or disgrace at all, but that was never really an option. He was of the generation that had been just too young for the First World War, Alec's war, and now he could again get even. Politically, the announcement of the Hitler–Stalin pact made the war acceptable to him, though as yet he had not completed his definition of that alliance as 'the Modern Age in arms' that impels Guy Crouchback into the battle. The clubman in Waugh could see that the infantry offered a membership that he very much wanted. Military – as opposed to civilian – service was a matter of honour. 'There is a symbolical difference between fighting as a soldier and serving as a civilian, even if the civilian is more valuable' (D 438). Most important, he could see that in the war life was offering him experience about which he would be able to write. 'Nothing would be more likely than work in a government office to finish me as a writer; nothing more likely to stimulate me than a complete change of habit'. Knowledge of himself as a writer was not, however, balanced by general self-knowledge. He did not know that his anarchic and in some ways defensive personality would make his military service an experience of frustration, bitterness, and disillusionment, and that it would push the changes he was effecting in his literary personality in unexpected and difficult directions.

Waugh's experience of the Second World War was skewed from the start by his interpretation of the nature of the conflict. In *Scott-King's Modern Europe* (1949), the protagonist expresses Waugh's view that the war had 'cast its heroic and chivalrous disguise and become a sweaty tug-of-war between teams of indistinguishable louts'. Waugh represented his enlistment as taking up the chivalrous and heroic cause, and then described how that cause came to grief when the Soviet Union became an ally. This was not a crusade but a brutal struggle for survival. In truth, only one team was fundamentally loutish, though the other had to do some very loutish things. Chivalrous and heroic assumptions permit no compromise, no merely expedient alliances, and do not accept that victory is the only thinkable outcome. Waugh could see this matter only from his religious point of view (which of course was the foundation of chivalry and heroism); from there, honourable defeat was far preferable to compromised victory. From the secular point of view of most of his countrymen and their allies, his view was unthinkable, hence the paradox that perhaps the best British fiction about the Second World War adopts an attitude that is strikingly out of alignment with the popular view of the war, both now and then. *Sword of Honour* is a minority view that has claimed such precedence as it has by literary power alone, not by coinciding with popular opinion.

Waugh was involved in three combat operations during his wartime service. As a marine, he took part in the expedition to Dakar, in French West Africa, in 1940, which was a total fiasco. When he was seconded to the Commandos, he went on a raid on Bardia, on the Libyan coast, in April 1941, and that too was a fiasco, though on a smaller scale. Then the Commandos were involved late in the defence of Crete, which meant in fact taking part in the nearly chaotic retreat and evacuation as the Germans got a victory that could have been denied to them. Surveying this sad list, one is struck by how every one of these operations seems to have been designed to contribute to the disillusionment of Evelyn Waugh and to the darkening of his outlook.

His individual career was a sequence of setbacks. When he first joined the Marines at Chatham in 1939, the considerable vestiges of peacetime soldiering and the friendly welcome offered by the regulars were quite enchanting, and he went through a brief 'honeymoon' of happiness and good feelings. But the elegance and ceremonial of Chatham were all too soon replaced by cramped and drafty improvised quarters at Deal and Bisley, where the younger subalterns in the mess played the 'wireless' that he abominated and generally confronted him with manifestations of the modern world and the younger generation that he openly loathed. The physical demands of the job were, he felt, degrading, and he found himself in a race to achieve steps in promotion before his physical limitations and deficient military skills brought him down. In this he succeeded; in April 1940 he was, after a stint as a platoon commander, promoted to captain (the only one of the temporary officers so elevated) and made commander of D Company, RM1 (Marine Infantry Brigade). But as training continued and was succeeded, as France fell and the Phoney War ended, by invasion scares wherein RM1 was shunted to Wales and Cornwall, he began to make his CO, Col. Lushington, regret the good report he had written when promoting him. At this time, and perhaps not coincidentally, Waugh began to angle for a transfer to one of the new 'independent raiding companies' he had heard about from Brendan Bracken.

In the event, he was pushed before he could jump. Lushington took away Waugh's company and gave it to a major from another unit. Selina Hastings offers an explanation, though without citing a source. At Plymouth, the train to Birkenhead was found to be without drinking water. The CO put a guard on the locomotive so that it should not leave until water was supplied.

> While this was being done, [Lushington] heard to his astonishment Captain Waugh giving his quartermaster sergeant, whom for some reason he held responsible for the waterless train, a ferocious dressing down. Such a public reprimand, in full view and hearing of the men, was unforgivable, and Lushington made up his mind there and then that Waugh must be removed from his command. (H 404)

It was Waugh's relationship with 'the men' that made 'plain regimental soldiering' an impossibility for him; 'the men' resonates like a knell throughout accounts of his career and his suitability – mainly unsuitability – for command. Brian Franks, commanding 2 SAS in Perthshire in 1944, discovered that he had somehow acquired Evelyn Waugh as one of his officers. Franks candidly informed him 'that he was a liability and on no account to be allowed near the men' (H 463). Waugh's inability to get on with the troops under his command (Sykes claimed that his life was endangered because the men hated him so much) was crippling for a man who wanted and expected to be a good officer. His unpopularity in the army has been declared to be a 'myth' (2S 27), but Franks's report of a conversation with Laycock is accepted as authentic.

> 'Evelyn's appointment will only introduce discord and weaken the Brigade as a coherent fighting force... And, apart from everything else, Evelyn will probably get shot'.
> 'That's a chance we all have to take'.
> 'Oh, I don't mean by the enemy' (SY 229).

Class consciousness, rooted in deep psychological insecurity about his own social standing, seems to have made Waugh incapable of a working, soldierly relationship with the men. 'He never hesitated to take advantage of the fact that while he was a highly educated man, most of them were barely literate. He bullied them in a way they were unused to' (SY 228). In the pattern of feelings and ideas that at this time were assembling themselves into Waugh's diatribe against the Modern Age, the way he saw and was seen by the soldiers he commanded played a considerable role.

An officer who continues on active service despite having proved to his superiors that he is unfit to command troops has to be assigned to staff duties at some level. After his six months as a company commander in the Marines, the only part of his service specified in the blurb, all the rest of Waugh's time in the Marines and in the army saw him as an intelligence officer, a liaison officer, as a personal assistant to his CO, or as part of a military mission supporting a political embassy. And his military employment continued mainly because Robert Laycock and Randolph Churchill maintained friendship with him and gave him posts.

It was as battalion intelligence officer that Waugh sailed to the capital of French West Africa. For a while, he was allowed to keep his captaincy. The purpose of the Dakar expedition, which forms the climax of *Men at Arms* (1952), was to support General De Gaulle and the Free French, who expected that the Vichy garrison would come over to them. The unfree French, however, did not prove amenable and gave substantial tokens of resistance. Despite the large force assembled for the expedition, the Allies abandoned their objectives and retreated. RM1 did not land. 'Bloodshed has been avoided at the cost of honour', Waugh told Laura, noting down for future use the 'oddities and follies' of the expedition (L 139,141). It was a fiasco that fitted perfectly into his evolving view of the whole war.

After returning to Scotland, Waugh went on leave to visit his wife, now eight months pregnant, and to chivvy along his transfer. On 12 November 1940, a lieutenant again, he was officially seconded to No. 8 Commando, at Largs, near Glasgow, for a period of six months. Lt Col. Robert Laycock of the Royal Horse Guards, Waugh's great friend, commanded and the officers were mostly drawn from the Brigade of Guards. 'Waugh was a small, irascible, middle-class writer not in his first youth. He was joining a set of aristocratic toughs largely recruited from the bars of White's and Buck's. Apart from anything else, the expense of life in such a unit promised to be exorbitant' (2S 22). The aristocratic toughs – one of them was Randolph Churchill – spent money freely and gambled for recreation. Waugh loved belonging to this outfit, but it was not only his monetary exigencies that kept him essentialy separated from the lords and dandies he wanted to be among:

he was always just beyond the secret society of those he most envied. He was liaison officer rather than gentleman killer. He could not afford their games or their meals. He was excluded from confidential policy decisions... Waugh's dream of upper-class life always circled round the same illusion: that he belonged, that he was a natural member of the clan. But he always knew, and Laura sometimes reminded him, that he didn't and wasn't. (2S 25)

In No. 8 Commando Waugh hoped to become a troop commander. He began as a liaison officer which 'really means being on the waiting list for a job' (L 146), but though Laycock's affection for Waugh went a long way, it did not go so far as to compromise the basic fighting efficiency of his command. Waugh could perhaps be useful at minor staff work but he would never be a troop leader. The commandos trained at various sites in Scotland. On 30 November 1940 Waugh was summoned to Pixton, where Laura had begun premature labour. He got there just after the child died. After more Scottish exercises and embarkation leave, No. 8 Commando sailed for Egypt via South Africa at the beginning of February 1941.

It was while based with the commandos in Egypt that Waugh experienced nearly all his fighting in the Second World War. He made literary use of all his military experience, however, from training and the Dakar fiasco with RM1 right through to the military mission to Yugoslavia in 1944 and early 1945. Egypt with the commandos gave him the material for Guy Crouchback's (and Brigadier Ritchie-Hook's) landing at Dakar in *Men at Arms*, and for Trimmer's 'raid' on the coast of France and the account of the Cretan débâcle in *Officers and Gentlemen*. The raid on the town of Bardia, just across the Egyptian border in what is now Libya, had more immediate if ephemeral literary fruit, an article for *Life* (November 1941) which in light of events that preceded it became fascinating in ways that Waugh never intended.

150 men from B Commando landed at Bardia on the night of 19–20 April 1941, with Waugh in his intelligence officer role ('noncombatant timekeeper', 2S 29). Intelligence had told them that there was a garrison of 2000 enemy troops and that the place was defended by large coastal guns. The commandos were to destroy stores and defences and cause the Germans to divert forces to Bardia. Intelligence was wrong. There was no garrison and the guns had already been destroyed. They were able to burn a dump of tyres and blow up a trestle bridge. The enemy did send forces to Bardia, but it is unclear

whether they permanently diverted reinforcements to the place, thus weakening their front line, as had been the plan.

The near total failure of intelligence was greatly compounded by B Commando's blunders. One officer was killed by 'friendly fire', one landing craft had to be abandoned, the only two enemy soldiers encountered, motorcyclists, got clean away, one of the landing parties descended to the wrong beach and was left behind to be captured. All in all, a near disaster. The disesteem with which temporary Captain Waugh had begun to view the army and the war increased. Crete, the 'island of disillusion' (SH 409), put paid in full to his love affair with the military, and added a torment of concealed guilt and pain to go along with disillusionment.

The British had occupied Crete in October 1940 to deny it to the Germans, who had attacked Greece. British naval supremacy made a seaborne invasion doubtful but the Germans, on a roll of victories, brought off a great gamble by launching a successful airborne invasion on 21 May 1941. After very hard fighting, the Germans began to prevail and the Allied forces (British, Australians, New Zealanders, Greeks) retreated. Two battalions of Laycock's brigade (A and D Commandos, denominated 'Layforce') were ordered to Crete and began arriving on 24 May. Their mission became that of covering the retreat to Sphakia on the southern coast. Waugh was Laycock's intelligence and liaison officer, following his CO around and trying to be helpful. His written accounts of the five days he was on the island state clearly and violently that he saw the whole business of the retreat and evacuation as a gigantic failure of nerve, gross cowardice, a totally unnecessary capitulation and a moral disgrace that enraged him because he was unafraid yet tainted by complicity. The violence of his denunciations, however, turns out to be given its almost hysterical note by what has emerged fairly recently of his own guilt and deception in the matter of the Cretan evacuation.

Waugh saw cowardice and the breakdown of order everywhere. He himself was simply fearless, and he never conceded that courage is most properly not the absence but the control of fear. The CO of A Commando in Laycock's brigade was Lt Col. Felix Colvin. Under attack from German dive-bombers, he cracked and displayed the symptoms of acute shell-shock. The sound of aircraft caused him to cower under tables and in culverts. At such times, he was irrational with fear and Laycock had to relieve him of command. Waugh was less sympathetic than George S. Patton would have been. For him, Colvin's case was explicable only within moral categories. Colvin had allowed his fear to overcome his reason, so he had abdicated his status as a rational man, one of God's special creatures. The relentless depiction of Major Hound in *Officers and Gentlemen* has its origins in Colvin's breakdown.

Layforce's participation in the battle of Crete was a measure of desperation, since commandos were trained for very different kinds of work than they were given there, but at the stage of their arrival there was nothing to do but withdraw, evacuating as many as possible. Because they were the freshest troops, Layforce became the rearguard for the evacuation from Sphakia, and just before leaving the island on 30 May, the commander of the British forces, General Freyberg, spoke what turned out to be troubling words to Laycock: 'You were the last to come so you will be the last to go'. Since evacuation of all of Creforce's troops proved impossible (5000 or so were captured by the Germans), it was from the first seen as strange and suspicious that about 200 of the commandos, including Layforce's brigade headquarters did get onto the ships and were evacuated. Stannard and Hastings, relying on Antony Beevor's *Crete: The Battle and the Resistance*, make it clear that it is likely that Laycock deliberately misinterpreted or disobeyed his orders and that those of his command who were evacuated with him used their power as a still disciplined unit to jump the queue ahead of other would-be evacuees, forcing their way onto the ships before a great rabble of the demoralized and wounded.

Waugh thus avoided imprisonment and was returned to Egypt, but though free and physically unharmed he had acquired a grave moral wound. He had not, of course, shared in Laycock's decision to get out and neither Laycock nor Waugh acquired any taint of cowardice by leaving – unless it was cowardice to wish to avoid imprisonment and to fight on. As far as Laycock's motives can be discerned, it was perhaps his view that the war effort could best be served by getting himself and as many of his men as possible back to Egypt, and in the confusion after the evacuation no one challenged him. But Waugh hero-worshipped Laycock, and if this calculus of ends and means had been shared with him, he would have despised it. Robert Laycock, in light of this action, was hardly better than the other officers he had scornfully observed failing in their duty and saving themselves.

Laycock's decision had presented Waugh with an acutely painful and swift decision of his own: should he speak out? should he declare Laycock's decision to be what it was? Perhaps hardly realizing in the turmoil of events that he had made a momentous choice, Waugh went along. Laycock had betrayed an ideal, but thereafter Waugh would never openly criticize him. As intelligence officer, Waugh's duties included keeping the Layforce war diary. For himself, he wrote the 'Memorandum on Layforce' that is part of his published *Diaries* (D 489–515). Martin Stannard has analysed the latter document, and Antony Beevor has commented on both. They leave no doubt that Waugh shaped these narratives to justify Laycock's actions but in his heart he knew that something had been destroyed. He lied in several ways after Laycock had betrayed both himself and Waugh's hero-worship. He lied in the diaries and he lied by saying nothing, by continuing to accept Laycock's patronage and by proclaiming him to be a *preux chevalier*. He lied to himself but finally he did so only in part. Eventually, in his war novels, he told not the whole truth but a significant part of it while simultaneously keeping up his lie.

And perhaps that is finally fair. Laycock's defection from Waugh's high ideal did not invalidate his whole career, his entire reputation. His was an agonizing case that in effect forced Waugh into seeing that absolutism can falsify, and that relativism, in matters of true and false, can bring one closest to truth.

It may be conjectured that the violence and absolutism of Waugh's attitude towards the Cretan débâcle were only increased by his own conduct and Laycock's in the matter of the evacuation. He never modified his earliest opinion that in the main the cause of all that went wrong for the Allies in Crete was cowardice. During his own time on the island he had behaved with such marked courage that Antony Beevor has suggested that it was owed to a death wish. In accusing just about everyone of something that he could not be accused of, he managed to spread a moral taint in general while knowing at least semi-consciously that he was accusing a mass of people as a substitute for the particular denunciation of the violation of the code of officer and gentleman that he would not make, a failure that gnawed at him until he got to writing *Officers and Gentlemen* a dozen years later. Waugh's railing against cowardice on Crete astonished other officers: 'I thought he was quite childish about it' (BV 230). The truth was that his proclamation of the cowardice explanation was childishly fervent because he was protecting the romantic idealism that was emotionally invested in the person of Robert Laycock. It was very important to Waugh that this ideal figure should not be tainted, but finally he saw that keeping up the pretence *in fiction* was a betrayal of one of the very few secular things that he held sacred.

The return of the defeated Creforce and its Layforce component to Egypt initiated a series of breakings up. Layforce was disbanded. Waugh's six-month 'contract' was at an end, and he became a marine again. In July 1941 he embarked for a 20 000 mile roundabout journey – to avoid U-boats – back to Britain. They sailed down the east coast of Africa to Cape Town, across the South Atlantic to Trinidad, up the east coast of the USA, across to Iceland and so to Liverpool. Waugh, however, had the perfect pastime; *en voyage* he wrote a novel, *Put Out More Flags*. It was finished in September 1941 and published in March 1942.

Back in Britain he was assigned first to 12RM Land Defence Force near Portsmouth, but his duties were merely administrative and petty, and he managed to get transferred, on his thirty-eighth birthday, to 5RM in Scotland. 5RM was not much better, however. His relations with his superiors were dismal, and the prospect of fighting seemed to recede. He was sent on a company commanders course near Edinburgh, but after completing it he was once more humiliatingly deprived of his company by his CO, backed up by the brigadier, who made the penetrating remark that he was fit only to command a company in battle. He was clearly not about to become the fighting man he wanted to be in the Marines, so he again set about angling for a transfer and was again rescued by Robert Laycock.

Laycock's career after Crete had included a long-distance raid behind enemy lines to try to capture Rommel. He was now commanding the Special Service Brigade and was willing to give Waugh a job at his HQ at Ardrossan in Scotland. Waugh had so successfully antagonized his Marine CO that, to bring off the transfer, Laycock had to persuade his old regiment, the Royal Horse Guards, to accept Waugh as one of its officers. By this strange route, he was permanently transferred from the Royal Marines to the army and moreover to an ultra-fashionable regiment, the Blues. Laycock's consideration for Waugh was extraordinary but as before it did not stretch to making him a company or troop commander. He was to serve as Intelligence Officer on Laycock's staff and stay away from the men, 'an acting temporary captain on lieutenant's pay, loyally kept on as a kind of regimental mascot' (2S 68).

The publication of *Put Out More Flags* (1942) initiated the period of Waugh's greatest popularity as an author, when he seemed – to his own surprise, certainly – to be able to match the mood of the public in novel after novel. While he was finding it hard to make a go of his temporary military career, therefore, he was succeeding very well indeed at his peacetime profession. When he was in London, as he often was when he served with Laycock's Special Service Brigade, he could spend a lot of time at White's, although his periods at the bar of the club made him all too visible to some who were not delighted to see him there. Mr Waugh the successful novelist co-existed uncomfortably with acting Captain Waugh, the military misfit.

His most recent novel was and was not a continuation of the writing that had established his reputation. *Put Out More Flags* was not a contemporary story, since it dealt with the events of a couple of years earlier, during the Phoney War (the novel's events are very carefully co-ordinated with historical events), and in wartime change was so rapid as to make a couple of years earlier seem a very long time in the past. Wartime put Waugh into a mood of retrospection, sometimes rising or sinking to nostalgia, that endured to the end of his career. With the exception of the two 'gifts' – novels based on unexpected events in his life, *The Loved One* (1948) and *The Ordeal of Gilbert Pinfold* (1957) – all his remaining fiction was to be 'historical' in the sense of being retrospective. (*Helena* was 'historical' in a quite different way.) In conformity with this attitude of mind, in the immediate postwar years, when he was in his forties, Waugh chose to become an old man.

Put Out More Flags was meant to be Waugh's farewell to comic fiction (though the suppressed did in fact return). The experiment of *Work Suspended* proved very influential on the book, albeit in form and manner it stands with the comic novels. It is usually spoken of as a 'transitional' work, showing Waugh in motion from his 'old' to his 'new' writing, and that is fair enough. It looks as if he decided that he must ask how the characters from his earlier novels would cope with the arrival of that war whose coming had been so often alluded to in those books. Most of all, the book was a way of clearing the decks for his future fiction. In 1950, he remarked in a letter to Nancy Mitford, 'You still have the delicious gift of seeing people as funny which I lost somewhere in the highlands of Scotland circa 1943' (L 343). The existence of *Work Suspended*, followed by *Put Out More Flags*, suggests that in 1941 Waugh expected and anticipated that his comic gift would be surrendered or lost in the not distant future, and that he would give it one more gallop while it was still with him. *Work Suspended* points forward; *Put Out More Flags* in the main points back.

This is true, moreover, in terms of narrative technique: *Put Out More Flags* is notable for a 'development' that is in fact a regression, though not a return. Its most striking technical feature is its omniscient narrator, a voice heard everywhere, quite dominating the narrative. The 'progressive' technical features of the earlier novels include a narrator who stays largely out of the way, letting the characters and events speak for themselves. By contrast, here the narrator has all the qualities that have been so abominated by modernist criticism and yet is undeniably the most successful aspect of the book. There is an element of Wavian self-indulgence in the narrator of *Put Out More Flags* as he lays bare for us the characters' hidden motives, yet it is handled so well that one may not complain. There is no narrator quite like this one anywhere else in Waugh's fiction, and the uniqueness may derive from Waugh's feeling that here he was bringing the world of his comic fiction to an end and passing judgement on it. The famous final line of the novel, the crushing judgement on the idiotic optimism of Sir Joseph Mainwaring's 'new spirit abroad' – 'And, poor booby, he was bang right' – is a final distillation of the narrator's attitude. That new spirit, the world coming into being, is most likely that which would make Waugh say that he had lost the ability to see people as funny about 1943. After that date, one thematic pillar of his work is the open detestation and indeed real fear of the modern world and modern people, not enjoyed for their awfulness, simply deplored.

'Awfulness enjoyed' perhaps explains the prominence of Basil Seal in the book. Before Atwater, Hooper, and Trimmer took over, as they were surely about to do, Waugh brought back an undeniably awful man whose monstrous misdeeds represented the world of style, panache, and *élan* that grey modernity would smother. It is the difference between Atwater begging from John Plant the cost of the flowers he had sent to John's father's funeral ('So I put a note in an envelope and sent it to the man who had killed my father'), and Basil Seal stealing his mother's emeralds (in *Black Mischief*). As a friend of John Plant's in *Work Suspended*, however, brought in to recount the story of Roger's courtship of Lucy, Basil seems like a thoroughbred pulling a milk-cart, created for nobler things. A book with Basil *primus inter pares* in the group of characters on which the novel centred would be a good farewell to the earlier Waugh, especially since Basil had been close to the centre of *Black Mischief*, where misunderstanding by an influential part of the public had forced Waugh to explain and defend his comic method. The great popularity of *Put Out More Flags*, this descendant of *Black Mischief*, permitted Waugh to take his departure, as he thought, from the territory of the professional humourist with acclamations of success. He was giving up the comic novel but *not* because he had failed with it.

Put Out More Flags has a number of characters from earlier novels taking prominent parts. This, too, was a stratagem of farewell. The novels that followed would forgo this Balzacian mannerism (except for a few very deliberate exceptions), but here, for the last time, it would be displayed extensively. The transitional nature of the book, however, is indicated by the introduction of a number of characters who point forward, not back. The 'three rich women' who, at the beginning of the book, are thinking about Basil – Barbara Sothill, his sister; Angela Lyne, his mistress; and Lady Seal, his mother – are largely a new departure for Waugh. Lady Seal is a sympathetically delineated fool, and Barbara, more than a little in love with her brother, helps the reader to feel how this in many ways monstrous egoist can be truly attractive. Angela Lyne's descent into alcoholism is preparation for Sebastian in *Brideshead* and is quite different from the drunkenness that occurs in the comic novels. (The taxonomy of drunkenness across the whole span of Waugh's fiction will repay study.) In Ambrose Silk, the homosexual aesthete, we have a finished character in himself who is also a preparatory study for Anthony Blanche in *Brideshead*. Martin Stannard is quite right to stress Waugh's perhaps reluctant sympathy for Silk and Blanche, who represent something very important in himself that he had to be cautious about confronting and confessing. It is telling that it is in his wartime fiction, while he was, so to speak, publicly a man of action, a soldier, that he introduces these characters from the other, more vulnerable, side of his personality.

A good understanding of *Put Out More Flags* requires a grasp of chronology. It is a comedy and a happy book because Waugh imposed careful restrictions upon himself. It deals only with the *drôle de guerre*, the Phoney War that ended with the German attack on France and the Low Countries. It has its military side but that is subordinate to civilian life during the period, involving of course the evacuation of working-class women and children from the cities to the countryside. (And just as Cyril Connolly found his name used for the General in *Black Mischief*, so the onomastic torment continued in *Put Out More Flags*, with the even more memorable Connolly children.) Waugh devoted *Men at Arms* (1952) to the Phoney War from the military perspective, and that book is correspondingly the most light-hearted of the wartime trilogy.

The experience of the battle of Crete was only two months in the past when Waugh began the voyage on which he wrote his novel. He was to interpret what he had seen on Crete as the betrayal of the aristocratic military ideal but even if he had not yet, in July 1941, formulated his disgust in those terms, he certainly knew that he could not write a comedy about Crete. He set the date on which he ceased to find people funny at 1943 but in May 1941 he had gone through an experience that gave him what he always held to be necessary for comedy, something to complain about, but that would never become a comic subject. He liked things to go wrong, but he did not like the wrong turn things had taken on Crete. His comic novel, written he said later for his own pleasure, took his mind off the great betrayal, and postponed for a few years his necessary facing up to it.

Waugh's service in Britain with Laycock's Special Service Brigade came to a nasty end in July 1943. Waugh was with them in Scotland, at Sherborne in Dorset, and at Combined Operations HQ in London. He had little of importance to do and did less. Laycock showed signs of disfavour when Waugh came drunk to dinner. Elements of the brigade were involved in the Dieppe raid (August 1942), but Waugh heard humiliatingly of the existence of the operation from the porter of the St James Club. In December 1942, *Work Suspended* appeared in a limited edition, its innovations admired only by a few friends, such as Henry Yorke (Green) and Edith Sitwell. On 23 March 1943, he wrote in his diary: 'Bob [Laycock] explained to me that I am so unpopular as to be unemployable. My future very uncertain'. His downfall came over Operation Husky, the invasion of Sicily from North Africa. Part of the brigade departed for the operation and Laycock left a letter indicating that Waugh should follow later when embarkation orders were sent. Then, with a timing that galled painfully, Arthur Waugh died and Evelyn had to spend two weeks in London winding up his father's affairs. He schemed to get his embarkation orders to come through, but at this time he fell foul of the brigade's Deputy Commander, Lt Col. the Lord Lovat, DSO, MC. He and Waugh were old enemies, the antagonism particularly painful for Waugh because Lovat was old aristocracy (the fifteenth baron), Roman Catholic and a genuine hero with an ego that at least matched Waugh's. Lovat was disgusted to encounter Waugh drunk at White's, and resolved that he should not go overseas with the brigade. He ordered Waugh to report to the Scottish base where the Royal Marine Commando was in training, to be passed physically fit for service. This was an impossibility for Waugh, as Lovat surely knew, and so Waugh launched a campaign of protests and complaints that rebounded on his head when an infuriated General Haydon, the Vice-Chief of Combined Operations, 'advised' him to leave the brigade. He had been sacked, and Laycock refused to get involved.

Waugh's only surviving affiliation with the army was, absurdly, the Royal Horse Guards. The regiment decided to send him to the Household Cavalry Training Unit at Windsor which turned out, as far as he was concerned, to be a holding tank for the unemployed and unemployable. He was financially well off and spent his time in London at his clubs, dining out in smart society, visiting Nancy Mitford, who was working in an upmarket bookshop, and angling for a post with Colonel William Stirling, who was then raising the 2nd Special Air Service Regiment.

Waugh had first gone over to Windsor with Hubert Duggan, an old friend and the brother of an old friend. Duggan was both a captain in the Life Guards and a Conservative MP, though he was not in good health and was not on active service either with the army or the House of Commons. In the autumn of 1943, though only thirty-nine, he was ill with tuberculosis and clearly dying. He was a lapsed Catholic and Waugh, being in London, decided to help Hubert save his soul. He visited the Catholic Forces chaplain for West London, who agreed to come if called. Hubert's sister, who was nursing him, opposed the giving of last rites; his mother did not know what to think. Waugh had, of course, no doubts, and saw the matter as one of greatest urgency. He got his way. When Hubert was near his end, and the Forces chaplain could not be found, Waugh went to Farm Street and brought back the Rector, Father Devas, who gave Hubert absolution. 'Hubert said, "Thank you father", which was taken as his assent'. Later Devas anointed him 'and Hubert crossed himself and later called me up and said, "When I became a Catholic it was not from fear", so he knows what happened and accepted it. So we spent the day watching for the spark of gratitude for the love of God and saw the spark' (D 552).

Waugh was certain that he had seen something close to a miracle and, as it turned out, he had a vitally important scene for his next novel. From a literary point of view, it matters not at all that he may have been not only the producer and director of this drama, but its part-author too. Yet one would dearly like to know when the idea of using this scene in *Brideshead Revisited* first entered his mind.

Waugh was now a Royal Horse Guards officer without employment, effectively on indeterminate leave. He wanted to write a novel but he also wanted to prove that General Haydon had been wrong to sack him. He did get an appointment from Colonel Stirling to 2 SAS but proposed operations for them were postponed and when Waugh took part in parachute training he broke his leg and was back on leave again. He then made a decision that seemed to be the renunciation of most of his military ambition. He wrote to his CO at Windsor (copies to the War Minister and to Brendan Bracken, now Minister of Information) requesting leave in order to write a novel. He described his situation without flinching. He was a forty-year-old lieutenant, physically unfit for the roles for which he had been trained, with little skill or aptitude for the duties that should be assigned to him. He went on to speak of his novel in terms that the bureaucracy might understand, much as he inwardly despised them.

> This novel will have no direct dealing with the war and it is not pretended that it will have any immediate propaganda value. On the other hand it is hoped that it may cause innocent amusement and relaxation to a number of readers and it is understood that entertainment is now regarded as a legitimate contribution to the war effort. (D 557)

The book had to be written now or it would never be written, and when it was finished perhaps there would be some way in which he might 'serve my regiment'. His several commanding officers during this period saw at once the advantages of giving Lieutenant Waugh leave. They would have been glad to give him leave to build sandcastles if that had been his request. The War Office, knowing him only on paper, made several attempts during the composition of the novel to find employment for him, but he was able to beat off what he called 'military frivolities'. He was now completely in aesthetic mode. He went off to Chagford, where he had not been to write since 1939 and professed total uninterest in the progress of the war.

Tuesday 6 June 1944

This morning at breakfast the waiter told me the Second Front
[the Normandy invasion] had opened. I sat down early to work
and wrote a fine passage of Lord Marchmain's death. Carolyn
came to tell me the popular front [?!] was open. I sent for the
priest to give Lord Marchmain the last sacraments. (D 567)

He had finished his manuscript by 24 June 1944. He received the
proofs in Yugoslavia and corrected them in late November 1944. The
first publication was a 'private edition' of about 50 copies, paper-
bound and at his own expense, that he sent as gifts to his friends at
Christmas 1944. The book was published by Chapman & Hall on 28
May 1945, an edition that incorporated many changes from the 1944
text. The American edition was published by Little, Brown in the
same year.

Brideshead Revisited was a success beyond anything else that Waugh
ever experienced; it made a fortune. When he visited the USA in
1948, he found that Little, Brown were holding $100 000 for him. The
Book of the Month Club had made it a main selection. For a considerable time, Waugh was rich enough to be under no compulsion to
write, a situation that was really not good for his morale. Success
brought perils. The new audience Waugh acquired with *Brideshead*
raised a variety of problems in his mind, the greatest one, from a literary point of view, being that the book's success with the public
might mean that it was popular for the wrong reasons and that his
message – and he really did have a message – was being missed or
mistaken.[1]

Brideshead Revisited is a novel with a religious theme and is therefore about two interrelated things: the world and the spirit. Waugh's
most helpful statement about his book is the text that he provided
for the dust-jacket of the first edition (CH 236). Reversing the notice
that had appeared on the cover of *Decline and Fall* sixteen years earlier, he emphasized that *Brideshead* was '*not* meant to be funny. There
are passages of buffoonery, but the general theme is at once romantic and eschatological'. These highly revealing terms refer to the
worldly and spiritual aspects of the book but the phrasing ('*at once*
romantic and eschatological') seems to suggest that Waugh saw no
conflict between the two terms. If that can be so, it was a basic con-
ceptual error that caused him genuine distress and had a major
effect on his literary life. The world, of the past especially, is seen

romantically and is evoked with a brilliancy of rhetoric that simply distracts from the book's eschatological side. The skull in Ryder's rooms labelled 'Et in Arcadia ego' should speak in two voices: 'I, Death, am in Arcadia' *and* 'I was once happy in Arcadia', but the second voice quells the first. Arcadia as Oxford and the lost paradise is rhetorically triumphant. What happened to the book's germinal scene tells all. Waugh wrote to Ronald Knox: '[The book] was, of course, all about the death bed. I was present at almost exactly that scene, with less extravagant decor, when a friend of mine [Hubert Duggan] whom we thought in his final coma and stubbornly impenitent... did exactly that, making the sign of the cross. It was profoundly affecting and I wrote the book about that scene' (L 206). Waugh's remarks emphasize the eschatological, exactly as one would expect in writing to a priest who had reservations about the sexual descriptions in the book, but he was quite sincere. He really wanted to believe that the eschatological balanced or indeed outweighed the romantic in the book. But the parenthetical phrase, 'with less extravagant decor', by which he attempts to put the romantic in its subordinate place, betrays him. The account of Lord Marchmain's return to Brideshead, of the Chinese drawing room and the Queen's bed, is not subordinate in the texture of the novel. Throughout, almost all that is 'romantic' is brilliantly realized and asserts itself irresistibly and the public enthusiasm was a response to the writerly power he manifested there. It took a long time for Waugh to admit it fully but he had thwarted himself. And until he did admit it, he expended a deal of energy in placing the blame elsewhere.

The novel ends with renunciation, not only of love but supposedly of the entire world. As the dust-jacket copy states, 'disaster lies ahead', and the disaster meant was the end of the world – literally and according to the Bible. Yet the rhetoric of the book, to which the public responded so enthusiastically, hardly emphasizes the world's ephemerality. The only hope, the religious hope, is that 'the human spirit, redeemed, can survive all disasters', but that survival can occur only in another world than this ('redeemed'), a message that the book renders ineffectual to all but a very specially formed group of readers. The logic of Waugh's argument in *Brideshead* calls for Charles Ryder to become, metaphorically at least, a monk, like Guy's nephew Tony in *Sword of Honour*. But how many readers have accepted or even seen that logic? The conclusion to be drawn will more likely be that happiness in any secular sense is not involved in conversion to Catholicism, which in some profound way Waugh surely did believe, for he always asserted that the greatest of happiness came from membership in the 'Household of the Faith', which not incidentally had been a working title of *Brideshead Revisited*.

Hubert Duggan's deathbed was what Waugh needed to get *Brideshead* started, but it was not the first thought of the novel. Waugh emphasized the deathbed because he wanted the book to have had eschatological beginnings, but his first vague conception of it seems to have been worldly or romantic. In a letter to his wife in 1940, he said, 'I think I shall start writing a book, for my own pleasure, probably not for publication – a kind of modern Arcadia' (L 146). His professionalism could not long tolerate writing not for publication, but it is fascinating that he ever expressed such an idea and it shows how personal and intimate his first thought of the book was. It began as self-indulgence and self-indulgence always remained part of its fabric, a fading stain that could never be quite obliterated. In all its versions, the novel remains autobiographical in a peculiarly intimate way. It is the intimacy of allowing the reader a view into the writer's daydreams and fantasies. The fantasy of a book not for publication also points to an apprehension in Waugh's mind as to how readers might react; his first impulse was to rule out readers altogether, as if to forestall the hostile comment he knew would come, and which he feared chiefly because he feared it would be just. He knew exactly and far beforehand how his novel would be taken by the reader he emphatically did not want. In a comic letter to Dorothy Lygon while he was writing the book, he set down the nightmare version of it.

> I am writing a very beautiful book, to bring tears, about very rich, beautiful, high born people who live in palaces and have no troubles except what they make themselves and those are mainly the demons sex and drink which after all are easy to bear as troubles go nowadays. (L 180)

No eschatology at all; Lady Dorothy was not a Catholic and neither were the masses of readers who bought *Brideshead Revisited* and read it wrong. The nightmare came true.

The doubts about the book's reception started early, but when he began it he had no doubts of any kind. He took to calling the book 'magnum opus' and wrote in his diary 'I think perhaps it is the first of my novels rather than the last' (D 566). The great esteem in which he held *Work Suspended* was extended, and more so, to *Brideshead*, and there came with it a corresponding dismissal, which really lasted for the rest of his life, of the 'light novels' he had published before. To Laura he openly stated the autobiographical attitude (strongly flavoured with self-justification) with which he began to compose the Prologue ('It is v. high quality about Col. Cutler and how much I hate the army' [L 176]), and as he moved from the Prologue to Oxonian Arcadia self-indulgent fantasy took a grip upon him. (In his autobiography, he said that the passages dealing with wine at Oxford were written 'in 1943 [really 1944] at a time of acute scarcity and in a mood of sentimental delusion' [LL 191].) His love affair with Alistair Graham became the basis of Ryder's friendship with Sebastian Flyte (several times in the manuscript Waugh wrote 'Alistair' for 'Sebastian' [H 484]), and he gave Sebastian a family whose history, particularly the father's self-exile, is derived from the Lygons and their father's involuntary exile. Brideshead Castle owes something to Madresfield and a lot to Waugh's love of baroque architecture. Ryder's view of the war, in Prologue and Epilogue, is Waugh's too. Catholicism and conversion to Catholicism are the book's spiritual stratum. To complete this great pudding of ingredients from his past, he included a loveless marriage for Ryder, betrayed by his wife, who has gone a step further than the earlier cuckolding wives in that she has fathered on him the child of her adultery.

The undoubted success of much of *Brideshead* seems to have as its basis Waugh's use of so much of his past for 'models', though he cast over it a romantic glow that seduced much of the reading public as it seduced him. With entirely fictional elements, those characters who seem to have had no models, he had mixed results. Following up his success with John Plant's father in *Work Suspended*, in *Brideshead* Waugh created a wonderfully feline, tormenting father for Ryder. Only in his essential alienation from all that is dear to his son does he faintly resemble Arthur Waugh. Lady Marchmain is a fine creation despite being finally a mystery to the reader, as she was to the author; Waugh told his agent, 'Yes, Lady Marchmain is an enigma' (L 185). He somehow conveys the succubus quality of her love, so that one recognizes without analytically comprehending why her husband hates her so and why Sebastian fears her.

Julia Flyte, Sebastian's sister, with whom Ryder falls in love, is the book's great failure. Waugh's discomfort in writing about the affair ('It is becoming painfully erotic' [L 185]) is palpable, despite the many alterations he made. Julia is there to provide a morally and socially acceptable consummation of the love between Sebastian and Ryder and to offer the possibility that through marriage Ryder might come to own Brideshead. Her father's return to the Church, his willed response to the 'twitch upon the thread', God's standing offer of grace ('the whole thing is steeped in theology' [L 185]), leads to Julia's own response, her return, which will entail giving up Charles Ryder. She expects him not to understand, but he has himself made the same motion of acceptance; he will become a Catholic, and so he, however painfully, must give up Julia. Their simultaneous acceptance of God's love means laying down the sin of their love for each other. The dilemma-and-resolution is tastefully understated and some will have failed to note that Waugh has produced an ending that could have come from a baroque opera. He did, however, notice it himself. In the 1959 Preface he says he had been 'in two minds as to the treatment of Julia's outburst about mortal sin and Lord Marchmain's dying soliloquy ['Better today' (BR 317)]. ...These passages were never, of course [!?], intended to report words actually spoken...I would not now introduce them into a novel which elsewhere aims at verisimilitude'. The speeches are virtually arias in the last act of a libretto for which Waugh's highly orchestrated prose supplied the setting. Between Julia and Ryder occurs a muted, tragic curtain scene, challenging the reader to come over to the side of the angels by accepting that the love of God makes human love literally negligible, though the renunciation of the lesser for the greater licenses the sadness in which Ryder's life is steeped as he makes his involuntary pilgrimage to revisit Brideshead. Some of the readers who observe what is going on will accept the dilemma on Waugh's terms, finding tragic feeling in what the logic of theology argues is no tragedy. But there will be others, far too many for Waugh's liking, who will respond with Mitfordian briskness: 'Goodness how sad'!

In the later part of his career, beginning with *Brideshead*, Waugh developed the proleptically self-defensive habit of describing to his correspondents what he thought his critics would say about his forthcoming novel. For the most part, he got it right but about *Brideshead* he was interestingly wrong. His first letter to his agent about the book (8 February 1944) says: 'It would have a small public at any time. I should not think six Americans will understand it'. Being wrong about general popularity meant a pleasant surprise as the sales figures mounted but the enormous sales in the United States gave him a shock. Strictly speaking, he had not predicted unpopularity with Americans, only that the 'yanks' would fail to understand. This was the escape clause. The Americans were obviously and eagerly enjoying his book but they did not, because as Americans they could not, understand what it was really about. As the book sold and sold, references to 'my humiliating success in U.S.A.' (L 224) multiply in his letters and in the memories of people who knew him. Perhaps the worst instance of the notorious Waugh rudeness is not accidentally associated with *Brideshead*. Lady Mary Lygon told Christopher Sykes about a dinner party to which she invited Waugh

> to meet some admirers who included a well-known American theatrical producer and his wife. The last-mentioned addressed him thus: 'Oh Mr Waugh, I have just been reading your new book *Brideshead Revisited*, and I think it's one of the best books I've ever read'. To which Evelyn replied: 'I thought it was good myself, but now that I know that a vulgar, common American woman like yourself admires it, I am not so sure' (SY 287).

The really crushing epithet in this last sentence was meant to be 'American'. Waugh had no strong objection to the public making him rich. What galled him almost to fury was that he had permitted the vulgar, the common, and most of all the Americans to enjoy a book which his ideological judgement of them declared that they could not understand. *Brideshead* in Waugh's view was in important part a denunciation and explosion of everything he meant by 'modernism', and Americans – secular, materialistic, uncultured, deracinated and, of course, vulgar and common (in the war, they were nearly as much 'the modern age in arms' as the German Nazis or Russian Communists) – Americans were the embodiment of modernity. And yet they were lapping up *Brideshead Revisited*! His first reaction was two-pronged. Nothing wrong with '*magnum opus*'; much wrong with Americans. These two points sufficed him for a while, but eventually he was compelled to modify both, and those modifications are major elements in his later postwar literary life.

With *Brideshead* in the publisher's hands, Waugh had to return to the colours. In June 1944, he was in Perthshire with Brian Franks's SAS unit, still the underemployed misfit with a CO perpetually uneasy about this difficult subordinate. Then came illusory salvation from an unanticipated quarter. Randolph Churchill asked Waugh to join him on a mission to Croatia to render military assistance to the Yugoslav Partisans. Waugh left for London immediately and less than a week later was en route to Bari on the Adriatic coast of Italy, where Brigadier Fitzroy Maclean had the Rear HQ of his military mission.

Their arrival in Yugoslavia was delayed for nearly two months by a plane crash at the end of their first attempt to fly in. Major Churchill and (now finally) Captain Waugh had to return to Italy to recover from wounds – burns, in Waugh's case. They were finally established in Yugoslavia in mid-September 1944.

The fact that Randolph Churchill was the prime minister's son perhaps explains why Maclean had recruited this bull for his Yugoslavian china shop. Waugh's invitation seems to have been Randolph's idea, and his motive may have been the delusion that he and Waugh would be good company for each other. Waugh was so desperate to find something interesting and 'honourable' to do that he ignored any reservations he might reasonably have had about a lengthy dose of Randolph's company at close quarters. Randolph thought that he had persuaded Waugh to join by telling him about Catholic–Orthodox enmities in Croatia and suggesting that he might be able to resolve them. Catholicism in Yugoslavia did prove of great interest to Waugh but a reduction of enmity was really not on his agenda. Maclean hoped Waugh might help keep Randolph in line.

The British had begun their Yugoslavian involvement by allying themselves with the royalist Chetnik forces of Drazha Mikhailovich. A mission to the country by Maclean in 1943, however, had discovered that the Communist forces of the mysterious Tito were far more effective in harrying the Germans than the Chetniks were, and as a result the British switched their support to Tito. Since Britain was already in alliance with the Soviet Union, it would have been hypocritical not to support the Partisans, especially when the wholeheartedness of Mikhailovich's anti-German commitment was suspect. Waugh, of course, when he found out what the situation was, became pro-Chetnik and anti-Partisan. His opposition to the objectives of his own mission took the form of embroidering and spreading the 'rumour' – it was not his own invention[2] – that Tito was a woman.

The British Military Mission was supposed to support the Partisans by arranging airdrops of supplies and weapons and by offering other forms of encouragement. Here again, there was really not much for Waugh to do. He proved to be no damper or emollient for Randolph Churchill's bumptiousness and he was soon yearning, in his letters to Laura, to be back home. The only worthwhile work he

did in Croatia (apart from correcting the proofs of *Brideshead*) was
in a civilian role. He was transferred as a one-man mission to Dubrovnik (Ragusa), where his main military duty was to act as liaison
between the Partisans and Floydforce, of brigade strength, that the
British had inserted to help cut off the now retreating Germans. But
there was little for him to do in a military way and his observation
of the way the Partisans treated the largely Catholic population of
Dubrovnik turned his initial prejudice against them to steady loathing. He neglected the Partisans as much as possible, tried to help
the local people and the many refugees in the city, and discovered
'for the first time the pleasure of charity' (2S 126). One of these
works of charity was to commission a bust of himself from a local
sculptor. (It eventually took its place among the decorations at Piers
Court.) In letters to Laura he described the surprising new role he
was playing.

> My work consists solely in doing good. I distribute food to the
> needy and get a sense of vicarious generosity in the process. . . . the
> bloodiness of the partisans and my uncertain position depress me
> continually; more than that there are so many unhappy people
> who look to me for help which I can ill supply. It seems to comfort
> them to come & tell me how miserable they are; it saddens me.
> But is it not odd? Would you have thought of me as having a kind
> nature? I am renowned for my great kindness here. (L 197)

The Partisans eventually asked for Waugh to be replaced and the
Bari headquarters recalled him. Yet he refused to move on the
grounds that the order had not come from Maclean and then got
Maclean's permission to stay until he had completed a report on the
condition of Catholics and the Church in Croatia. So Waugh hung
on a while longer, gathering material, and finally left Dubrovnik on
20 February 1945. He began writing his report in Bari and finished it
in London.

'Church and State in Liberated Croatia', some 7500 words in
length, is not available in print and has to be consulted in the Public
Records Office (2S 138–43). This fact defines its nature and explains
why Waugh's efforts to publicize it and to make it public policy so
embroiled him in difficulties with the government. He treated the
document as if it were a piece of investigative journalism, whereas
it was in legal fact a report by a serving officer and so within the jur-
isdiction of the Official Secrets Act. Yet it is impossible to see the

report as the work of Mr Valiant-for-Truth wickedly suppressed by a corrupt government, which is undoubtedly how Waugh saw it. The perspective that the 1980s and 1990s have given us on Yugoslavian affairs totally endorses Martin Stannard's view that Waugh told the truth about certain aspects of the relationship of the Catholic Church and the Communist regime aborning but that overall he falsified by omissions and partiality. The report was an act of Catholic advocacy by a man who would not accept that politics, especially the politics of wartime, required compromise and deal-making with people whose principles were alien to one's own. Fitzroy Maclean was able to escape the task of refuting Captain Waugh on a technicality. The Foreign Office sent the report to the British ambassador in Belgrade for comment and his devastating reply, accepting Waugh's truths but pointing out their massive inadequacies, gave the government all the case it needed to shelve the thing. Waugh made one further attempt, getting a Catholic MP to ask a question in the House of Commons, but the Foreign Secretary effectively shrugged it off.

This was not the end of Waugh's crusade against the Yugoslavian Communists. It is an important element in the wartime trilogy, particularly *Unconditional Surrender* (1961), and it got a few gallops outside literature, particularly in November 1952 when Tito came to London on a state visit and Waugh sniped at him in the press.

Waugh had spent the later part of his time in Yugoslavia conducting the first stages of a campaign against the policies of the government he served, for 'he preferred the interests of the Church to those of the British Government' (2S 137). It is in several ways a characteristic end to his military service. But before following him home, this account must take up one more point about the Yugoslavian episode. In August 1949, the *Month* published a short story by Waugh, 'Compassion'. This is the story of a Major Gordon, serving in Croatia in 1944, and how his attempts to aid a group of refugee Jews inadvertently lead to the execution by the Partisans as 'spies and saboteurs' of the couple he comes to know best, the Kanyis. The story is obviously the first version of the culminating episode of *Unconditional Surrender*, published twelve years later, and its appearance in 1949 shows that, despite his extensive involvement with Catholic matters in the last stage of his Yugoslavian stay, Waugh had decided that in fiction Jewish refugees were to be the objects of his protagonist's frustrated acts of compassion, despite the fact that his own contacts with Jews in Yugoslavia were not at all extensive and his diary shows his attitude to them to have been distant, even faintly hostile (D 584–6).

On his birthday in 1944, Waugh had prayed that next year he might be 'at my own home, at my own work, and at peace' (D 588). One year later he was back at Stinchcombe; he had written some of *Helena*, was at work on the abortive 'Charles Ryder's Schooldays' and had prepared the excerpts from his travel books that make up *When the Going Was Good* (1946). The war was over and he had been officially 'demobilized' on 18 September 1945 – but it may be doubted that he was ever 'at peace'.

In London, on his return from Yugoslavia, he found himself living a very different life from that of most people in the immediate postwar period. He was suddenly rich, thanks to *Brideshead*'s sales in both Britain and the USA, but these circumstances in no way restrained his bitter complaints about postwar austerity and the Labour government, which he compared to the German occupiers of France, 'the grey lice'. Spending money on what others would have called luxuries was essential to the style of life that Waugh now made his own. He had not lived long enough at Piers Court really to establish himself there. After the war he made that his first priority. Adornment of house and grounds absorbed much of his disposable income and his attention; he bought pictures and furniture, predominantly in the Victorian style that, in addition to their inherent charms, possessed the great attraction of unfashionability. The grounds were landscaped with grotto and folly. Several servants were employed, including a butler and an estate carpenter. Laura's small farm included a herd of cows.

Waugh's houses were to be his places of refuge, where his order would reign and from which, as much as possible, the modern world would be excluded. The objective of near-isolation was fairly easily attained, whereupon Waugh found that its fearsome side-effect was boredom. Hardly a week passed by without some excursion to keep Giant Boredom at bay, usually day-trips to London, ostensibly to get his hair cut or to visit the London Library. It is true, however, that from 1945 on the events in Waugh's life were mainly the writing and publication of his books and family occasions. He made many excursions but his way of life was settled and his writing was mainly retrospective. His life was more literary than ever, though the quality of the work was more uneven.

In a life that is, to the joy and despair of biographers, lavishly documented, the period after 1939 is by far the better half as regards diary entries, letters, and especially public pronouncements, including that later twentieth-century phenomenon, the recorded interview. From that mass of documents, recurrent themes emerge and one of them is money. In imitation of his own father, Waugh was what Americans call a 'poormouth', loudly advertising imminent ruin. He added to these paternal theatricals a view of taxation as the work of the devil, or more accurately of fiendish and envious politicians ideologically determined to steal what was rightfully his. Resistance to such criminals was bound to be morally vindicated. When the great success of *Brideshead* made it worth while, he began to adopt schemes of tax avoidance and dodgy manoeuvrings that take up considerable space in Stannard's second volume. His accomplices in this, not always willing, were his literary agent, A. D. Peters, and various others – lawyers, agents, accountants.

In truth, Waugh did not know after the war what poverty was. At one stage Peters was trying, without success, to get Waugh to agree to live on £5000 a year, which in 1950 was five times the average professional wage (S2 253). Yet still the laments rang out.

> It is no good trying to live decently in modern England. I make £10,000 a year, which used to be thought quite a lot, I live like a mouse in shabby-genteel circumstances, I keep no women or horses or yachts, yet I am bankrupt, simply by the politicians buying votes with my money. (L 365)

To keep this important client out of the poorhouse, Peters dreamed up a scheme which quickly acquired the nickname of 'the Save the Children fund'. In 1949, after learning the true value of the Penguin Books deal mentioned earlier, Peters suggested that a trust be created for the benefit of Waugh's children into which the proceeds from Penguin should be paid. 'You save tax, ensure [your children's] future to some extent, and can also draw on the income from the Trust for their education and maintenance if the Deed is skilfully drawn up' (S2 255). The deed was drawn up by a lawyer unforgettably named Wilfred Ariel Evill, who, however, planted a time-bomb of bad advice by declaring that the income from the trust was tax-free, an estimated saving of £700 per year. The £1000 advance from the Penguin deal was the first deposit in the trust and there followed all the existing copyrights that Waugh owned. Peters and Evill were the trustees; the children were the only beneficiaries; the money in the trust no longer belonged to Waugh and his wife: 'all interest in the father was eliminated in perpetuity'. Waugh had evaded the tax man but seemed to have put most of his income quite out of reach. He planned to live instead on what future writings brought him and on his American earnings. Little, Brown had been banking that money and paying it to him in annual instalments (on which the taxes due were largely evadable). This was Waugh's explanation to the Internal Revenue. What he did not tell the Commissioners was that he had also worked out how to get access to the trust's capital. Property he had withheld, such as his manuscripts, was sold to the trust as investment and the luxury items that he had to buy for his house and grounds were paid for by the trust, since such items were 'improvements' to his children's patrimony: 'during the year after the Trust was executed, bills began to arrive: from silversmiths and art dealers, interior decorators and Universal Aunts. Waugh had discovered that he could buy whatever he wanted and charge it to the Trust.... Basil Seal might have been proud of the scheme' (2S 256).

The 'Save the Children Fund' was a main pillar of Waugh's financial structure until January 1965. Cracks started to appear in September 1963, when he was told that sales of his manuscripts to the trust *were* taxable; they stopped. In early 1964, Evill had been replaced as co-trustee and the new trustee seems to have reappraised the trust's legal position. Peters sent Waugh the bad news that 'it now appears that Evill was mistaken in his view that...this revenue...was not subject to tax' (2S 485). Peters did quite well in saving what he could from the wreck of this gravy-train (Waugh was liable for fifteen years' back taxes, but got away with paying only six), but this financial catastrophe contributed its mite to the despondency of Waugh's last months. The buccaneering approach to twentieth-century taxation had met its usual end, though the final accounting of all Waugh's schemes would probably show that he came through, as in this case, with a profit. That it was not the profit he hoped for was the justification for his gloom and lamentation.

One unexpected aspect of Waugh's financial problems after the war was the contribution made to them by his acts of charity. His rebarbative public persona of those years is so well established that Martin Stannard could surprise the readers of his second volume of biography by revealing that privately Waugh performed many acts of kindness for individuals and donated large sums of money for charitable purposes. These gifts were enough to be a considerable factor in Waugh's finances. And in doing good by stealth, he effectively presented a distorted image of himself to the world; he acknowledged that he could not fulfil the obligation of charity of feeling towards mankind in general, yet there were many individuals and groups beyond his many personal friends who, unlike mankind in general, saw Evelyn Waugh as a man of 'great kindness'.

After *Brideshead*, Waugh's next published novel was the nugatory *Scott-King's Modern Europe* (1947), after which came *The Loved One* (1948). Yet this sequence was not what Waugh had expected. On 1 May 1945 he was at Chagford. The war in Europe was about to end, *Brideshead* was to be published on 28 May, and he was at the Easton Court Hotel to begin his next novel, *Helena*, about the finder of the True Cross, the canonized mother of the Emperor Constantine. To write about Helena was a longstanding ambition, and now, confident of his mission as a Catholic apologist in fiction, he began his novel eagerly but very quickly ran into difficulties. After a week he abandoned work on the book for seven months; it would not be published complete until 1950.

He had congratulated himself in 1944 on becoming a stylist rather than a prophet, but in both his pre-war and postwar fiction there is a notable if minor prophetic element. It had appeared in 'Out of Depth' (1933), but after the war, as his alienation from modern Britain increased, it got a more extensive allowance of liberty with increased emphasis on the dystopian element. *Scott-King's Modern Europe* is retrospective in its subject matter but in spirit it is prophetic, since its climax is the schoolmaster's declaration that 'it would be very wicked indeed to do anything to fit a boy for the modern world', a conclusion the narrative is designed to endorse. In the summer of 1946, Waugh had accompanied Douglas Woodruff, then editor of *The Tablet*, to Spain to attend a celebration of the quatercentenary of the Dominican, Francisco de Vittoria, pioneer theorist of international law, a festivity organized by the Franco government for purposes of image-improvement. Waugh and Woodruff treated the occasion as purely a junket, and the difficulties of postwar travel and currency restrictions, combined with inefficiency of organization in Spain, gave Waugh material for a diatribe against the horrors of modernity. To lessen the blow upon Spain, a Catholic country with a hard right-wing government, of which he approved more rather than less, Waugh gave his 'Neutralia' a number of features borrowed from Tito's Yugoslavia. As a vent for his prejudices, *Scott-King* no doubt worked well, but as fiction it is flat. When the book was published in the USA in 1949, it was reviewed by George Orwell, shrewdly and sympathetically, while in no way yielding on his own principles. In April 1946, Waugh published just such a review of Orwell's *Critical Essays* (EAR 304) and so the Yin and Yang of twentieth-century British writing had the meeting of minds that would eventuate in a face-to-face meeting at the Cotswold Sanatorium in January 1949. (And symbolism is all we get, since no record exists of what this pair of carefully self-constructed opposites said to each other.)

Scott-King's Modern Europe is a tepidly comic description of an inoffensive schoolmaster in the toils and trammels of the modern world. The Spanish expedition provided its plot and atmosphere, but the writing was given impetus by the Labour general election victory of 1945, since Waugh saw it, apparently without affectation, as the first stage of the establishment of socialist totalitarianism in Britain. At this time he was thinking seriously of emigrating to Ireland, a resolve that held during his American journey and which he gave up in the summer of 1947.

The expedition to Hollywood, of which the literary result was *The Loved One*, is best appreciated in the context of his career as a pendant to *Brideshead Revisited*. He had transferred to Americans much of the dissatisfaction with himself that the novel had occasioned and he now planned to take all the advantage he could of American wealth while surveying American society for targets of opportunity. On his return, he made in his diary a pair of apparently contradictory remarks. 'America seems very remote and the diary I had meant to keep in detail, to be a store of literary material, is a blank'. This reveals the literary intention of the journey. He planned to write about the United States but he had no idea of where his point of focus would lie. Until he found that focus, he had no principles for the collection of data; hence the blank diary. When he did find his focus, his imagination was so tenacious of it that he needed no notes, being well supplied with documents, including Dr Hubert Eaton's *Embalming Techniques*, which he most carefully read and annotated. Thus, later in the same diary entry he wrote, 'I found a deep mine of literary gold in the cemetery of Forest Lawn and the work of the morticians and intend to get to work immediately on a novelette staged there' (D 674). The use of 'novelette' is a good sign; he had used it first of *Decline and Fall*.

The book would be brief and comic, the product of that need to complain that he knew was requisite for what he now denied was his best work.

When Hollywood had opened discussions about filming *Brideshead*, Waugh had responded with a duplicitous eagerness. He had no intention of letting Americans film the book; they would only distort it, since they were avid for romanticism but blind to eschatology. He, however, wanted a trip to California for himself and his wife. Laura was most unhappy about the prospect of exile in Ireland; the hardships of wartime, postwar austerities, and repeated pregnancies (Septimus, the sixth surviving child of seven – hence his name – was not born until July 1950) had so lowered her morale that even her husband began to feel he should act to help. He therefore let MGM believe that he might agree to sell the rights to *Brideshead* but only if he was transported with his wife to Hollywood and accommodated with every circumstance of luxury. The deal that Peters negotiated involved MGM paying Waugh $2000 a week (these were 1947 dollars!) for approximately four weeks of 'discussion' over the sale and adaptation of the book. The terms for the rights would be $140 000 *if* agreement was reached. Knowing full well that he would never agree, Waugh was careful to have it understood that the payment for the weeks of 'discussion' was not dependent on the sale. Expenses incurred in bringing the Waughs to California would be deducted from the $140 000 but if there was no agreement MGM would still pick up the tab.

The Waughs arrived in New York on 31 January 1947 and after fêting and business went on to Los Angeles via Chicago, arriving in Pasadena on 6 February. There was much that was new for Waugh to be happy complaining about: ice water, air-conditioning, insufficiently servile servants, and smog: 'Since the war they have succeeded in spoiling even the climate by inducing an artificial and noxious fog' (D 675). (There were things he liked, too: Masson's Pinot Noir, some of the restaurants, Charlie Chaplin and Walt Disney – 'the two artists of the place'.) Negotiations with the studio went nowhere fast, much to Waugh's satisfaction. He could not fully enjoy himself while 'the danger of the film' existed, meaning until he had conveyed unmistakably to MGM that he would agree to no proposal. That point came when Waugh explained to Leon Gordon, MGM's negotiator, 'what *Brideshead* was about' (which must mean its eschatological aspect). Gordon, according to Waugh, 'lost heart' after the explanation 'until in the end when the censor made some difficulties he accepted them as an easy excuse for abandoning the whole project' (D 675).

The film industry's own censors must have responded to a 'treatment' since it seems that MGM never got so far as drafting a script of *Brideshead*, and Waugh is probably right that the studio used the Hays office's reaction as its escape clause, since if they had read the book (admittedly, Waugh says they had not) they must have expected trouble from the censors. But the reasons did not matter. Waugh got what he wanted: MGM dropped its option, *Brideshead* was whisked away from the studio's clutches and Waugh was free to explore the necrological subculture of southern California.

He was in California in part to exact revenge for the Americans' ignorant enthusiasm for *Brideshead*. They had barbarously missed the eschatology, in effect death in the book, and Waugh had seen now how to nail the nation that embodied secular humanism to the cross of its brainless, pagan optimism. Forest Lawn, where euphemism and avoidance of reality were elevated into a philosophy, explained both why the Americans had misread *Brideshead* and how they could be punished for it. Waugh's heart must have leaped when he realized that, with complete religious orthodoxy, the misprision of *Brideshead* could be revealed to be a single aspect of the multifaceted religious error of humanism. The Americans had failed the test on death; Waugh would now anatomize and publish their failure before the world – and get them a good laughing-at too.

'Research' for *The Loved One* took the form of Waugh's ingratiating himself with the owner and operators of Forest Lawn; Dr Hubert Eaton and his staff seem to have been delighted by the English author's keen interest in their work. These hapless innocents gave Waugh tours of the place and initiated him into the arcana of their business. They pressed the serpent to their bosom and he voyaged back to the Old World flexing his jaws expectantly for the bite he was about to give them.

Begun in May, *The Loved One* was put through a couple of drafts and was finished in September 1947. Its first publication was a complete issue of *Horizon* (February 1948), a decision that involved Waugh and the editor, Cyril Connolly, in one of the *rapprochements* of their love and hate relationship. There was some fear, particularly on the part of Waugh's agent, A. D. Peters, that American publication would be disastrous, but it went ahead most successfully in terms of sales and without the lawsuits Waugh feared. To protect

himself were he sued, he had dreamed up a nearly incredible stratagem with his friend 'Ed' Stanley.

> Lord Stanley of Alderley, with all the prestige of a peer of the
> realm, agreed to add a codicil to his will stating that he wished to
> be buried at Forest Lawn as he understood it resembled the beau-
> tiful cemetery so movingly described by Evelyn Waugh in *The
> Loved One*. (The clause was revoked after ten years as the danger
> was past and Lord Stanley was afraid it would involve his heirs in
> great expense.) (H 520)

It was surely just as well that Waugh never had to rely on this
defence in a lawsuit. Plaintiff's counsel would have enjoyed themselves immeasurably.

Many people at the time of publication were so happy to believe
that Waugh had returned to his old ways with *The Loved One* that
they over-valued the book. It is a fine comic novel with a truly Wavian subject, but no masterpiece. Its plot is the ancient 'choice' topos,
as in the Choice of Hercules between virtue and pleasure, or as here
in parody, Tannhäuser's choice between sacred and profane love.
Aimée cannot choose between Dennis and Mr Joyboy, the chief
mortician of Whispering Glades, and so, on the 'advice' of the Guru
Brahmin – 'I told her to go take a high jump' – chooses instead her
ancestral lover, Death. The nomenclature is another reliable indic-
ator. Given the amazing variety of American names, Waugh could
have done so much better than 'Joyboy' and 'Slump'; he could have
had names both meaningful *and* realistic. As a name, Aimée (Loved
One) Thantagenos (Born of Death) is perhaps a tad programmatic.[3]

The facts about the mortician's trade that went into the book make
the most impact, especially upon British readers, Waugh's principal
audience, and that they were facts, true history, was emphasized by
Waugh's publication of an essay on Californian burial customs just
before publication of *The Loved One* (EAR 331). Although some of his
agents, such as Cyril Connolly in his introduction in *Horizon*, tried to
argue that Waugh was not being anti-American, Stannard is quite
right to emphasize that that was exactly his object (2S 205), and if
one asks oneself what the 'lessons' or 'moral' of the novel are, one
has to say that a prominent one is that Americans are infantile idiots
and that the term 'American civilization' is an oxymoron. In the eyes
of British readers, therefore, Waugh certainly attained part of his
objective in writing the book. Americans' ideas about death are shown

to be euphemistic and self-deluding; no wonder they got *Brideshead* wrong.

With regard to Americans themselves, however, Waugh's book failed to have the punitive effect he hoped for and against which he protected himself by such devices as the absurd arrangement with Lord Stanley. He claimed that the American morticians had agreed that, should he die in the United States – as they devoutly hoped – they would refuse to touch him, and serve him right. But Waugh failed to understand a lot about America, including the fact that Americans are self-critical people. *The Loved One* got generally excellent reviews in the USA and sold well, and although *The New Yorker* had refused to publish it, they did not do so because the book was anti-American or shocking or because they had never much liked his books, but because they saw it as old hat:

> far from being shocked by his sending up of Hollywood and of Californian burial customs, they felt this was stale stuff, had already been done before, by Nathanael West, Sinclair Lewis, Aldous Huxley, S. J. Perelman among others. 'The freshest part of Mr Waugh's story is that part which refers to the English in Hollywood, and we wish, wistfully, that he had concerned himself more exclusively with that theme' (H 520).

The reader who comes to *The Loved One* from a reading of Waugh's most recent fiction, *Work Suspended*, *Put Out More Flags* and *Brideshead*, will note another imperfection. Dennis Barlow clearly issued from the mould that had produced Atwater and Hooper (and would later produce Trimmer). The marks of the beast are upon him. He has been a non-combattant officer in the RAF, for example. ('I never count the R.A.F. as English' [L 263].) Yet Waugh compromises on Dennis to the extent of blending the narrator's viewpoint with his, and of permitting a degree of identity to exist between Dennis and himself. The narrator of *The Loved One* is a close relation of the narrator of *Put Out More Flags*, elegantly witty and withering in judgement: 'Liturgy in Hollywood is the concern of the Stage rather than of the Clergy' (LO 62). But Dennis speaks in this voice too. When Mr Joyboy laments the death of his 'honey-baby', Dennis says, 'I must beg you not to intrude these private and rather peculiar terms of endearment into what should be a serious discussion' (LO 153). Most striking of all, and in anticipation of the ending of *The Ordeal of Gilbert Pinfold*, where there is no uncertainty about the identification of author with character, Waugh in *The Loved One* seems finally to confer the status of artist on Dennis. As he plans to return to England, he knows he will be 'carrying back a great, shapeless chunk of experience, the artist's load; bearing it home ... to work on it hard and long, for God knew how long – it was the moment of vision for which a lifetime is often too short' (LO 163–4). Irony here is hard to assess; one possibility is that there is hardly any. Could *The Loved One* be the work of Dennis Barlow? 'I have been planning an opus on the subject [of Whispering Glades]' (LO 142).

What seems to have happened is that Waugh began with the concept of a protagonist *à la* Atwater or Hooper, a character clearly separate from the narrator, whose voice would be essentially that of Waugh himself. As the book progressed, with Dennis working at the pet cemetery, the Happier Hunting Ground, and coming under pressure from the various twits of the English 'exile' community in Hollywood, Waugh moved close in sympathy to his protagonist. The narrator's voice and Dennis's grow to resemble each other. The reader is allowed hardly any freedom to reprobate Dennis's conduct and sentiments; the critical distance between novelist and protagonist has disappeared. In fact Dennis Barlow, carefully made unprepossessing in the 'factual' details of his 'life', becomes Waugh's prophet in the denunciation of American ways, especially the American way of death. When the character of Basil Seal 'took off' for Waugh in *Black Mischief*, he forgot that part of the original conception (based on the character of Peter Rodd) was that Basil was a terrible bore. Waugh came to like Basil Seal a lot (in his last work of fiction, as we shall see, he adopted the persona of Basil for himself, with no visible reservations) and the same thing happens with Dennis Barlow in *The Loved One*. Unlikely as it would have seemed at the conception of the character, Dennis ends up as a version of Basil Seal rather than as a better-educated Hooper. His final act before leaving Hollywood is to arrange for Mr Joyboy to get a postcard from the Happier Hunting Ground each year on the anniversary of Aimée's cremation; 'Your little Aimée is wagging her tail in heaven tonight, thinking of you'. Pure Basil Seal.

The anti-American objectives of *The Loved One* are perhaps too well served by the recruitment of Dennis to the narrator's point of view. Waugh's other great objective for his book, what he called 'memento mori old style, not specifically Californian' (L 266), is hardly communicated at all to a reader not alertly Christian. The conclusion that a 'secular' reader draws is that the Californian/

American euphemistic attitude towards death is silly and that properly one should acknowledge that 'human' means 'mortal'. But Waugh's Catholic fundamentalism required more than such proper reasonableness. For him, we should not only remember that we will die, we should remember it every day, if not every hour: 'a complete life can only be lived when the fact of death is kept steadily in mind...In the greatest & smallest human affairs remember that Death is at the elbow' (2S 182). Our death will involve the rotting of our bodies in the ground, which is a reality that emphasizes the greater reality that 'our ultimate destiny is elsewhere'. This point was no doubt taken by devout Catholic readers such as Katherine Asquith, who surprised Waugh by approving of the book (L 275) but it is a postulate of Waugh's conception of himself as a Catholic novelist that he was *not* writing for mostly Catholic readers. His *memento mori* purpose allowed him to justify the book as a Catholic novel, but he surely persuaded few readers not already persuaded to adopt his view of the place of death in life.

The Loved One had been conceived as a scourge for the criminally tender backs of Americans, who were guilty of bad taste and secular humanism. As with *Brideshead*, though in this case the critics were unable to sniff out the failure, Waugh had achieved only half his purpose. The public misconceived *The Loved One* as the resurrection of the former areligious or crypto-religious novelist of the comic novels, whereas Waugh in no way wanted to conceal his religious attitude towards death. The book, however, succeeded with the public on the same terms that *A Handful of Dust* had done. *The Loved One*, too, permits itself to be read without specific religious judgement, and that was not a situation that Waugh would let continue. He wrote to Nancy Mitford: '*Loved One* is being well received in intellectual circles. They think my heart is in the right place after all. I'll show them' (L 273). His next novel was to be *Helena*.

Helena was hard to get written. Like *Scoop*, its writing was interrupted and its completion in March 1950 came five years after he had started on it. Unlike *Scoop*, the delay in getting it finished did not lead to a dislike of the book; to what is surely widespread astonishment among those who read his work closely, Waugh insisted, later as well as at the time of publication, that *Helena* was his best novel, by which he must have meant that it applied his strongest talents to the most important subject he had undertaken. There is a great deal of respectful commentary on the novel that travels a fair way along the road towards Waugh's estimation of his book but not much of it arrives there. Very few critics have declared that the parts add up to much of a whole. Yet critics are very interested in *Helena*. Martin Stannard, for instance, devotes ten ingenious pages of his critical biography to the novel (2S 272–82), which emerges as a post-modernist subversion of literary realism and 'a technical experiment towards creating a new kind of theological realism'.

So from a critic's point of view, *Helena*'s great attraction is that it offers much to say. Such as this. *Helena* is Waugh's anti-Gibbon. On the last page he mentions that St Helena's remains now lie in the church of Ara Coeli in Rome. 'Within a few yards of her, on the steps of that church, Edward Gibbon later sat and premeditated his history' (HL 158). The remark is simultaneously a stab at Gibbon and a tribute to him. 'Premeditated' suggests crime, here the intellectual crime of foreordained conclusions; Gibbon set out to write a history that would sneer at Christianity, the Church of Rome. But the pun in *premeditated* is a Gibbonian deftness, literal versus metaphorical. What Waugh has learned from reading Gibbon is to be used against him, and when Gibbon has been employed in defence of Christianity, the old pagan Gibbon can be dismissed.

Waugh's choice of genre is highly anti-Gibbonian. *Helena* is a saint's life, a work of hagiology, a form of writing without importance as history in Gibbon's view. Waugh adopts it defiantly, and then writes the saint's life according to the conventions of the not-quite-realistic novel as he had adopted them. He even followed his customary procedure in using one of his friends as the model, in some aspects at least, for his protagonist. Penelope Betjeman, wife of the poet (both were longstanding friends of Waugh's) was becoming a Catholic convert at the time he was writing the book. She was an enthusiastic horsewoman and the systematic 'horsey' traits of Helena's character were derived from her. Similarly, he said that he had based Constantius Chlorus, Helena's husband, on Fitzroy Maclean (LWC 83).

In general, however, *Helena* is the least autobiographical of Waugh's novels. Its intellectual concerns are his own, but to dramatize ideas without the embodiment of personal experience cut his fiction off from its greatest source of vitality. Martin Stannard argues that 'In many respects it is Waugh's (displaced) spiritual autobiography, a dry-run for the *Sword of Honour* trilogy'. But the actors seem very uninvolved with the events. In one notable place where he should have been able to bring autobiographical experience to bear, he is silent; he gives no account of what led Helena to become a Christian (HL 89).

Waugh's triumphant feelings about his book seem to be owed chiefly to the belief that he had found out how to write the Catholic novel that was his religious *raison d'être*, his vocation. To comprehend this, one must grasp the meaning of sainthood in the novel. Waugh's ideas about this were evidently quite orthodox – none of his Catholic correspondents ever hinted otherwise – but they do seem highly individual. Helena becomes a saint because

> She had done what only the saints succeed in doing; what indeed constitutes their patent of sanctity. She had completely conformed to the will of God. Others a few years back had done their duty gloriously in the arena. Hers was a gentler task, merely to gather wood. That was the particular humble purpose for which she had been created. (HL 156)

He explains further in a letter to John Betjeman.

> Saints are simply souls in heaven. Some few people have been so sensationally holy in life that we know they went straight to heaven and so put them in the calendar. We all have to become saints before we get to heaven. That is what purgatory is for. And each individual has his own peculiar form of sanctity which he must achieve or perish. It is no good my saying: 'I wish I were like Joan of Arc or St John of the Cross'. I can only be St Evelyn Waugh – after God knows what experiences in purgatory. (L 339)

Achieving sainthood, therefore, is the task and hope of every Christian. Waugh remained devoted to this definition; it is a fundamental theme of *Sword of Honour*. And his high opinion of *Helena* is owed in the main to his conviction that his humble purpose was to write the novels that only he could write and that would propagate the Faith. *Helena* for him was a major step along his road to becoming Saint Evelyn Waugh.

The Catholic novelist that only he could be had to do even more than propagate the Faith; he should see if he could not defeat the Faith's English literary enemy. As part of his preparation for writing *Helena*, Waugh had bought the early (perhaps second) edition of the

Decline and Fall of the Roman Empire that is now among his books at
the University of Texas. Gibbon, however, mentions Helena so briefly
that she is evidently beneath his serious notice and so little was possible by way of argument against his treatment of the Inventor of the
True Cross. Since Gibbon was a historian and an empiricist, Waugh
made history and empirical fact into his own postulates. His own
basic reason for believing Christianity to be true had always been
that its foundation events, the Incarnation, the Crucifixion and the
Resurrection, were *historically* true. They really happened. Helena
says to Lactantius,

> 'If I asked you when and where [this god of yours] could be
> seen, what would you say'?
> 'I should say that as a man he died two hundred and seventy-
> eight years ago in the town now called Aelia Capitolina in Pales-
> tine'.
> 'Well, that's a straight answer anyway. How do you know'?
> 'We have the accounts written by witnesses. Besides that, there
> is the living memory of the Church' (HL 85).

(One advantage of being a novelist was that Waugh did not have to
say whether *he* believed the evangelists to have been 'witnesses' or
what that weasel word might mean.) Waugh accepts the truths of
Christianity on faith but he puts public emphasis on the supporting
facts of history. He goes on to imply that for those, like Gibbon,
without faith, there is still enough historical evidence for conviction.
Gibbon in being unconvinced is untrue to his profession of faith as a
historian.

His power over the public mind, moreover, is owed to his style.
The paragraph in which Waugh sees Gibbon off is spoken by Lactantius, early historian of the Church, himself 'the greatest living
prose stylist'. ('Form' here again seems to mean 'form of words',
style.)

> 'One might combine two proverbs and say: "Art is long and will
> prevail". You see it is equally possible to give the right form to the
> wrong thing, and the wrong form to the right thing. Suppose that
> in years to come, when the Church's troubles seem to be over,
> there should come an apostate of my own trade, a false historian,
> with the mind of a Cicero or Tacitus and the soul of an animal',
> and he nodded towards the gibbon who fretted his golden chain

and chattered for fruit. 'A man like that might make it his business
to write down the martyrs and excuse the persecutors. He might
be refuted again and again but what he wrote would remain in
people's minds when the refutations were quite forgotten. That is
what style does – it has the Egyptian secret of the embalmers. It is
not to be despised' (HL 80).

Waugh's over-estimation of the importance of style thus continued
at least into *Helena*. But in reality it is not Gibbon's style that makes
him an effective enemy, unless the term means mainly scepticism
and irony. Yet to counteract Gibbon's style, Waugh seems in *Helena*
to crank up his own.

> But, out of sight on the shores of Propontis, where the vested
> chamberlains stood like dummies, motionless as the stuffed thing
> [the corpse of the emperor Valerian] that had hung in the Persian
> court, and the eunuchs scuttled like pismires when a soldier passed
> them; in the inmost cell of the foetid termitary of power, Diocle-
> tian was consumed by huge boredom and sickly turned towards
> his childhood's home. (HL 70)

The aim seems to be to out-Gibbon Gibbon. And for scepticism and
irony there is the personality of Helena; Waugh conceives her as a
near-caricature of the British empiricist. She is utterly impatient
of all mystery and obfuscation; her Church, when it comes, will
obviously be that which was revealed to Waugh at Debra Lebanos,
'a triumph of light over darkness consciously accomplished', whose
theology will be 'the science of simplification'. Helena's great word
is 'Bosh'! She dismisses mystification and subtlety as obscurantism
and hair-splitting. If it were not for the fact that she is seeking to
establish her version of religious truth, she could be mistaken for an
utter sceptic. Waugh has given her the intellectual features he saw in
Gibbon, and makes the discovery of the cross, and the foundation of
truth he claims it supplies, result from an investigation that could be
one of scientific archaeology. To distinguish the cross-beam of the
True Cross from those of the crucified 'thieves', 'The beams were
carried up to the room of a dying woman and laid one at a time
beside her on the bed. Two made no difference. The third effected a
complete recovery.' "So now we know", said Helena' (155). Miracles
occur scientifically. The pleasures a reader gets, according to Waugh,
from Gibbon are here sanctified and serve religion.

Waugh worked hard on *Helena*, and it shows. Every rift is laden with what he took to be ore. His purpose in this studious application was to draw all the attention he could to his art as a novelist. By stressing in the style the extent to which this book was *written*, he could conquer by embracing it the always anticipated response that the story of Helena and the Cross was, as he laconically and defiantly proclaims it at the end of his Preface, 'just something to be read; in fact a legend'.

How this works in practice can be seen in an episode Waugh was clearly proud of, Helena's encounter with the Wandering Jew.

> The Wandering Jew has no previous connexion with Helena. I have brought them together as a device for reconciling two discrepant stories of the invention: one, that Helena was led to the spot in a dream; the second and less creditable version, that she extorted the information from an elderly rabbi by putting him down a well and leaving him there for a week. (HL [11])

On the night of Good Friday, 'the most desolate night of the year', Helena has 'a dream that she knew was of God'. She dreams that she meets the Wandering Jew and that he tells her where to dig for the crosses. Having told 'the Galilean' to 'move on' when he stumbled on the doorstep of the shop, the Jew has been quietly cursed by Jesus to live on unaging until the *parousia*: 'Tarry till I come'. He is presented as the epitome of 'rootless cosmopolitanism', earning his living as a seller of incense and relics, totally indifferent to every form of religion, including Judaism, except for its commercial possibilities. 'I always respect religion. It's my bread and butter' (149). He is happy to show Helena where the crosses are buried because he foresees a huge increase in business. 'One wants a few genuine relics in thoroughly respectable hands. Then everything else will follow. There won't be enough genuine stuff to meet the demand. That will be my turn'. Helena contemplates the pollution of fake relics that her 'invention' will cause. 'She saw all this, considered it and said: "Show me the cross"'. In her dream, the Wandering Jew leads her to the spot. Next day, she goes to the place 'where she had stood with the business man. Where she had seen him set his heel there was a print in the dust that looked as if it had been left by a goat's hoof. Helena gently rubbed it out and set in its place her own mark, a little cross of pebbles' (152).

Most of all one wants to know why Waugh congratulated himself upon this restrained viciousness. His Wandering Jew is a stereotype caricature. His statement in the Preface (quoted above) indicates that he thought it desirable to reconcile two stories of the invention, the dream and the tortured rabbi. But why did he think so? Why did he not ignore one of the legends? Is he stating that these tales have some kind of authority that he ought to respect? Perhaps his persona as author of *Helena* takes a collegial interest in stories, tales, legends. He certainly has a lot invested in the blurring of the categories of fiction and history throughout the book. By combining the two stories into one and co-opting the Wandering Jew to boot, he was putting on a display of professional deftness and thickening the layer of literariness that lies heavy all over *Helena*. He was not here especially – and rarely ever – in the mood to worry about the sensibilities of heretics, schismatics, pagans, historians or literary critics. Publish and be saved. What he thought of as his best book is the best for only a tiny part of his customary audience. By sticking rigidly to his self-defined criteria for a Catholic historical novel, he had shrunk both himself and his book into conformity.

5

Small Acts to Redeem the Times: 1951–66

I have two shots in my locker left. My war novel and my autobiography. I suppose they will see me out.

(24 October 1946, L 238)

When Waugh wrote this letter to Nancy Mitford, he had begun his extended work on *Helena*, so presumably he was thinking of projects as yet unbegun. He sees his future as a writer solely in terms of his personal experience and retrospectively. Since he was in his early fifties, his survey of future production seems thin, even when one factors in that both war novel and autobiography were to be multi-volume works. In the event, though the war novel did appear in three volumes, only one volume of the autobiography was written, yet compensation came in the form of a second 'gift' to go with *The Loved One*: *The Ordeal of Gilbert Pinfold*. The list of postwar publications is filled out by some short(ish) fictions: *Scott-King's Modern Europe* (1947), *Love Among the Ruins* (1953), and *Basil Seal Rides Again* (1963); a biography, *The Life of the Right Reverend Ronald Knox* (1959); and a feeble travel book, *A Tourist in Africa* (1960). (There are also some items of interest to collectors: *Wine in War and Peace* [1947] and *The Holy Places* [1952].)

Helena was published in 1950, both in Britain and the USA, and in the late summer of that year Waugh and his wife were in New York for what amounted to a holiday. For more than a fortnight they enjoyed being admired and fêted. Before leaving for New York, he had written, 'It is the most wonderful health resort in the world. I look to it to revivify me' (L 336). Since in these pages Waugh's opinions of the USA have hitherto been those derived from his *Loved One* journey of 1947, where the keynote was clearly not revivification, we should go back to discover what had occurred to change his mind.

165

Stannard calls it 'Waugh's American Dream', and it has to be deduced from his actions rather than from his statements. On the trip to Hollywood, Waugh had received some surprises that worked on him in a delayed-action manner. He was astonished to discover that the position of the Roman Catholic Church and of Catholics in the USA was very different from what prevailed in Britain. American Catholics, both in absolute numbers and as a percentage of the population, were far more numerous. Catholics, identified and acknowledged as such, played prominent parts in public life, and their politics were very much to Waugh's taste, particularly in the anti-Communist 1950s. (He was, however, very suspicious of Joe McCarthy and kept McCarthy's defender, William F. Buckley, at a long arm's length. 'Has he been supernaturally "guided" to bore me? It would explain him' [L 542].) Most of all, American Catholicism had given rise to an extensive and vigorous literary culture, supported by and supporting a system of Catholic higher education that impressed Waugh no end. He never lost his love for Oxford but he could not help wondering if the United States, with its prominent Catholic universities and colleges, was not the way of the Catholic future.

That, in fact, was his conclusion. Even while he was giving the United States as a whole a pen-lashing by means of *The Loved One*, he was deciding that he had blundered massively by slighting American Catholicism and this was an injustice, born of imperceptiveness, that he could not shrug off; an *amende honorable* was necessary. He got in touch with Clare Boothe Luce, prominent Catholic convert, wife of the proprietor of *Life* magazine, and was soon explaining to the staff of *Life* that he wanted to make a study of American Catholicism because 'the history of the Church for the next four centuries will be determined in America'. He would inform European Catholics 'about their future leaders . . .' (L 282).

Life agreed to commission a long article from him and to pay the expenses of a research trip to the United States. He sailed alone to New York at the end of October 1948 and travelled widely in the eastern states, visiting Catholic establishments from Boston to Baltimore, where Loyola University awarded him his only honorary degree, to New Orleans. He was back in England in January 1949; later that month he left for New York again, this time with Laura, for a lecture tour (he lectured on Chesterton, Ronald Knox, and Graham Greene) arranged before his *Life* tour, that took him again to Baltimore and New Orleans, and also to Ontario, Chicago and

Milwaukee. The Waughs arrived back in England at the end of March 1949.

It is not too fanciful to see these journeys as a penitential pilgrimage – by Pullman, with champagne and cigars – undertaken to compensate for his ignorance of the world of American Catholicism. The article for *Life* (September 1949), 'The American Epoch in the Catholic Church', was perhaps a 6000-word over-compensation. Stannard makes clear Waugh's genuine struggle at this time – it is visible in the essay – to confront his deeply rooted and maybe hitherto cherished prejudice against the Common Man. The hierarchic principle of the link between Catholicism and European high culture was given a damaging blow by the vitality of American Catholicism and Waugh struggled to make prejudice conform to reason.

> No humanist argument could ever convince him of the merits of egalitarianism, but he had to accept that all men were equal in the eyes of God. 'A youth who is inarticulate in conversation may well be eloquent in prayer. It would be an intolerable impertinence to attempt to judge.... The Church and the world need monks and nuns more than they need writers'. Nothing could be further from the implicit connection between high culture and Faith which permeates *Brideshead*.... (2S 249)

This was not a firm determination that Waugh attained and thereafter held unwaveringly. It was the attitude that a large part of him *wanted* to attain and hold unwaveringly; he never succeeded, but it is impressive and moving to contemplate his efforts.

It is hard to put a name to this impulse of Waugh's towards kinder and gentler attitudes. It cannot be described as a remorseful impulse and he was rarely able to apologise. And a literary critic becomes entangled in problems of aesthetic versus moral judgement. One should unreservedly applaud Waugh's efforts to be a less intolerant person, one who could feel more charity towards humankind in general, but a reservation does nag: the suspicion that the best novels did not come from the best person that Waugh could have been. Humour cannot escape cruelty, and to set a high value on humour implicates one in ways that – for a moment or two – give pause.

This is perhaps the time to attempt a summary of the imperatives and the blocked routes that Waugh faced when he came to write his later fiction. After *The Loved One*, the fiction confirms what he seems to have known but could never quite accept: his comic talent was worked out. *Brideshead* represents his first major effort not to be funny, to be other than a comic novelist. In his career after *The Loved One* he did find occasional nuggets of Wavian comedy but he also – to change the metaphor – sank some very dry holes. It was imperative that he be a Catholic novelist, openly, not clandestinely or cryptically. The approach, and particularly the style, of *Brideshead* could not be repeated. *Helena*, like *Brideshead*, was a singular experiment, though received very differently by the public. Each of these paths was barred. The future fiction must be based on Waugh's life history and since he had arranged, as he thought, that nothing novel was to happen to him for the rest of his life, it would have to deal with his past, and the only stretch of that past not yet fully treated in fiction was the war. The changes thus forced on him for his war books would be in style – not that of the comic fiction nor that of *Brideshead* – and in the character of the protagonist. Guy Crouchback was to be a new and quite unexpected version of Evelyn Waugh.

The 'war novel' has a complicated and confusing textual history. Three volumes were separately published dealing with the wartime experiences of Guy Crouchback. Waugh began writing the first, *Men at Arms*, in June 1951 and had it finished in December of that year. It was published in Britain and the USA in 1952. The second volume, *Officers and Gentlemen*, was begun in March 1953 and finished in November 1954. It was published in June 1955 in Britain and in the same year in the USA. He began the third volume, *Unconditional Surrender*, in May 1960 and finished it in February 1961. It was published in Britain in October 1961 and in the USA in the same year but under the title of *The End of the Battle*. In the summer of 1965, Waugh edited the three novels into a single volume, making cuts and some changes. This reshaping of the three into one was published in Britain as *Sword of Honour* in September 1965 and in the next year and under the same title in the USA.

With consideration of the 'recension', *Sword of Honour*, principles of textual criticism come into collision with judgements of literary value. Generally speaking, the last edition of a work that was supervised by the author is assumed to represent his final intentions and should become the base text for future editions. When an author rewrites and makes excisions, his involvement is undoubtable and the implicit claim of that text to be the authoritative one is strongly reinforced. Textual principles support Waugh's intention that the text of the recension should be the future text of his war novel, and that it should be a single volume called *Sword of Honour*. Yet there is widespread agreement that, with some exceptions, the changes that he made in fashioning the three into one were unfortunate, that most of what he cut was worthwhile stuff, and that the unrecensed three volumes are better as a work of art. His literary executors seem to share this opinion. The re-formed Everyman's Library, publishing in both Britain and the USA, in 1994 incorporated (as its 173rd title) Evelyn Waugh's *The Sword of Honour Trilogy*, which gives, in a single volume, the texts of the three separately published novels without most of the cuts and changes made for the 1965 recension, although the title of that version is now the title of the whole, with 'Trilogy' tagged on. (The Everyman edition includes a detailed chronology of Waugh's career, making no mention of the 1965 *Sword of Honour* recension [p.xliv].) Both Waugh and textual principle have therefore been overruled, and by and large that seems a sensibly pragmatic outcome. One major exception to the general condemnation of Waugh's cuts and changes comes on almost the last page of the trilogy. Guy Crouchback is married for the second time and is bringing up as his own child the boy that he knows was fathered on Virginia, his first and deceased wife, by Trimmer. In the *Unconditional Surrender/End of the Battle* (1961) version of the text, Guy and his second wife also have 'two boys of their own'. It is in every way an improvement that, in the 1965 recension, this is changed to read 'they haven't any children of their own'. But the recent Everyman edition, sticking with the 1961 text, has restored the two boys to the Crouchbacks. (Discussion of this change by Waugh will be found in the consideration of *Unconditional Surrender*, for the procedure here will be to examine the volumes as they appeared in the context of Waugh's life.)

On publication of *Officers and Gentlemen* in 1955, Waugh made the claim on the dust-jacket that he was finished with his Crouchback novels: 'I thought that the story would run into three volumes. I find that two will do the trick'. This, like his claim that 'each was to be regarded as a separate, independent work' was a 'less than candid assurance (dictated by commercial interest)'. In itself this petty – and naïve – deception deserves little consideration but it does offer an opportunity to examine Waugh's concept of the whole of his last ambitious fictional enterprise. When he began writing *Men at Arms* in 1951, the overarching structure of the three volumes was in place in his mind, and, as things worked out, architectonic power – of structure beautifully carried through to completion – was to be the principal aesthetic triumph of the book.

When he started, much of the ending, or what was to be almost the last word, was already written. 'Compassion' ('its title...suggesting both a major theme of *Sword of Honour* and the object of its author's spiritual struggle' [2S 235]) had been published in 1949 and was to be tailored and fitted into place as Guy Crouchback's final experience of the Second World War. As with 'The Man Who Liked Dickens' and *A Handful of Dust*, Waugh knew his protagonist's destination and was now about to begin his account of how and why he got there. The procedure had been used before, but the hero's 'journey' would follow a very different path.

When about to leave New York in 1949, Waugh had given an interview to the *New York Times*. Attempting to be both accomodating and sphinx-like, he gave the interviewer a mercilessly accurate, pseudo-ironical account of his life ('a vacation, occasionally interrupted by work'), and casually revealed what became one major theme of *Sword of Honour*: 'I suppose I do want to write a novel about the war. It would be a study of the idea of chivalry' (2S 240). His definition of this term, as it can be deduced from the novel, has little to do with secular romance. The knightly ideal, encompassing courage, honesty, courtesy, the protection of the weak and respectful gallantry towards women, is both used as a criterion and is itself critically examined in the novel. The wartime setting allows the examination to take place in a specifically military context, particularly in the second book, where chivalry appears as the code that should govern the conduct of officers and gentlemen. But Waugh never lets the reader forget that chivalry for him is foremost a code of religious conduct and that the crusader, ideally conceived, is its noblest type. As his novel moves towards its close, the code that should lead the individual to sainthood, as he had already embodied it in *Helena*, brings chivalry to its most searching test. All of this is brilliantly prepared for in the Prologue to *Men at Arms*, which from the first was titled 'Sword of Honour', when Guy Crouchback stops at the tomb of Roger of Waybroke, Knight, an Englishman, in the parish church of Santa Dulcina delle Rocce, before returning to England to serve in the war.

Guy has lived for years in exile. He is of an old Catholic family and is divorced. His wife's infidelity has brought about a change in him. The 'wasteland where his soul languished' is indescribable.

There were no words in any language. There was nothing to describe, merely a void. His was not an 'interesting case', he thought. No cosmic struggle raged in his sad soul. It was as though eight years back he had suffered a tiny stroke of paralysis; all his spiritual faculties were just perceptibly impaired. (SH 12)

This is a new representation of the cuckolded husband in Waugh's writing, and a new kind of protagonist, with religion as an essential element, though it is dominated by an alienation from humankind, not a vigorous misanthropy but a settled and wearing lack of communal feeling, absence of charity towards humankind in general, that puzzles and saddens him. This is well captured in Guy's understanding of himself in the Italian village as 'not *simpatico*'. Every other foreign resident and regular visitor – some of them rather revolting characters – is *simpatico* to the Santa-Dulcinesi. 'Guy alone, whom they had known from infancy, who spoke their language and conformed to their religion, who was open-handed in all his dealings and scrupulously respectful of all their ways... Guy alone was a stranger among them' (SH 13). The probing of Guy's various spiritual and emotional conditions that Waugh prepares us for here will extend his scope as a novelist and offer proof, obtainable from no other source, of astonishing spiritual growth. His greatest autobiography was always his fiction.

The coming of war in 1939, or rather the announcement of the Russian–German alliance, has brought Guy a spiritual revitalization and the power to act.

He expected his country to go to war in a panic, for the wrong reason or no reason at all, with the wrong allies, in pitiful weakness. But now, splendidly, everything had become clear. The enemy at last was plain in view, huge and hateful, all disguise cast off. It was the Modern Age in arms. Whatever the outcome there was a place for him in that battle. (SH 10)

Guy can see the war as a crusade, and so his visit to the tomb of Sir Roger of Waybroke is apt. But the ironies of Sir Roger's tomb will prove even more apt as the novel unfolds. Sir Roger set out for the Second Crusade (1147–9 AD), which was a disastrous failure. (St Bernard of Clairvaux, who had preached it in 1145, attributed the failure to the lack of purity and commitment of the crusaders.) Sir Roger was shipwrecked on the coast near Santa Dulcina. 'There he enlisted under the local Count, who promised to take him to the Holy Land but led him first against a neighbour, on the walls of whose castle he fell at the moment of victory' (SH 11). This failed crusader has, however, received unexpected canonization, 'despite all clerical remonstrance', from the local people, 'who brought him their troubles and touched his sword for luck'.

> All his life, but especially in recent years, Guy had felt an especial kinship with 'il Santo Inglese'. Now, on his last day, he made straight for the tomb and ran his finger, as the fishermen did, along the knight's sword. 'Sir Roger, pray for me', he said, 'and for our endangered kingdom' (SH 11).

The biggest twist of irony is that Guy's prayer to a thwarted crusader, killed by fellow Christians, and a 'saint' of unorthodox sanctity, is going to be overfulfilled, since the path that Guy is forced along, with frustrations and thwartings quite equal to Sir Roger's, will bring him, too, to an unlikely sanctity.

The main lesson of Guy Crouchback's experience of war is that his view of the meaning of the struggle is distorted and that in any case almost no one else in Britain or in Britain's army shares it. This lesson is conveyed definitively only in the third volume; he called *Men at Arms* 'the first volume of four or five, which won't show any shape until the end' (L 363). After the Prologue, where Sir Roger's sword of honour is set up to wait for its dishonourable twin, the 'State Sword' of Stalingrad in *Unconditional Surrender*, 400 pages later, there comes the greater part of two volumes where Guy's experience of the army and the war signally fails to approximate to the ideals that motivated him to leave Santa Dulcina. The Modern Age is in arms, all right, but it is in arms on both sides of the battlefield.

Men at Arms deals with the Phoney War from a military point of view, that of bored and frustrated soldiers. In a letter to his wife from Yugoslavia in 1944, Waugh developed the metaphor that would govern the narrative of *Men at Arms*. 'We grow backwards in war time. First it was public school life in the Marines, then prep school at COHQ, now [on the mission to Tito] nursery...' (L 192). When he came to write *Men at Arms*, he cast his experience of service with the Marines, from the delights of Chatham to the debacle of Dakar, in the mould of a school story, a genre that seems to have had a strong grip upon him. He had suggested that the book's jacket be designed to look like 'a school story or P. G. Wodehouse wrapper', but Chapman & Hall rejected the idea (2S 306). Waugh's time in the Marines reminded him of being at school, particularly because he himself had been so much older than his fellow entrants and so more sensitive to the feeling of being taken back, of having everything prescribed, as if returned to adolescence. Then there was the intense competition, to become a captain and a company commander, so similar to being a house captain and a school prefect. In the early days there had been the ceremony and tradition that for a while had prevailed at Chatham and gave him one of his best experiences of belonging, as one belongs to a house or a club or a team. This too could be approximated to the school metaphor. He combined the eccentric character of his Brigadier, St Clair Morford, with the appearance and style of a famous and revered fellow-member of White's, Lt-General Sir Adrian Carton de Wiart V. C., a one-eyed, one-handed, fire-eater, threw in a reminiscence or two of Captain Hook from *Peter Pan*, and had his Brigadier Ben Ritchie-Hook, who could take simultaneously the roles of gung-ho headmaster and over-achieving head boy. The school story metaphor, in other words, provided a vehicle to get the story told, keep it true to Waugh's own early feelings about the Marines, and present Guy's developing but largely mute disaffection with this schoolboy world – it cannot be called alienation – as a note of criticism that avoids heavy reliance on his own profounder alienation from the military life.

This much was well judged and effective, but Waugh then made a big mistake. He himself had been a very poor soldier, and what eventually became his disgust with the army was to a large extent his reaction to the army's disgust with him. Guy Crouchback quite understandably is not the misfit that Waugh had been. Waugh commiserates with himself strikingly in that Guy became a perfectly sound and efficient officer who is the victim of circumstance, malevolence, and conspiracy. The blighting of his military career was not to be his own fault and Waugh put his inventive powers to work to provide mechanisms to present Guy as the victim of anything but his own personality and conduct. In *Men at Arms* that mechanism is Apthorpe. Like Guy, Apthorpe is older than the other entrants into the Halberdiers (the fictional equivalent of the Royal Marines), so the pair become known as 'the uncles', and from this beginning their fates are intertwined. The event that causes Guy to be ejected from what he had originally thought to be the Eden of Halberdier soldiering is Apthorpe's death. After the Dakar fiasco, the Halberdiers are stationed in what is clearly Sierra Leone in West Africa (Waugh borrowed the locale, as he obliquely indicates in the novel,

from *The Heart of the Matter* [1948] by Graham Greene, who had
become a friend after the war [SH 218].) Apthorpe becomes ill after
going on leave upcountry 'for sporting purposes'.

> This talk of Apthorpe brought back tender memories of Guy's
> early days in barracks. He asked permission of the brigade major
> to visit him.
> 'Take a car, Uncle'. Everyone was anxious to be agreeable. 'Take
> a bottle of whiskey' ...
> 'Will that be all right with the hospital'?
> 'Very much all wrong, Uncle. That's your risk. But it's always
> done. Not worth calling on a chap in hospital unless you bring a
> bottle. But don't say I told you. It's your risk if you're caught'. (SH
> 221)

And so it proves. The whiskey kills Apthorpe and Guy is thrown out
of the Halberdiers 'under a cloud', but it is not, we know, a cloud of
his own making. It is Waugh's invention, not his history.

Apthorpe as Guy's double and as the means of his downfall is a
very fine conception. Those functions of the character were no mistake. Waugh's large and nearly crippling misconception was
Apthorpe as a personality. He seems to have believed that Apthorpe
proved that his powers as a comic writer were undiminished but
this was a sad delusion and a sizeable failure of critical judgement.

Apthorpe takes a large role in *Men at Arms*. The three 'books' into
which the novel is divided bear his name: *Apthorpe Gloriosus*, *Furibun-
dus*, and *Immolatus*.

> Apthorpe alone [of the officer entrants] looked like a soldier. He
> was burly, tanned, moustached, primed with a rich vocabulary of
> military terms and abbreviations. Until recently he had served in
> Africa in some unspecified capacity. His boots had covered miles
> of trail. (SH 40)

Apthorpe turns out to be a plausible sham. He is deviously ambitious and given to one-upmanship, almost totally devoid of common sense, and possessed by strange obsessions, the most notable of
which is the 'thunderbox'. As a veteran bush-hand (or so he claims)
Apthorpe has a huge array of 'gear', one item being this chemical
portaloo. He hides it for his private use in the grounds of Kut-al-
Imara House school, where the Halberdiers are billeted, and there

develops a contest between Apthorpe and Brigadier Ritchie-Hook for exclusive rights to it. Contest and thunder-box come to an end when the Brigadier rigs an explosive booby-trap and Apthorpe is blown up, though not seriously hurt.

All of this is underwhelmingly funny, and it is positively embarrassing that Waugh never seems to have seen how dull Apthorpe is. Christopher Sykes said it: 'Apthorpe is a bore who bores' (418). Waugh claimed that the whole of *Men at Arms* should have been regarded as 'the first comic turn of a long music-hall show, put on to keep the audience quiet as they are taking their seats' (L 379), which suggests that his illusion of the longevity of his comic talent was firmly established at this stage. There are good things in *Men at Arms*, but they are not funny, and Apthorpe is not one of them. When it is revealed in *Officers and Gentlemen* that Apthorpe is not a 'bush-hand' at all but a tobacco company employee who hardly ever got out of town, the revelation is so unsurprising that it seems like pointless cruelty to expose so feeble a sham. Against his own intention, Waugh turns Apthorpe into a figure of pathos.

Waugh claimed that Apthorpe had threatened to take over *Sword of Honour* and that he had had to kill him off to prevent that hijacking. The remark makes sense if we see comedy as only incidental, although importantly incidental, to the conception of the trilogy as a whole. Waugh's failure with Apthorpe could not be radical, despite his prominence in *Men at Arms*. Had the character been the great comic success that Waugh imagined he was, he would have derailed the trilogy; as it stands his success is confined to his role as hapless Guy's hapless nemesis.

With two other characters in *Men at Arms*, Waugh was successful so as to more than balance the failure with Apthorpe. Both Guy's ex-wife, Virginia, and his father represent signal advances in his fictional repertory and in his human sympathies. Crouchback senior, Gervase, like his dead son, is a good, even saintly, man and an attractive, endearing character. His view of his family's history in the history of England is

> not an entirely sane conspectus but it engendered in his gentle breast two rare qualities, tolerance and humility . . . He had a further natural advantage over Guy; he was fortified by a memory that kept only the good things and rejected the ill. Despite his sorrows, he had had a fair share of joys, and these were ever fresh and accessible in Mr. Crouchback's mind. (SH 31)

His greatest importance to the work as a whole is to come in *Uncon-ditional Surrender*. In *Men at Arms* he is established as a believably human ideal whom Guy will later discover the possibility of faintly emulating, remote though that possibility seems in the first volume. His success as a character is an earnest by Waugh that he could see the beauty and power of tolerance and humility, even if he could rarely attain them.

The existence of Mr Crouchback is one of several reasons Waugh had for not making Guy a convert to Catholicism. Presumably he did not wish to explain or to dramatize a conversion by Guy and he did want Guy's father to be a Catholic. Conversion in the novel is to be left for a most unlikely candidate: Virginia, Guy's ex-wife.

Virginia indicates a quite startling advance in Waugh's attitudes. She is the first of his unfaithful wives, in the She-Evelyn role, so to speak, to be married to a Catholic, though no Catholic herself, and she is the only one to whom he extends any sympathy. The divorce came about with the usual abruptness. Guy recalls how Virginia, claim-ing ill-health, had gone back to England from their farm in Kenya, and then had written 'still affectionately' that she had fallen in love with an acquaintance of theirs, Tommy Blackhouse, and that she wanted a divorce. Guy has clearly been shocked by this but the effect is less shattering than it had been in the case of Tony Last. Guy's lowness of spirits seems owed to a variety of causes, merely including the divorce, or is perhaps constitutional, and whether Waugh planned it or not, the reader, knowing Guy, is likely to feel a fair degree of understanding and sympathy for Virginia. (Tommy Blackhouse is a similar development along the lines of the 'other man'. Guy does not hate or despise him; he is not an awful man. Later he becomes Guy's admirable commanding officer in the Com-mandos.) And in the only part of *Men at Arms* where Virginia is a principal player, Waugh seems to at least one reader to take a satir-ical jab at the wronged husband and his religion. Guy has fallen in with a Mr Goodall, a retired schoolmaster who is a rather dotty con-vert to Catholicism, fascinated by the genealogy of the old English Catholic families. But it is remarks of his on theology and canon law that prove in the short run painfully beguiling to Guy, although in the very long run ironically saving. Mr Goodall recounts an anec-dote of 'the extinction (in the male line)...of an historic Catholic family', distantly connected to the Crouchbacks (SH 112). The wife deserted the husband and the couple divorced. She remarried. Some years later the husband and his ex-wife met again abroad. 'A kind of

rapprochement occurred but she went back to her so-called husband and in due time bore a son. It was in fact your kinsman's'. The
genealogical implications are uninteresting to Guy but he is struck
by the moral situation.

'You mean to say that theologically the original husband committed no sin in resuming sexual relations with his former wife'?
'Certainly not. The wretched girl of course was guilty ... But the
husband was entirely blameless. And so under another and quite
uninteresting name a great family has been preserved. What is
more the son married a Catholic so that *his* son is being brought
up in the Church. Explain it how you will, I see the workings of
Providence there' (SH 112).

Virginia has returned to London with her third marriage on the
rocks, and she has shown herself amiably disposed towards Guy
(and towards Tommy Blackhouse too). With Mr Goodall's declaration insistent in his ears, Guy sets out for London in the hope of
achieving his own 'blameless and auspicious pseudo-adultery'. The
conditions, notably ill-timed telephonic interruptions by Apthorpe,
prove inauspicious, and when Guy explains that his proposition
would not be considered sinful by the Church ('You're my wife ...
you asked what the priests would say. They'd say: "Go ahead"'),
Virginia is appalled.

Tears of rage and humiliation were flowing unresisted.
'I thought you'd taken a fancy to me again and wanted a bit of
fun for the sake of old times. I thought you'd chosen me specially,
and by God you had. Because I was the only woman in the world
your priests would let you go to bed with. That was my attraction.
You wet, smug, obscene, pompous, sexless, lunatic pig' (SH 124).

It seems clear that if Guy has legalism on his side, Virginia gets the
emotional verdict. Waugh has found a literalism that he does not
like, though he certainly recognized its attractiveness for minds con-
stituted like his own. Unless one adopts the Goodall attitude whole
hog, it is hard to see how Waugh is not targeting the way some
Catholics, including not infrequently E. Waugh, attitudinized about
their faith.
Though of great thematic importance in *Sword of Honour* as a
whole, Mr Crouchback and Virginia are minor characters in *Men at*

Arms. Most of the novel is the account of Guy's service, mainly train-ing, with the Halberdiers. Waugh, of course, attempted to enliven this fundamentally undramatic material by weaving Apthorpe into it, with rather lamentable results, and by giving a fair amount of space to Ritchie-Hook. He too will reappear in the later volumes, but in his case there are signs that the author changed his functions from the original conception. At the end of *Men at Arms*, but before the death of Apthorpe, Guy is already in trouble because of Ritchie-Hook. As the expeditionary force prepares to turn back from Dakar, the Brigadier orders Guy and men from his company to make a noc-turnal beach reconnaissance. The Brigadier secretly accompanies the patrol, armed with 'a weapon like a hedging implement', for his real purpose is to use the reconnaissance as an opportunity for head-hunting – quite literally. He gets back to the boat wounded, but car-rying 'the wet, curly head of a Negro ... French colonial infantry' (SH 214).

This expedition gets Ritchie-Hook into trouble. He is the wrong age, apparently, for such piratical exploits and he is recalled. Guy, by some species of injustice, is implicated with the Brigadier. 'You're in the clear legally. But it'll be a black mark. For the rest of your life when your name comes up, someone is bound to say: "Isn't he the chap who blotted his copy-book at Dakar in 40?"' Apthorpe's death then comes along to be a more substantial but similarly unjust blot, and Guy travels back to England with the Brigadier, a halberdier no more. Waugh thus re-enacted his own separation from the Marines while keeping his hero blameless. Moreover, at this stage, it seems likely that Ritchie-Hook is making his final exit, clutching the sev-ered head that proclaims him a Great English Eccentric. When Waugh reintroduces him in *Unconditional Surrender* (after a very brief appearance in *Officers and Gentlemen*) he will be somewhat uncomfortably playing a part in the chivalry theme.

After *Men at Arms* in 1952, Waugh's next work of fiction was the brief dystopian novel *Love Among the Ruins* (1953), with a hero called Miles Plastic in love with a lady with 'a long, silken, corn-gold beard', living in the apotheosis of the nanny state where the social services are principally sterilization and euthanasia. Writing to Gra-ham Greene, he said, '*Love among the Ruins* was a bit of nonsense begun 3 years ago and hastily finished & injudiciously published' (L 204). Let that be its epitaph. It is a tiny skirmish in his war against the Modern Age and almost the exception to the rule that nothing he wrote is unreadable. The time of its publication was one of mounting mental stress that was about to come to a crisis. The sequence of events requires a narrative of his literary life to make a choice of order in which events will be recounted.

The chronological sequence is that Waugh began writing the second of his war novels (working title 'Happy Warriors') in March 1953 but could not get very far with it. In August 1953 he allowed himself to be interviewed at Piers Court by the BBC radio Overseas Service. In September and October of that year he took part in two sessions at Broadcasting House in London for a second interview that was broadcast in Britain. His state of mind during the latter part of 1953 was such that he saw these interviews, especially the first, as figures in a pattern of persecutions; they became an important component of the plot against him that was devised by his subconscious, and so they play a large role in *Pinfold*. To get his book going again, he decided to make a voyage to Ceylon to work in warmer and more relaxing surroundings. The *Staffordshire* left Liverpool at the end of January 1954 and Waugh, who had realized some time before he left that he was harming himself by self-prescribed and self-administered doses of bromide and chloral, began at once to suffer from vivid auditory hallucinations, 'voices', which plagued him and led him into some very bizarre behaviour until the ship reached Port Said. He believed he was being psychologically attacked by broadcasters who had, as we would now say, 'bugged' the ship. But when he flew to Ceylon from Egypt, he found the voices 'waiting' for him. He flew back to England and was met by a greatly shaken Laura, alarmed by his letters describing what he thought was going on, and was persuaded to talk to a psychiatrist, Catholic of course, who diagnosed narcotic poisoning. The diagnosis was a huge relief to Waugh, who had serious fears for his sanity. The voices had stopped once he was shown that his assumptions about these happenings were impossible. Narcotic poisoning could be handled by changes in medication; the whole thing was an episode, all over, quite separate from the rest of his life, and moreover by its episodic nature – as something that had happened and was over – perfect material for a novel: a 'gift', in fact.

The experience aboard ship became the narrative of *The Ordeal of Gilbert Pinfold*, but despite what that novel itself suggests (Mr Pinfold on the last page sits down to write the novel we have just read), he did not set about 'writing up' his experience immediately. First, after a period of three months, he set out to finish 'Happy Warriors'.

We shall consider that book, published in June 1955, next and then move on to *Pinfold*, published in 1957.

Officers and Gentlemen begins like *Men at Arms* in Britain, with Guy Crouchback unemployed after his departure from the Halberdiers. Because the prime minister is an admirer of Ritchie-Hook (as Churchill certainly was of Carton de Wiart), the Brigadier is rescued from disgrace and assigned to HOO (Hazardous Offensive Operations, Waugh's version of the SOE, Special Operations Executive), and – lifted up himself – he lifts Guy and gets him assigned to Tommy Blackhouse's X Commando, training in Scotland, where he is given administrative duties. As part of 'Hookforce', X Commando with Guy is sent to the Middle East, and from Egypt is thrown into the battle for Crete. Guy escapes by small boat from Crete instead of surrendering but finds that he has been ordered back to Britain rather than reassigned in the Middle East.

As X Commando leaves for the Middle East, the novel begins to alternate scenes of military life abroad involving Guy with accounts of goings on back in Britain, involving principally Guy's ex-wife Virginia and Trimmer, last in the line of Atwater and Hooper. Trimmer, like Guy, had been an officer entrant into the Halberdiers and had been rejected by Ritchie-Hook. He turns up on the Isle of Mugg (fictional neighbour of the quite real islands of Rhum, Muck and Eigg) under the name of McTavish as an officer in a Highland regiment, attached to the Commando for defence duties. On leave in Glasgow, Trimmer recognizes Virginia as one of his former customers on the transatlantic liner where before the war he had been a hairdresser known as 'Gustave'. Waugh handles very well the combination of Virginia's depression and loneliness and Trimmer's irrepressible assurance that leads to their having what seems to be a one-night stand, 'Trimmer's idyll'. By an administrative quirk, Trimmer is also assigned to HOO and gets sent on a farcical raid, 'Operation Popgun', staged entirely for publicity purposes, which eventuates in a Military Cross and promotion to Colonel (*à la* T. E. Lawrence). He is then employed as an example of the 'new officer emerging from the old hide-bound British Army', to be sent on morale-raising tours. He, however, is love-sick for Virginia, undeterred by her forthright rejections.

Trimmer is a figure of major importance in *Sword of Honour*, with a clearly defined thematic role. He is Modern Man, the embodiment of all that is shameful and meretricious in the system of values that has replaced the old codes for which the nation would formerly have gone to war. Waugh's contempt for the character is quite clear but it is not so clear that most readers will unhesitatingly go along. One whose memory includes Grimes and Basil Seal will perhaps feel that Trimmer, like Atwater in *Work Suspended*, only more so, has an effrontery that the younger Waugh might well have admired. It is possible, however, that Waugh's miscalculation about the impression Trimmer might make is owed to his private feelings. In his autobiography Auberon Waugh states that Lord Lovat 'had been ridiculed as "Trimmer" in the war trilogy' (WTD 49). This is certainly not deducible from the book itself and no one else who has written about Waugh has made the identification, as far as I can discover. Waugh's son presumably relied on information from his father, and once the claim is made one can see points of similarity. Waugh called Lovat a 'Palais de Danse hero' (L 172); he had the Military Cross and had taken part in the Dieppe raid (but that was not quite Operation Popgun). Lovat was a well-publicized hero. But the dissimilarities are so huge that if Waugh intended Trimmer to be identified as Lovat he can only have failed to plant clues that would lead that way. It seems most likely that privately he worked off a deal of animus in Trimmer but decided that if he made his readers connect the character with Lord Lovat then Trimmer would not be able to fulfil his thematic role in the book. In that case, Waugh sacrificed the pleasures of lampoon for the architectonic integrity of his trilogy.

Martin Stannard speculates acutely that what brought Waugh to a stop in his composition of 'Happy Warriors' was the difficulty of revisiting his military career for the purposes of his novel. Stannard points to the futility of his military employment in the period leading up to Crete. 'Is it fanciful to suggest that Waugh's imaginative saturation in his *alter ego*'s military irrelevance had contributed to the breakdown'? (2S 350). Pinfold's voices accuse him of doing 'pretty badly' in the army. 'Did he dare confront this? It seems unlikely'. I would add, and perhaps give more weight to, the fact that in his writing Waugh was likely getting ready to deal with the circumstances of Laycock's and his departure from Crete, and that the psychological strain of reviewing that morally traumatic experience made its own contribution to the 'Pinfold' breakdown of February 1954.

When, with the Pinfold business behind him, Waugh turned back to 'Happy Warriors', he resolved his Laycock dilemma very neatly. The horns of that beast were – left – that he was firm in the purpose of confronting 'Laycock's & my ignominious flight' (H 573), and –

right – that he should describe that flight without indicating that it involved Laycock, whom he wished to continue to worship. Guy Crouchback was to be deprived of the illusion of military chivalry. The idea that the war had an honourable purpose, that it was 'a time of glory and dedication' (SH 57), was to be thrown away with the abandoned weapons and the prisoners of the 'island of disillusion'. Yet moral depravity could not be handled abstractly, but must be embodied in characters. There Waugh's imaginative dexterity gave him a saving strategem. He divided Laycock into two. The leader of X Commando, the man who holds as regards Guy Crouchback the position that Laycock held as regards Waugh, is Tommy Black-house, a Guardsman but a Coldstreamer, friendly towards Guy despite (or because of) having been the man for whom Virginia left Guy. Tommy is a no-nonsense professional with no panache about him; the panache of Laycock Waugh embodied in the figure of Ivor Claire.

The first officer that Guy encounters when he joins X Commando on the Isle of Mugg is the temporarily injured Claire, 'a Captain of the Blues who reclined upon a sofa, his head enveloped in a turban of lint, his feet shod in narrow velvet slippers...He was nursing a white pekinese; beside him stood a glass of white liqueur' (SH 276). Guy recognizes him as a fellow member of Bellamy's club and as a 'show-jumper of repute' whom he had seen competing in Rome. The dandiacal note is usually heard when Claire is present but the initial impression of effeteness is only fleeting. As with Tommy Blackhouse, an unlikely friendship grows of Guy and Claire. Guy 'had recognized from the first a certain remote friendship with this most dissimilar man, a common aloofness, differently manifested – a common melancholy sense of humour; each in his way saw life *sub specie aeternatis*; thus with numberless reservations they became friends...' (SH 315). The friendship between Waugh and Robert Laycock is thus divided into two aspects of two characters and when one friendship is destroyed, one friend can be eliminated, leaving the other intact. In life matters were much more complicated, since two characters seemed to inhabit Laycock's person. Waugh had found a way in his book to denounce one side of that complex figure, or really one episode in that figure's life.

Guy Crouchback's feelings for Ivor Claire go beyond reserved friendship. At Cape Town, en route for Egypt, Guy recalls a description of X Commando.

'The Flower of the Nation', Ian Kilbannock had ironically called them. He was not far wrong. There was heroic simplicity in Eddie and Bertie. Ivor Claire was another pair of boots entirely, salty, withdrawn incorrigible. Guy remembered Claire as he first saw him in the Roman spring in the afternoon sunlight amid the embosoming cypresses of the Borghese Gardens, putting his horse faultlessly over the jumps, concentrated as a man in prayer. Ivor Claire, Guy thought, was the fine flower of them all. He was quintessential England, the man Hitler had not taken into account, Guy thought. (SH 342)

Only the repetition of 'Guy thought' hints at the instability of this judgement. It is to crumble to bitter ashes on Crete.

The account of the Cretan débâcle is one of Waugh's greatest passages, and his stage-management of the situation superbly allows Guy's disillusionment to unfold. First, since with him in command there could be very little demoralization, Waugh effects the disappearance of Ritchie-Hook on a flight from Brazzaville (SH 341). 'Hookforce' is Hookless. For much the same reason, Tommy Blackhouse is not in command when his outfit lands on Crete. He breaks his leg on the voyage there, and so when his command lands it is without him and effectively without direction (SH 392). After the wonderfully delineated account of Guy's wanderings among the various formations (most utterly formless, others – like the Halberdiers – well disciplined and of high morale) fighting the Germans and retreating to Sphakia, he is with Hookforce holding the perimeter for the evacuation and under orders to surrender next day. There he is visited by Ivor Claire, whose conversation runs on the theme of surrender and imprisonment. He begins and ends with the word 'honour'.

'I was thinking about honour. It's a thing that changes, doesn't it? I mean, a hundred and fifty years ago we would have had to fight if challenged [to a duel]. Now we'd laugh. There must have been a time a hundred years or so ago when it was rather an awkward question ... And in the next war ... I expect it will be quite honourable for officers to leave their men behind ... I reckon our trouble is that we're at the awkward stage'.

Guy could see him clearly in the moonlight, the austere face, haggard now but calm and recollected, as he had first seen it in the Borghese Gardens. It was his last sight of him. Ivor stood up

saying: 'Well, the path of honour lies up the hill', and he strolled
away. (SH 449)

After Guy's escape in the boat, in effect captained by the theatrically
sinister and creepy Corporal-Major Ludovic, who is from Ivor Claire's
troop, he discovers in Egypt that Claire has in fact got out of Crete
leaving his men behind to be taken prisoner. As Waugh's 'Synopsis
of Previous Volumes', (included in the Everyman edition [483–5])
states bluntly, 'That night Claire deserts his troop and insinuates
himself into the disembarkation [sic. ?embarkation]'. Guy's duties
on Crete included keeping the Hookforce War Diary, so when he
arrives in Egypt he has documentary evidence with him of the order
to surrender.

By creating two characters to represent what he no doubt saw as
contradictory aspects of Laycock, Waugh came as near as he could
to telling the whole truth about the Cretan episode. Without naming
Laycock as the man implicated, Waugh made betrayal – or treason
in fact, a capital crime – a major topic of his account. And then he
took steps that he thought would keep his readers from seeing that
Laycock's features were behind the masks of both Tommy Blackhouse and Ivor Claire. He dedicated *Officers and Gentlemen* 'to Major-
General Sir Robert Laycock KCMG, CB, DSO that every man in arms
should wish to be', followed by an elaborate assertion of 'this story
as pure fiction', in no detail 'identifiable with the realities of those
exhilarating days when he led and I lamely followed' (SH 234).

That, he must have thought, would wipe out the scent. When the
book appeared, however, he received 'to my horror' a telegram from
the dauntless Ann Fleming: 'Presume Ivor Claire based Laycock
dedication ironical'. It seems that she was simply teasing and had
not realized how true her presumption was (D 728). Waugh wrote to
her on 4 July 1955,

> Dear Ann, Your telegram horrifies me. Of course there is no pos-
> sible connexion between Bob and 'Claire'. If you suggest such a
> thing anywhere it will be the end of our beautiful friendship...'.
> Near the end of the letter he came back to the subject. 'For Christ's
> sake lay off the idea of Bob = 'Claire'...Just shut up about Lay-
> cock. Fuck you. E. Waugh' (SY 376)

In his diary, however, he made a revealing entry. 'I replied that if
she breathes a suspicion of *this cruel fact* it will be the end of our

friendship' [Italics added] (D 728). 'Fact' may have been a slip, but if so none more Freudian was ever made.

The Laycock difficulty shows Waugh striving to tell the truth under a veil. But when Guy arrives back in Egypt, Waugh made a decision that is truly astonishing and morally impressive. From *Scoop*, last of the pre-war comic novels, he introduces into *Officers and Gentlemen* Mrs Stitch, the character unambiguously based on the most famous and prominent of his 'sisters', Lady Diana Cooper. Duff Cooper had been made British Representative in liberated Algiers in 1943 and Waugh had visited the Coopers there. In *Officers and Gentlemen*, Algernon Stitch and his wife are transferred to Egypt, where Julia Stitch befriends Guy, whom she had met before the war. She is, however, much firmer friends with Ivor Claire and it is from her that Guy is initially delighted to learn that Claire, 'that young prince of Athens sent to the Cretan labyrinth', has in fact escaped from the island. But Mrs Stitch is evasive about the details. Claire has already been spirited off to India and Mrs Stitch is clearly making a defending counsel's case for him. 'Obviously by the end there *weren't* any orders'. But Guy knows otherwise, and reveals that he has those orders in writing. Mrs Stitch gives him what is evidently the cooked-up version of Claire's departure from Crete. He went to the beach to verify the order to embark, was himself ordered to get aboard at once:

> guides had been sent back and . . . Hookforce was already on its way. His ship was just leaving. There was another staying for Hookforce . . . Until Ivor reached Alexandria he thought the rest of Hookforce was in the other cruiser. When he found it wasn't, he was in rather a jam . . . So you see no one can blame Ivor, can they'? (SH 463)

But everyone does blame Ivor, Guy most of all. Tommy Blackhouse rejects the Stitch account: 'No one believes it, least of all Julia'. But Tommy's military professionalism and careerism urge him to a conclusion very different from that which Guy has supposed: 'Now the best thing is to keep quiet and forget the whole business. It's far too big a thing to *do* anything about'. Only Ritchie-Hook would *do* something, and he has disappeared. Guy looks at his war diary notes: 'This was his contribution to History; this perhaps the evidence in a notorious trial'. Julia Stitch and Tommy Blackhouse are guided by simple rules of conduct. For her 'there was no problem.

An old friend was in trouble. Rally round'. For Tommy, the precept was 'never cause trouble except for positive preponderant advantage . . . Ivor had behaved abominably but he had hurt no one but himself'. Guy alone cannot give up the big question. Is not the war, is not all they have gone through, 'for Justice'? Then, on 22 June 1941 – 'a day of apocalypse for all the world for numberless generations' – comes news of the German attack on the Soviet Union and the consequent alliance of Britain with Russia.

Guy gives up. The fight against 'the modern age in arms' was hallucination.

> he was back after less than two year's pilgrimage in a Holy Land of illusion in the old ambiguous world, where . . . gallant friends proved traitors and his country was led blundering into dishonour.
>
> That afternoon he took his pocket-book to the incinerator . . . and thrust it in. (SH 468)

Mrs Stitch, however, believing that Guy still has the notes, and having heard that Ritchie-Hook has survived his plane crash and is on the way back to Egypt, pulls strings to get Guy sent back on a very slow boat to England. As Guy takes farewell of her, he asks her to see that an envelope he gives her, marked 'GHQME', gets to the right person. He tells her that it is 'a bit of unfinished business from Crete'. The envelope contains the identity disc Guy had taken from the body of a young Catholic soldier he had to leave unburied in a Cretan village. Mrs Stitch, of course, believes it is the war diary. 'As he drove away she waved the envelope; then turned indoors and dropped it into a waste-paper basket. Her eyes were one immense sea, full of flying galleys' (SH 472).

In transporting Mrs Stitch from *Scoop* to *Officers and Gentlemen*, Waugh was making a large exception to his rule that the two worlds of his fiction were to be almost totally separate. That is mildly astonishing. What is more so is that to many of his readers Mrs Stitch was known to 'be' Diana Cooper, that she herself accepted the identification and rather gloried in it and that Waugh in this reintroduction of her undeniably darkens her character. He told her so in a letter on 1st November 1954: 'My work nearly finished . . . Rather good though Mrs Stitch turns out rather unscrupulous and uncharacteristic', and in another about two weeks later: 'I have finished my book at last and is O.K. although Mrs Stitch rather lapses from her high original and becomes a sort of Cleopatra of intrigue (not amorous)' (LWC 198, 200). He was giving her warning but did not expect much trouble and he was right. Lady Diana told at least one interviewer that she would certainly have behaved as Mrs Stitch did in the matter of Ivor Claire (and therefore in the matter of the 'notes' too?). Her rather slight religious sensibility probably prevented her feeling much anguish over the soldier's identity disc thrown away.

Having 'split' Laycock into two characters, Waugh repeated the procedure for himself. Two strong conflicting emotions were prominent in his attitude towards Laycock and the escape from Crete. One was the conviction that he had become Laycock's accomplice in a moral crime, amounting in legal terms to treason. The other was that he had supported Laycock, and profited by that support, out of friendship and that in doing so he had given friendship something like spiritual value. He realized that he had confronted in actuality E. M. Forster's famous hypothetical dilemma, what might be called the liberal doctrine of friendship: 'If I had to choose between betraying my country and betraying a friend, I hope I would have the courage to betray my country'. But Waugh was not happy with his decision. He had made Forster's courageous choice only to discover that it did not feel like courage and so he turned his hostility onto the doctrine of friendship. By choosing Diana Cooper as Mrs Stitch to be its advocate, Waugh enacted a varied scenario of desiderata. First of all, Diana Cooper assigned the highest value to friendship and was quite unlikely to accept or pursue his strongly implied denunciation of it. And in consequence of that, their friendship would not be harmed by Waugh's indirect statement that he valued friendship differently, that there were occasions when friendship counted for less than other considerations. She was known to a significant part of the public as Mrs Stitch and so as someone linked, in part identified, with Waugh, so he came as close as he dared to identifying her values as (once) his own. Guy Crouchback by means of this stratagem is allowed to repudiate his brief friendship with Ivor Claire and to think very differently from Mrs Stitch about friendship. The character who represents in several ways the person that Waugh wished he could have been, Guy, is allowed to voice the arguments that a less confused Waugh, one hardly entangled in his web of friendships and conflicts, would make.

The process of fission that Waugh used to get out of his dilemma permitted him, of course, to have it both ways. He kept his friendships with Robert Laycock and Diana Cooper but in his novel he excoriated the betrayals and the perverse system of values that he saw embodied in their (and his own) conduct. Moralists of a rigid inclination may see this as evasion. Why did he not tell the truth and be damned? Less severely, it reveals the seriousness of Waugh's commitment to the novel, that he would only there tell as much of the truth as this, having in other forums, such as the 'Memorandum on Layforce', maintained the rightness of what he and Laycock did. The crucial factor of difference is almost certainly time. He thought that the trilogy would be his last work of fiction and when he came to it he had thought long about the Cretan experience. His mature conclusions were not those of his younger self, and finally he was as true as he possibly could have been to the truth in the form of writing he valued most.

Officers and Gentlemen is clearly not the end of Waugh's engagement with his wartime experience. Virginia and Trimmer, for example, are left awaiting further development. But in Guy Crouchback's experience at the book's end there is a terminal quality that perhaps suggested – very briefly – to Waugh that he should not go forward with a third volume. At the tomb of Sir Roger of Waybroke, Guy had committed himself to battle for two interrelated motives: personal honour and the crusade against the Modern Age. The latter motive is dominant, especially in *Officers and Gentlemen*, and its overthrow, with the inception of the British alliance with Russia, coincides with the loss of honour involved in the escape from Crete, and so both of Guy's motives seem to have been frustrated. It should be objected that Waugh had exonerated Guy from loss of personal honour by putting the onus entirely on Ivor Claire and by allowing Guy to leave the island by boat in a quite acceptable way. But there is one sentence that seems to indicate that Guy himself felt that his escape was *not* honourable. On the night before he embarks, Guy 'had no clear apprehension that this was a fatal morning, that he was that day to resign an immeasurable piece of his manhood' (SH 449). This sentence was in the first edition of 1955 and so reappears in the Everyman edition of 1994. But Waugh excised it from the *Sword of Honour* recension in 1965, and this, like the excision of Guy's two sons at the end of the third volume, is a change that should be definitive. When *Officers and Gentlemen* first appeared, therefore, Waugh had not finally decided that, with personal honour as the sole surviving motive, Guy should soldier on for one more volume and until that motive itself surrenders in the moral squalor of Yugoslavia.

*

Waugh began to write *The Ordeal of Gilbert Pinfold*, his 'mad book', before *Officers and Gentlemen* was published. He began it on a visit to the Flemings in Jamaica in January 1955 and worked at it on and off until October 1956. At that time he had arranged to sell Piers Court and was getting ready to move to Combe Florey House near Taunton, Somerset, farther into the West Country, deeper into seclusion. The book was in the publisher's hands in January 1957 and appeared in July of that year. The events of his life at this time that are of importance to his writing were a couple of law suits.

The action for libel that he brought against Nancy Spain and the *Daily Express* is well known and fully treated by all biographers. The Beaverbrook press had been conducting a vendetta against him for some time. The libel by Nancy Spain was the statement that Alec Waugh's novels had consistently outsold Evelyn's on first publication. Alec loyally testified in court to his literary inferiority to his brother and Waugh was awarded £2000 damages plus costs. The more interesting case, described only by Martin Stannard, also involved the *Daily Express*. The paper had attacked Waugh in October 1965 by running a story with quotations from a revised and reissued version of Rebecca West's *The Meaning of Treason* (USA 1947; UK 1949). In the additions she had made, West had argued that Waugh and Graham Greene 'have created a climate of crack-brained confusion between virtues and vices... a climate in which the traitor flourishes'. Stannard concludes that 'The suggestion was that Waugh and Greene *encouraged* treason' (2S 377, 379). In addition to his personal interest in the idea of treason, Waugh was sensitive on the subject – as the country was sensitive – because of the Burgess and Maclean case which had begun with the disappearance of the two in 1951. Waugh sued, and the case came to court in December 1956. Pan Books climbed down, admitting that the words were indefensible and unfair. All unsold copies would be withdrawn. Waugh agreed to settle for costs.

In December 1956, *Officers and Gentlemen* had been published for more than eighteen months and had the case come to trial, Waugh could have pointed out that in his latest book treason was a major topic and that the authorial attitude towards it was unambiguously censorious. Yet this defence would probably not have attracted him because, apart from Ivor Claire's great treason, the theme is elsewhere rather problematical. It is introduced in the scenes on the Isle of Mugg that involve the laird's loony niece, Miss Carmichael, who is a Scottish Nationalist supporting the Germans to advance her cause. Her activities draw the attention of the counter-espionage service to Guy Crouchback. His harmless activities become of interest to Colonel Grace-Groundling-Marchpole, head of an ultra secret counter-intelligence unit who is clearly paranoid and has delusions of grandeur. There is even an ecclesiastical side to the theme of treason in *Officers and Gentlemen*. Waugh gives to Guy his own true experience of going to confession in Alexandria and deciding that the priest's questions about tanks and troop movements are those of a spy (SH 351). Guy's report of this eventually becomes an item in his own counter-intelligence file (SH 369), for one important function of this element of the book's structure is to provide explanations for some of the unusual postings and transfers that Guy receives. They are not owed, as in Waugh's case, to personal friendship or to his incompetence and the desire to be rid of him, but to the machinations of real and clandestine enemies of both himself and his country. This topic comes to the fore in *Unconditional Surrender*. The element of persecution and paranoia in the latter half of *Officers and Gentlemen* derived immediately from the 'Pinfold experience', and once the war novel was finished, Waugh set to work on the book wholly devoted to his 'madness'. What was for him a 'gift', however, is something of a disappointment for his readers.

The idea of a great novelist writing with objectivity about an uprising of his subconscious wherein his own mind employs his powers of fictional creation against him is excitingly promising. This should be an unruly masterpiece. That it is not is owed to the function that Waugh decreed that the book should have in the life of his fiction. Three formal details help make clear that role he had assigned to it.

At the very end of the novel, Mr Pinfold sits down in his study. He looks at his unfinished novel, but, unlike Waugh with *Officers and Gentlemen*, does not resume work on it:

> there was more urgent business first, a hamper to be unpacked of fresh, rich experiences – perishable goods.
>
> He returned the manuscript to the drawer, spread a new quire of foolscap before him and wrote in his neat, steady hand:

The Ordeal of Gilbert Pinfold
A Conversation Piece
Chapter One
Portrait of the Artist in Middle-age[1]

The purpose of adopting this device was to put the serpent's tail in its mouth, to give the book the most visible shape of completion possible. The experience was finished, encapsulated in this very controlled short novel. It was the effect of poisoning, an episode, not strongly rooted in the past and never to recur in the future. Waugh was not exploring his psyche but reporting events, quite real events. The only struggle would be that depicted in the novel between Mr Pinfold and his enemies, his quite real enemies. A second formal feature underlines this assertion of reality.

The sub-title of the book, repeated on the final page, is 'A Conversation Piece'. Since the book is about Mr Pinfold's 'voices', the assumption might be that Waugh is making a sort of pun on 'voices' in 'conversation', but I doubt that he would invest so much in so feeble a joke. He was a connoisseur of British painting and it is impossible to believe that he did not think first of 'conversation piece' as a group portrait of family or friends engaged in some favourite activity in their familiar surroundings. The novel begins with a 'portrait' of Mr Pinfold, but the whole is an ironic 'conversation piece' in which the hero is shown with the enemies who pester and persecute him, not friends but 'familiars', and all as real as those very solid citizens who populate the ungrandiose canvases of the painters of 'conversations'.

The third formal feature Waugh employed to define his book's purpose is simply that he refers throughout to his undoubted *alter ego* as 'Mr Pinfold'. When negotiating with the BBC for the second of the interviews in 1953, Waugh had written that there was to be no 'bandying about of Christian names' (2S 334), and the absence of such familiarity in the relationship between the author and his fictional self indicates that even here distance will be kept. There will be no probing in depth. Mr Pinfold is an actor among other actors, most of whom, though real, are invisible, and the book is the record of the drama they perform.

Most of all, *Pinfold* is the account of a victory. The protagonist is truly the hero, and Waugh has him flirt with the idea that he has overcome Satanic possession (GP 258), but even if it is not the Devil he has overcome, it is at least a devilish temptation. On his flight back to England from Columbo, Mr Pinfold considers a deal that the voice of Angel offers him. 'I'll switch off the apparatus. I promise on my honour we'll none of us ever worry you again. All we ask is that you don't say anything to anyone in England about us'. Mr Pinfold is tempted but finally turns down the deal. He will exact retribution

for his own sufferings and he declares the voices to be 'a public men-
ace that has got to be silenced...Angel was a beaten man and he
knew it'. After this the story is swiftly wound up, and as Mr Pinfold
recounts its details to his wife he is 'like a warrior returned from a
hard fought victory'. Had he accepted the angelic offer, 'I should
have lived in fear that at any moment the whole thing might start
up again'. Unlike Waugh himself, Mr Pinfold declines to see even a
Catholic 'psychologist' and is not eager to accept his GP's diagnosis
that his experience has been owed to 'a perfectly simple case of poisoning'.

> He knew, and the others did not know – not even his wife, least of
> all his medical adviser – that he had endured a great ordeal, and
> unaided, had emerged the victor. There was triumph to be cele-
> brated ... (GP 268)

The trouble is that Mr Pinfold's victory doesn't seem like much of a
triumph. Waugh's objective was to tell his story in such a way as to
insist on its utterly anomalous, over-and-done-with nature. The narrative is always too firmly controlled. The brilliant 'Portrait of the
Artist in Middle-age' with which the book begins has been praised
for its frankness but it is a limited and tactical frankness. Waugh
gives a fine account of the persona, the mask worn in public, 'a front
of pomposity mitigated by indiscretion, that was as hard, bright, and
antiquated as a cuirass', that he developed to protect his face but
which showed signs of becoming his face. But he suppressed
any effectively formulated mention of the powerful and dangerous
impulses and prejudices out of which his subconscious was to man-
ufacture the accusations against himself in the role of Pinfold. Mr
Pinfold cannot understand why the voices make such ridiculous
accusations. 'If I was supplying all the information to the Angels,
why did I tell them such a lot of rot? I mean to say, if I wanted to
draw up an indictment of myself I could make a far blacker and
more plausible case than they did' (GP 267). What seems to have
happened is that his subconscious was never the utterly free agent
that he showed it to be. When it settled on anti-semitism as material
for an accusation, for example, the accusation emerged in absurd
form.

> 'He's a Jew'.
> 'Is he? I never heard that'.

'Of course he is. He came to Lychpole in 1937 with the German refugees. He was called Peinfeld then'. (GP 181)

Control was exercised to divert a plausible accusation – anti-semitic attitudes – into absurdity, and that is how the book is kept from being the revelation that it might have been. All of Waugh's biographers have seen through the screen he erected to keep himself from getting a sight of the fact that the novel is unlikely to have been the total and final exorcism of the malign spirits that chloral and bromide set free to torment him.

In one way, however, Waugh did have a triumph in *Pinfold*, though it is unclear if this is simply one reader's idiosyncratic response or a response shared by many. However often I read *Pinfold*, I in effect forget, as soon as the voices start, all that I know about them as hallucinations. One part of me knows quite well that what Mr Pinfold is hearing aboard the *Caliban* is the product of his own mind but that knowledge never affects my response to the voices. Every time I am captured by the drama. The 'characters' who address Mr Pinfold are as real to me as they are to him. If this was a 'reality' Waugh wanted for his novel, then he did triumph. But this success has its down side. When the revelation of the voices' hallucinatory nature is made, I always feel a sense of anticlimax, even disbelief. I suspect Waugh of mental reservations about his final acceptance of them as hallucinations.

With *Pinfold* published, the programme of composition could be resumed; one final volume of 'war novels' and several volumes of autobiography lay ahead. In the event, two unexpected additions were made to the programme, and though neither is likely to alter by more than a scruple Waugh's reputation with posterity, the two books and the circumstances of their composition say quite a bit about his life as a writer at what turned out to be this late stage.

On 24 August 1957, Ronald Knox died, and Waugh, who had spent some rather purgatorial weeks keeping his friend company in the later stages of his illness at Torquay and Sidmouth, was Knox's literary executor and had chosen to take on the task of writing the biography. He worked very hard at this, going through Knox's papers, rereading his works, and interviewing those who had known him, including Daphne Acton, who lived in what was then Rhodesia. Waugh's determination of purpose is indicated by the fact that, loathing air travel, he flew there and back early in 1958. Another interview became in several ways a source of vexation to

him. As a young Anglican priest, Knox had been tutor to Harold
Macmillan, but their friendship had been broken up by Macmillan's
parents, who feared the Roman tinge Knox seemed to be giving to
young Macmillan's religious fervour. In *A Spiritual Aeneid*, Knox had
written of Macmillan under the initial 'C'. In 1958 Macmillan was
the British prime minister. Waugh was invited to Downing Street to
discuss Knox, was given permission to use Macmillan's letters, but
was asked to maintain his anonymity, and of course agreed. When
the book was published, however, there was something of a contest
among writers in the weeklies to uncover the identity of 'C', and
Malcolm Muggeridge in the *New Statesman* made the revelation.
This triumph alone was enough to ensure Waugh's enmity but his
ire was stoked by his fear that Muggeridge's scoop would put paid
to the knighthood that Waugh had come to hope for after his meeting with the prime minister. In the event, and apparently uninflu-
enced by the blowing of his cover, Macmillan offered Waugh the
CBE, which he declined 'out of side [conceit]', as he said later when
he had come to regret his rejection.

The biography of Knox was published eighteen months after his
death in early October 1959. This rapidity of execution would not
have been possible, however, had Waugh not refused to allow himself to be distracted by an event that would have utterly distracted
most men: the accidental machine-gunning of his eldest son, doing
his National Service with the Horse Guards in Cyprus. On receipt
of the news early in June 1958, Laura left for Cyprus at once to be
with Auberon, who had six bullet wounds and was not expected to
live. Despite the loss of a lung, he did survive and was eventually
flown to London for operations and a long convalescence. His
father's sang-froid during this episode was astonishing. He would
go to Cyprus only if Bron died. When Bron was carried back to London, it was three weeks before his father, who had an appointment
in Munich, came to visit, although he had rounded up others to
visit, pray for, and write to his son. More astonishing is the attitude
of the family and two of the biographers towards this distance of the
father from his son. Sykes and Hastings seem to consider it nothing
extraordinary. Laura's criticism, if there was any, can hardly be detected in her letters. Waugh stopped the allowance he had been paying to Bron, 'explaining that I did not need the money in hospital
and that he was skint. I wept bitter tears of rage on reading his letter'
(WTD 109), but he, like everyone close to Waugh, was well trained,
and what he wrote to papa was, 'Far from being upset by your

action, I am enormously grateful that you should have been so generous as to continue my allowance up to this moment. I hope that you soon overcome your financial difficulties' (WTD 110). Only Martin Stannard is willing to face the truth of Waugh's response to Bron's near death. 'Strangely unmoved' he says of Waugh's first reaction. Of his refusal to leave his book for Bron's bedside: he 'could not bear the disruption of well-laid plans'.

> Nor did he advertise Bron's misadventure. Friends heard about it late and, writing to offer sympathy, would receive curt notes of thanks as though they had mentioned the onset of congenital syphilis. Waugh was, it seems, not simply impatient but embarrassed. (2S 409)

Waugh felt little love for his son. One can easily imagine how differently he would have reacted had his adored daughter Margaret similarly come to harm. The energy and commitment that were going into *Knox* must not be dissipated by the side-show that Bron had staged. Waugh was a hypocrite less often than most men; he acted according to his true feelings. Interestingly enough, it was after his experience with the Browning machine gun that Auberon records, 'About this time I began to be quite fond of my father, never having liked him much in childhood or early youth . . . in the last five years of his life we enjoyed a distinct cordiality' (WTD 112). Bron wounded was competing for his father's interest with the biography of Knox and the book was an easy winner. To his credit, he accepted his place on this scale of values.

The investment Waugh made in the biography was enormous, yet when all is said and done one wants to put a question in the form in which one was famously put in the nineteenth century: 'Who was John Sterling that Carlyle should have written his Life'? Waugh, as Stannard remarks, tried to present Knox as a latter-day Newman, but the character could not sustain the weight. There was a degree of self-identification between Waugh and this convert to Catholicism whom he presented as wronged and thwarted by his Church, a judgement not widely accepted. Most of all, Knox to Waugh was a great writer who happened to be a Catholic, a judgement that the public then and now steadfastly refused to accept. (Christopher Sykes claimed that Waugh in his heart knew Knox to be a philistine and a *petit maître* but that this was his *secret du roi* [SY 399].) Knox's chief claims to fame were his book on the religious phenomenon of imagined and delusional religious inspiration, *Enthusiasm* (published in 1950, dedicated to Waugh) and his translation of the Bible complete. In print, Waugh declared that '*Enthusiasm* should be recognized as the greatest work of literary art of the century' (EAR 479). Professor Harold Bloom has lately written admiringly of it, but even his enthusiasm will not soar to that height. Knox's translation of the Bible is almost entirely flavourless, and in a period which has surprisingly become a great age of Biblical translation is one of the duds. *The Life of the Right Reverend Ronald Knox, Fellow of Trinity College, Oxford, and Pronotory Apostolic to His Holiness Pope Pius XII, compiled from the original sources by Evelyn Waugh* is admirable for its author's *pietas* and for its prose, in the mandarin style, but it is not nearly the *magnum opus* Waugh wanted it to be.

A Tourist in Africa (1960), the second unexpected addition to the programme of composition, stood quite otherwise in its author's esteem. He inscribed a copy, 'A Potboiler by Evelyn Waugh Presented with shame to Christopher Sykes by the Disgraced Author' (SY 402). But Sykes was not made privy to the real nature of its origins; he thought Waugh's trip to East and Central Africa was financed by articles commissioned by the *Sunday Times*. (Several excerpts appeared in the *Spectator* in 1960 as Waugh as usual maximised profit from his work; the deal seems to have been made after the book was written and the *Sunday Times* does not seem to have been involved.) Hastings gives the true account. Waugh had asked his agent if it would be possible to make a deal to get him a free passage to 'places of beauty & people of charm'.

> Peters came up with the perfect proposal, a promotional deal with the Union Castle line: Evelyn would travel to Africa and back on two of their ships, and write a book about his experiences disguised as an independent travel book and published by his usual publisher. This, their managing director hoped, would stimulate interest in Africa while sowing in the mind of the reader that Union Castle was the best means of going there. The company would have final approval of the text, would pay a fee of £500 as well as £1500 expenses, with a free cruise to Madeira for Mr and Mrs Peters thrown in. (H 590)

Waugh's shame may have had as much to do with this sleazy deal as with the writing that went into *A Tourist in Africa*. Yet it is one reader's opinion that there is more pleasure and profit to be had from reading the potboiler than the *magnum opus, Ronald Knox*, but both books are reserved for what record collectors call 'completists'. In 1958, Waugh had written to John MacDougall of Chapman & Hall: 'Soon I shall have to jump at every chance of writing the history of insurance companies or prefaces to school text-books ... But meanwhile while I have any vestige of imagination left, I must write novels' (L 507). The experience of writing *A Tourist in Africa* confirmed the rightness of the judgement. As it happened, however, there was to be only one more novel; there was enough imagination left to make it a good one.

In a letter to Cyril Connolly in 1952 (L 383) in response to his review of *Men at Arms*, Waugh had made an informative remark about the next volume. He briefly described his plan for the book – in the event much changed – and added, 'Anyway the theme will see me out – that is, the humanizing of Guy'. The chivalry theme, wrapped up with the theme of the war as crusade against the Modern Age, is effectively completed when Ludovic goes to Westminster Abbey to view the Sword of Stalingrad, the Modern Age's counterpart to the crusader's sword of Sir Roger of Waybroke. (The theme makes its last appearance as an almost parodistic coda when the senile Ritchie-Hook – momentarily rejuvenated – makes his single-handed attack on a strongpoint in Yugoslavia late in the novel with the clear – and successful – intent of getting himself killed in tilting at this lethal windmill.) For the most part, *Unconditional Surrender* focuses on Guy's reduced ambition of somehow acquitting himself honourably in a degenerate conflict. What happens to Guy in the novel certainly 'humanizes' him, but the meaning of that word for Waugh was not something he could expect Connolly to understand; humanity for Waugh depended on the realization of a religious purpose in the individual's – here Guy's – life.

The notion of a special religious purpose for each individual went back for Waugh to the time of *Helena*. The purpose for which his heroine there had been created was to 'gather wood' or to 'invent' the True Cross. Guy Crouchback's purpose in life will be shown to him only when he makes the positive effort to act on and develop the stirrings of compassion that come to him on two separate occasions in the narrative. Guy's general spiritual condition – stirrings apart – was described by Waugh in a piece he wrote for a book on *The Seven Deadly Sins* in 1962 (EAR 572). Waugh wrote on *accidia*, Sloth, which he hastens to define as *not* indolence. Instead he follows Aquinas: Sloth is 'sadness in the face of spiritual good'.

Man is made for joy in the love of God, a love which he expresses
in service. If he deliberately turns away from that joy, he is denying the purpose of his existence. The malice of Sloth lies not merely
in the neglect of duty (though that can be a symptom of it) but in
the refusal of joy. It is allied to despair.

If this is not exactly Guy's condition, it is close enough. His refusal of
joy in God's service is certainly understandable and well motivated
but it is a sin and dehumanizes as all sin does. Before he can take his
few steps away from that dehumanization, however, he must be
chastened by words from his father.

On the occasion of the Salerno invasion and the flight of the king
of Italy, Guy vents some vigorous and so rather startling opinions
about Church and State in Italy: 'That looks like the end of the Pied-
montese usurpation. What a mistake the Lateran Treaty was' (SH
489). His father's line, however, is quite different. 'My dear boy,
you're really talking the most terrible nonsense, you know. That
isn't at all what the Church is like. It isn't what she's *for*'. To settle
the brief disagreement, he writes a letter to Guy:

> The Mystical Body doesn't strike attitudes and stand on its dig-
> nity. It accepts suffering and injustice. It is ready to forgive at the
> first hint of compunction.
>
>   When you spoke of the Lateran Treaty did you consider how
> many souls may have been reconciled and have died at peace as
> the result of it? How many children may have been brought up in
> the faith who might have lived in ignorance? Quantitative judge-
> ments don't apply. If only one soul was saved that is full com-
> pensation for any amount of loss of 'face' (SH 491).

These are in effect Mr Crouchback's last words, for he dies soon
after. Guy's reaction to the letter is to be deduced from the fact that
'Quantitative judgements don't apply' becomes rather his mantra
for the remainder of the book. Spiritual values predominate over
secular concerns as the trilogy comes to a close.

Mr Crouchback's formulation, of course, is more absolutist than
anything Guy has hitherto said. It totally subordinates everything
secular to the spiritual; it is the credo of a saint, and it is his efforts to
become a saint, according to Waugh's definition, that now govern
Guy's actions until the end of the novel. Sainthood, however, is not

to be equated with happiness, and before he was finished with *Sword of Honour* Waugh took steps to quash that assumption.

In the wake of his father's death, Guy comes to an understanding of the apathy that has gripped him for years. His prayers to God have begun: 'I don't ask anything from you. I am here if you want me'. He realizes now that '"I don't ask anything from you" ... was the deadly core of his apathy'.

> his father had tried to tell him, was now telling him.
>
> That emptiness had been with him for years, even in his days of enthusiasm and activity in the Halberdiers. Enthusiasm and activity were not enough. God required more than that. He had commanded all men to *ask*.
>
> In the recesses of Guy's conscience there lay the belief that somewhere, somehow, something would be required of him... One day he would get the chance to do some small service which only he could perform, for which he had been created. Even he must have his function in the divine plan. He did not expect a heroic destiny. Quantitative judgements did not apply. All that mattered was to recognize the chance when it offered. (SH 540)

When the chance does offer itself, Guy might be expected to miss it but his father's letter has alerted him. Virginia tells him that she is pregnant by the revolting Trimmer. She is divorced, broke, and desperate. Since in religious terms she has never ceased to be his wife, he 'remarries' her in a civil ceremony, having failed to explain himself to Kerstie Kilbannock, who thinks he is crazy. She accuses him of 'being chivalrous – about *Virginia*. Can't you understand men aren't chivalrous anymore and I don't believe they ever were'. But Guy's motives are chivalrous in a way, a religious way, that Kerstie could never understand. 'Can't you see how ridiculous you will look playing the knight-errant'? she demands.

> The question she had asked was not new to him. He had posed it and answered it some days ago. 'Knights-errant', he said, 'used to go out looking for noble deeds. I don't think I've ever in my life done a single positively unselfish action. I certainly haven't gone out of my way to find opportunities. Here was something most unwelcome, put into my hands ... not the normal behaviour of an officer and a gentleman; something they'll laugh about in Bellamy's'.

But his greatest motive he cannot really explain to Kerstie: the soul of the unborn child. She can only speak in secular terms: 'What is one child more or less in all the misery'?

> 'I can't do anything about all those others. This is just one case where I can help. And only I, really. I was Virginia's last resort. So I couldn't do anything else. Don't you *see*?'
> 'Of course I don't. Ian was quite right. You're insane'.
> And Kerstie left more angry than she had come. It was no good trying to explain, Guy thought. Had someone said: 'All differences are theological differences'? He turned once more to his father's letter: *Quantitative judgements don't apply. If only one soul was saved, that is full compensation for any amount of loss of 'face'.* (SH 624, original italics)

Trimmer's child, legally and in religion now Guy's and named by his sister Gervase, for their father, is born while Guy is in Yugoslavia. Virginia has no feeling for the child, and Angela takes it to the country, ostensibly to protect it from the buzz-bombs, one of which kills Virginia and Guy's Uncle Peregrine in whose flat she has found shelter.

Guy's second chance comes in Yugoslavia, where he has been moved by the plight of Jewish refugees. He has been manoeuvring ineffectively for their evacuation to Italy.

> Guy had not dismissed the Jews from his mind . . . he felt compassion; something less than he had felt for Virginia and her child but a similar sense that here again, in a world of hate and waste, he was being offered the chance of doing a single small act to redeem the times. (SH 663)

News comes that the Jews are to be flown out, a signal received by Guy 'with joy'. This time, however, his act of redemption is to be partly frustrated. The weather makes flying impossible; the Jews seem to be stuck in Begoy. The spokesman for the refugees is a Mme Kanyi, a woman of acute intelligence and sympathy with whom Guy forms a tenuous friendship whose danger to the Kanyis he does not appreciate. Mme Kanyi's prominence, her contacts with Guy, and her husband's job as the engineer who has to try to keep the run-down electrical system in Begoy working, make her vulnerable to the politically paranoid suspicions of the Communist partisans.

When Guy is transferred back to Italy, he learns that the Jews of Begoy have been brought there by truck and he goes to seek out the Kanyis in their latest refugee camp. They are not there and he learns from a Communist fellow officer that they were arrested, tried and killed by a 'People's Court', the husband for sabotaging the electrical system and the wife because she was the mistress of a British liaison officer and for possessing 'counter-revolutionary propaganda'. Guy's brief visit to the Kanyis' hut and his gift of 'illustrated American magazines' have been the pretexts for these fatal accusations. Even though the rest of the Jews have escaped and Guy could feel that most of his efforts have been successful, quantitative judgements do not apply. Compassion has been perverted by hideous circumstance and has brought death to the Kanyis and misery to Guy Crouchback.

The similarity of the circumstances of the Kanyis' fate (and of Guy's innocent responsibility) to that of Apthorpe at the end of *Men at Arms* is perhaps unfortunate, but the differences are real and very significant. Apthorpe's death mainly gives Guy a lesson in military careerism and offers a benevolent explanation for the blight that affects his army career. The judicial murder of the Kanyis is the Modern Age malevolent, ideological politics crushing helpless individuals while justice exists in name only. Moreover, Waugh intended the episode of the Kanyis to be the culminating revelatory experience of Guy's wartime experience, so nothing was attempted to mitigate the gravity of the episode. Apthorpe's death has overtones of comic absurdity; in the case of the Kanyis it is an absurdity of grim blackness.

To make Mme Kanyi into the voice of revelation for Guy, Waugh had to make some changes to the story 'Compassion' that he had published in *The Month* in 1949 and that he had been following very closely as he wrote the latter part of *Unconditional Surrender*. Section 7 of the story ends with Major Gordon telling Mme Kanyi that he is being recalled to Bari but promising that he will help get the Jews out of Yugoslavia. No reaction of hers is given and in the last paragraph of the section Gordon sends her the fatal gift of magazines and departs for Italy. In the novel, after Guy's promise, 'We'll get you all out', he and Mme Kanyi leave the hut and see Bakic, Guy's partisan 'minder' and translator, who has followed him there and who, we assume later, reported Guy as Mme Kanyi's lover. She then delivers a speech of which there is no hint in the short story. She speaks first of the illusion that one can move away from evil.

Is there any place that is free from evil? It is too simple to say that only the Nazis wanted war. These communists wanted it too. It was the only way in which they could come to power. Many of my people wanted it, to be revenged on the Germans, to hasten the creation of the national state. It seems to me that there was a will to war, a death wish, everywhere. Even good men thought their private honour would be satisfied by war. They could assert their manhood by killing and being killed. They would accept hardships in recompense for having been selfish and lazy. Danger justified privilege. I knew Italians – not very many perhaps – who felt this. Were there none in England? (SH 702)

The answer is the most telling sentence that Waugh ever wrote. ' "God forgive me", said Guy. "I was one of them." '

The gift of compassion has brought with it the painful bonus of self-knowledge. The crusade against the Modern Age ended in defeat; progress is unstoppable, however monstrous, degrading and absurd it may be. And now, as the consequence of his discovery of compassion, Guy Crouchback has to give up the illusion of honour. That motive for his participation in the war has gone too. His 'fathering' of Virginia's and Trimmer's child and his efforts on behalf of the Jews of Begoy will be the only worthwhile things to come out of his war, but it should be noted that these acts will place Guy on the road to sainthood according to the Waugh doctrine. At least his wartime service has not shut him out of the company of the saints. That Guy's perhaps prosperous spiritual state has little to do with earthly happiness should not surprise readers of *Brideshead Revisited*.

It will also be noted that Mme Kanyi's interview with Guy is a rewriting of Helena's encounter with the Wandering Jew near the end of that novel. In both cases the protagonist gets vital information from the Jewish character leading to a revelation on which the book's meaning turns: Helena finds the crosses and Guy faces a truth about himself. The change in the nature and authority of the Jewish character, however, is enormous. When Waugh first wrote of Major Gordon and Mme Kanyi, which may have been *before* he wrote of Helena and the Wandering Jew ('Compassion' appeared before *Helena*), he had decided that the Yugoslavian victims who were to represent the 'displaced persons' of modern history should be Jews, rather than the Catholics of Croatia on whose behalf he had striven in Yugoslavia and afterwards. The most likely motive for this adjustment is not fashion or popularity but truth. In this case, his personal experience and his prejudice could not be allowed to dominate because he saw that they were not nearly as true to history as was the fate of the Jews. Yet it took him twelve years more to raise Mme Kanyi, herself apparently a non-observant Jew, from the status of victim to that of prophet, speaking God's truth in an age of faithlessness and destruction.

Waugh never said elsewhere that the scathing assessment of his role in the war that Guy is forced to accept was his own assessment of his own role but that is the conclusion to which his fictional recreation of his own experience inescapably leads. Martin Stannard states it memorably:

> All the reviewers missed this: that the shame, the guilt at complicity and pride, the withdrawal from the struggle into the silences of religious contemplation and humdrum domesticity, all rewrite Guy's life as a history of egotism. It was the nearest Waugh came to a public apology for his own selfishness, although he felt the issue as deeply as his hero. The problem was that Guy Crouchback was a better man than he. (2S 443)

Or to put it another way, Waugh neither could nor wished to be Guy Crouchback in life. The form of apology he had chosen allowed him to make his confession in the secular forum he held most sacred, his fiction, but it had the added advantage of implicit 'deniability' and so he could live and speak as if he were *not*, in the deepest recess of his mind, Guy Crouchback.

Unconditional Surrender is built of apologies of this very Wavian kind. The parts of the book that are not devoted to Guy in England, Italy and Yugoslavia are concentrated mainly upon two characters, Virginia and Ludovic. Each involves an apology.

When Virginia begins her manoeuvrings to get Guy to remarry her, she talks about becoming a Catholic because 'it might help'. And though this possibility seems to play no part in Guy's decision, Virginia persists in taking instruction and is received into the Church. She is perhaps a naïve convert: 'The whole thing is as clear as daylight to me. I wonder why no one ever told me before'. After her first communion, she says, 'Why do people make such a *fuss*? It's all so easy. But it is rather satisfactory to feel I shall never again have anything serious to confess as long as I live' (SH 643). The dottiness of this is mitigated by the fact that it is almost certainly true, since she is killed not very much later. In turning to the Church, Virginia acquires a kind of innocence and a new happiness. The simplicity and matter-of-factness of her acceptance of the articles of the faith are very similar to Waugh's own attitude at his conversion. These qualities and the fact of conversion itself are bestowed on the last of Waugh's faithless wives, the final incarnation of the She-Evelyn. So while never having to declare it *in propria persona*, he moves away from his earlier presentations of those women as a species of monster and confers on Virginia the literally saving graces of real humanity. Her conversion to Catholicism has no function in the novel other than to represent one more Wavian apology.

Ludovic's part in *Unconditional Surrender*, which is extensive, culminates in a really astonishing apology. His character and his role are highly problematic, and it is hard not to feel that Waugh had got into rather a mess with him. In *Officers and Gentlemen* he is a member of Ivor Claire's troop who keeps a kind of journal commenting sardonically on his superiors. (In this respect he was based on 'Sergeant L----' of Waugh's *Memorandum on LAYFORCE* [D 514].) On Crete, Ludovic is Brigade Corporal Major. He and Major 'Fido' Hound, the coward, 'severally desert and meet in a cave on the south coast . . . Nothing more is ever heard of Hound. It is to be supposed that Ludovic perpetrated or connived at his murder'. Guy and Ludovic escape with others in a boat. 'They suffer acutely from privation and exposure. Ludovic alone remains capable. The delirious sapper officer who was originally in command disappears overboard during the night. It is to be supposed that Ludovic precipitated him' (SH 484). But Ludovic carries Guy ashore and is decorated and given a commission. He turns up as the major commanding the parachute school where Guy is sent for training. Guy's appearance there terrifies Ludovic, for he thinks that Guy knows that he murdered Hound. Though Guy breaks his leg parachuting and is clearly unsuited for cloak-and-dagger work, Ludovic passes him fit for action in the hope that he will be killed.

The character's and author's motives for these actions are far from clear. Waugh seems to make Ludovic into a murderer to indicate that he is not only creepy but wicked. Yet Ludovic is suave and intrepid, so why he should be so afraid of Guy is ineptly mystifying. The lengths to which he goes to rescue Guy are more incomprehensible than the murders. Moreover, there seems to be a systematic but incomplete attempt to make Ludovic into Guy's, and perhaps more, Waugh's, spiritual and moral *doppelgänger* in reverse. He is very tall, plebeian, and homosexual – if anything. (His nauseatingly sentimental affection for a Pekinese seems to strike at Ivor Claire, but would someone terrified of being exposed as the murderer of a 'Fido' give the name to his dog as Ludovic does?) To make Ludovic murder Hound could be another Wavian apology or more likely a displacement of guilt if Waugh knew somewhere in his mind that his fury over the 'cowardice' shown by Colvin had dubious motives.

But all these tenuous and hypothetical parallels and oppositions of Ludovic to Waugh are replaced with a startling certainty when one comes to consider Ludovic's literary career. The publication of his *pensées* gives Waugh the opportunity to lampoon Cyril Connolly's book *The Unquiet Grave*, and Connolly, editor of the wartime magazine *Horizon*, himself appears as Everard Spruce, editor of *Survival*. It is the second of Ludovic's publications, however, that is the shock. In 'Fan-Fare' (1946), Waugh had made a grand announcement of his recently developed love for the English language: 'It is the most lavish and delicate which mankind has ever known'. Style has now become a preoccupation and writing a pleasure. ('I have never, until quite lately, enjoyed writing' [EAR 302]). In *Unconditional Surrender*, Ludovic, in his *pensées* phase, has 'become an addict of that potent intoxicant, the English language', a sentence that suggests that it was composed by a recovering addict. Attributing his earlier infatuation to Ludovic passed a severe judgement upon it, and greater severity is to come. Ludovic writes a novel, orgiastically, Balzac rather than Flaubert.

> His manner of composition was quite changed. Fowler and Roget lay unopened. He felt no need now to find the right word. All words were right. They poured from his pen in disordered confusion. He never paused; he never revised. He barely applied his mind to his task. He was possessed . . . (SH 632)

The book becomes a huge best-seller; one of Spruce's acolytes calls it 'pure novelette' although it is 'twice the length of *Ulysses*'. Waugh's description points unmistakably to the model he had in mind.

> It was a very gorgeous, almost gaudy, tale of romance and high drama set . . . in the diplomatic society of the previous decade. The characters and their equipment were . . . more brilliant than reality. The plot was Shakespearean in its elaborate improbability. The dialogue could never have issued from human lips, the scenes of

passion were capable of bringing a blush to readers of either sex and every age.

Half a dozen other English writers, the narrator tells us, though we can think of only one, were at work on such books, turning from 'the drab alleys of the thirties into the odorous gardens of a recent past transformed and illuminated by disordered memory and imagination'. The book deals primarily with the wife of an ambassador, Lady Marmaduke Transept '(that was the name which Ludovic had recklessly bestowed upon her)'.

> She was extravagantly beautiful, clever, doomed; passionless only towards Lord Marmaduke; ambitious for everything except his professional success. If the epithet could be used of anyone so splendidly caparisoned, Lady Marmaduke was a bitch. Ludovic had known from the start that she must die in the last chapter
> ...he realized that the whole book had been the preparation for Lady Marmaduke's death – a protracted ceremonious killing like that of the bull in the ring... Lady Marmaduke, in the manner of an earlier and happier age, fell into a decline. Her disease was painless and unspecified. Under Ludovic's heavy arm she languished, grew thinner, transparent, the rings slipped from her fingers among the rich coverings of her chaise-longue as the light faded on the distant, delectable mountains. (SH 659)

And the title of this hilarious confection is not *Brideshead Revisited Again* but *The Death Wish*.

The deftness of this particular 'apology' is amazing. The description has great 'deniability'. There is no religious element, first of all. There is no great house, no young lovers. But that Waugh was sending up his own portly best-seller is quite undeniable; the emphasis on the death-bed makes the case. Unconscious self-parody has signalled the end for many authors; Waugh's is conscious, deliberate, and proclaims that his self-critical judgement had ultimately been bribed by none of the many offers it had received. It was not in his power to make a more direct apology but none could be better than Ludovic's *magnum opus*.

When *Unconditional Surrender* was published, Waugh was annoyed by the assumption that he had arranged a happy ending for his trilogy. It is easy to see why the assumption had been made. Guy has retreated into the West Country. He has married Domenica

Plessington, a Catholic of course, who had looked after Virginia's baby after her death. They live on a farm which is a remnant of Guy's mostly vanished family lands. In addition to the child of Trimmer (Guy seems to keep its parentage to himself), they have 'two boys of their own'. When Guy's brother-in-law says 'not without a small, clear note of resentment, "things have turned out very conveniently for Guy,"' it is hard not to agree. But Waugh seems to have meant this as a statement of bitter irony. He intended the focus to be on the fact that the child of Trimmer had dispossessed 'the real heirs of the Blessed Gervase Crouchback [Guy's ancestor] ...but I plainly failed to make that clear. So no nippers for Guy & Domenica' (L 579) in future (the change made in the *Sword of Honour* recension and reversed after his death in the Everyman's Library version).

The parallel with *Brideshead*'s ending clarifies the problem. Charles and Julia's decision not to go against religion by marrying is in the secular context an unhappy ending, but in the more important context of religion is right, though not conventionally 'happy'. By not sinning in a form of marriage, Charles and Julia have not disqualified themselves from what Waugh called 'sainthood'. But it seems that Waugh would not use 'happy' to describe this outcome; a 'happy ending' must have meant to him secular happiness only. As Martin Stannard says, 'The book concerns Guy's slow discovery of terrestrial impotence and spiritual vocation, his relationship to God, not man' (2S 441), and why should not the discovery of spiritual vocation be a happy ending? Waugh seems to be in the peculiar position of resenting the dispossessor, Trimmer's child, more than Guy and the reader do. (There might be a good 'nature versus nurture' novel to be written about the coming of age of Trimmer's and Virginia's child in the nest of Guy's family.) Waugh thought that the elimination of Guy and Domenica's sons would correct his readers' mistake of the happy ending, but that was to miss the point. The 'inheritance theme' at the end of the trilogy, whereby Ludovic takes over the Castello Crouchback and Trimmer's son will inherit what is left of Broome, is less bitter in context than Waugh wanted it to be. He had forgotten that quantitative judgements do not apply. The soul even of Trimmer's son is worth a lot more than the loss of face of his inheritance of the Crouchback name and lands. Making that boy Guy's 'only son' is the right literary decision for quite other reasons. Guy's sacrifice in remarrying the pregnant Virginia has given him an heir of his name and his faith, and as Mr Goodall said 'a great family has been preserved'. Things have turned out more conveniently for Guy than his author wanted to perceive.

Unconditional Surrender should have been Waugh's last work of fiction; it has a fine valedictory air. But in fact the last fiction he wrote was a long short-story or tale, *Basil Seal Rides Again, or, The Rake's Regress*. This was a mistake, but given the intense and dynamic relationship between Waugh's life and his art, it was perhaps inevitable.

In 1962, Waugh's second daughter, Margaret ('Meg') told her father that she wanted to be married to Giles FitzHerbert. The announcement pained Waugh greatly and made him miserable, all the more so because he could not reasonably forbid the marriage or do anything but feign acceptance and express, if not delight, acquiescence. Margaret had long been his adored favourite; in his letters, particularly to the 'sisters', he claimed to have a sexual passion for her, though no one ever rose to the bait. But everyone who knew him well realized that the engagement would be a secret wound to him. He then took elaborate steps to publish his hurt.

He was occupied at that time in writing his first volume of autobiography, but he broke away from it and rapidly wrote *Basil Seal Rides Again*. The now elderly and outwardly respectable Basil is the husband of Angela (Lyne) and the father of an adored daughter, Barbara, 'Babs'. Barbara brings home a revolting modern young man, Charles Albright, and announces her hope of marrying him. Basil thwarts the proposed marriage by 'confessing' to his daughter that he had had a brief affair with Albright's mother and that Charles is her brother. The 'revelation' quite obliterates the sorrowful Barbara's interest in Albright; Basil has effectively killed off his rival.

Waugh had never before made his fiction autobiographical in so crude a manner. The technique was the same but his feelings about Margaret's engagement were powerful enough to distort his critical judgement; on this occasion he abused his fictional authority. It is not bad writing and its professionalism is superb, but following *Unconditional Surrender*, where the autobiographical elements had been used impressively for self- criticism, it is a lamentable backsliding. The Basil Seal we have known hitherto (apart from his small and ill-judged role in *Work Suspended*) gained much of his power from the continuously varying distance from which his author viewed him, at times standing close to him in self-identification with this 'man of the world', at others seeing him with nearly dispassionate coolness from a great distance. This latter-day Basil Seal is all Waugh, held uncritically close; it is an eruption of sentimentality.

Worse, it is a betrayal of Waugh's loyal reader. V. S. Pritchett wrote of *Basil Seal Rides Again*, 'Sequels rob fictions of their immortality and reintroduce them to the vulgar stream of time' (CH 452). By 1963, Basil had been an immortal for more than twenty years and Waugh had lost his right to subject him to distorting change. 'The real Basil Seal can never be in his fifties. His place is on that beautifully cock-eyed old Grecian urn where age never wearies and the chase is never up'. Sometimes a writer's contempt for 'fans' is invigorating, but fans have rights, too; one such is the right not to admit this self-indulgent mis-step as the last word on Basil Seal.

In the time left to him, Waugh completed two pieces of literary work. He published *A Little Learning: The First Volume of an Autobiography* in 1964, and in 1965 (1966, USA) brought out his single-volume 'recension' of the war novels, *Sword of Honour*. Neither of these met with much of a response from the public. As discussed already, the 'final version' of the trilogy has been in effect rejected by critical opinion and by Waugh's literary executors, and his autobiography was and is a disappointment, though no one should have been surprised that it was.

A Little Learning disappoints, certainly. But one should say first that it is beautifully written in the late, rather mannered prose of which he had become a master. For biographers, and for anyone interested in Waugh outside his books, it is obviously indispensable. And there are passages here and there as good as anything in his best fiction. (Some of them, it is true, may *be* fiction.) Why then does it disappoint?

One minor reason is that Waugh was reticent, a quality that can make an autobiography comforting to oneself and one's nearest and dearest but that is rarely or never even a minor presence in great autobiography. He was also apprehensive. The second volume would have to include an account of the disaster of his first marriage, a wound that he had perhaps brought to heal or something like healing in his last novel but that would have to be revisited, and perhaps torn open, in the next book. It is probably the wisdom of hindsight, but apprehension seems to grow as *A Little Learning* comes to its end and the second volume looms. (Its title was to have been *A Little Hope*.)

But the great reason for the autobiography's disappointment is that Waugh the novelist had spent his career revisiting and analysing in fictional terms the great episodes of his life. The changes involved in moving from his habitual mode of camouflaged autobiography with the freedoms of fiction to 'straight' autobiography where he would be assumed to have employed none of those liberties were inhibiting. Readers of the autobiography would surely be readers of his fiction and they would expect some discussion of the relationship of art to autobiography. They would be disappointed. Hints, and some of them misleading, were all they got from Waugh. To have been a great book, *A Little Learning* would have had to show throughout how truth was stranger than fiction, and it is notable that when it infrequently does so – as in the final suicide episode, for instance, or in the account of the brief encounter between 'Grimes' and Knox minor (227) – its power is owed either to the fact that it *was* fiction or to censorship outwaited (Waugh realizing that he could not use the episode in *Decline and Fall* and waiting for times to change – as they eventually and emphatically did). Generally speaking, *A Little Learning* reminds its reader forcefully how much more preferable fiction can be to fact.

Waugh's last years were not happy. He wished and prayed for death – 'All fates are worse than death' – and the infrequent notes he kept in place of a diary are often bitter with the record of what were for him defeats, such as the happy marriages of his three eldest children or Bron's beginnings as a novelist. He had physical ailments, too, such as some deafness, lumbago, and rheumatism. When Ann Fleming told him some pitiless home truths about the condition of his teeth, he had them all out without anaesthetic. These griefs and pains, however, are best understood as the results, not the causes, of Waugh's condition. It is evident that he had suffered for years from depression, a disease that is made worse by alcohol and that seems to find an unusual proportion of its victims among writers. And his depression could only have been deepened by his refusal to attribute it to any but spiritual causes. In the mid-1960s, Church matters and their implications for his own spiritual condition hugely compounded his depression.

Waugh was plunged into anger and misery by 'the buggering up of the Church' (L 633), the *aggiornamento* of Pope John XXIII. The idea that the Church could change was a radical shock to him, whose hatred of the changes, particularly the mass in English, led him to use a word that had hitherto been unthinkable: 'I find the new Liturgy a temptation against Faith, Hope and Charity but I shall never, pray God, apostasise' (L 631). He never had to. On Easter

Sunday 1966, 10 April, Father Caraman celebrated a mass in Latin and returned with the Waughs (Evelyn, Laura, Hatty, James and Septimus, together with Margaret, her husband and two children) and friends to Combe Florey. Waugh went to the gentlemen's downstairs lavatory where he was found a little later to have died. Those who recalled his last day of life noted that he had seemed unusually affable and benign, and that his last mass had been said in the form he loved.

Literary lives usually end with the decay and failings that attend bodily lives. In that respect Waugh was lucky. The main stream of his literary life had ended in *Unconditional Surrender* with writing that displayed largely undiminished powers and true moral progress. His had been an unpredictable career, not at all easy for literary history to categorize even when it had come to a close. When he had visited the Acton family in Rhodesia, young Richard Acton had asked him what he thought of Jane Austen. His answer applies well to his own work: 'Very complete'.

Notes

Chapter 1

1. In 1951 Penguin issued simultaneously ten of Waugh's books in paperback. This arrangement was of huge importance to his finances and to his reputation but it also involved him in autobiography. On the back of each book appeared a photograph of the author, sleek and slender, above a biographical description or 'author's blurb' of about 340 words. Waugh's blurb for the Penguin mass publication is his most widely disseminated autobiographical statement (none of the authors so far republished in this way had sold less than a million copies in the first year), and since it reveals him presenting a retouched and restored picture of himself to the public, most telling in its omissions and silences, its statements, taken piecemeal, will provide useful points of reference and return for this short life.
2. See n. 1 above.
3. 'But even those familiar with the eternal dotage of our Universities, will scarcely believe that at Oxford, as late as 1924, Gibbon's *Decline and Fall* was still presented as a set book to candidates, about to embark on a two years' study, not of literature, but history'. Robert Byron, *The Byzantine Achievement* (London: Routledge, 1929).
4. In 1955 Waugh took his daughter Teresa to Oxford for an admission interview; his diary reveals that he did not know where Somerville College was (D 748).

Chapter 2

1. 'Whether or not this incident really took place is almost irrelevant; what matters is that Evelyn was miserable enough to have thought that he wanted to die, even if not quite miserable enough to pursue the ambition to its end' (H 136).
2. Waugh's biographers have adopted from the couple's friends the convenience of labelling him and his wife 'He-Evelyn' and 'She-Evelyn'.
3. See Paul Fussell, *Abroad: British Literary Travelling between the Wars* (New York, Oxford University Press, 1980).

Chapter 3

1. 'I can only be funny when I am complaining about something' (H 590).
2. One serious and surprising work of fiction from this period is his short story 'Out of Depth' (CRS 121–38) written in July 1933, his first openly Catholic story. 'Two months after denying, in his "Open Let-

ter", that as a Catholic novelist he was "required to produce overtly propagandist art" he did precisely that' (1S 347). Oldmeadow did have his effect.

Chapter 4

1. The most important date in the publishing history of *Brideshead Revisited* may actually be 1960, when Waugh issued a revised version considerably cut and rewritten with an explanatory preface. This text appears in the Penguin Modern Classics edition and in the Everyman's Library edition of 1993.
2. See Vane Ivanovíc, *LX. Memoirs of a Yugoslav* (New York: Harcourt Brace Jovanovich, 1977) p. 262.
3. His bestowal of the name 'Hinsley' on one of his characters led to the only recorded rebuke that this form of tease ever occasioned. Cardinal Hinsley's niece wrote to protest the use of her uncle's name for the suicidal pseud for whom Dennis composes his only original albeit derivative poem. The letter is in the files of Waugh's agents now at the University of Texas.

Chapter 5

1. *Pinfold* is dedicated to Daphne Fielding. She had ended her memoir *Mercury Presides* (1954) by depicting herself on the last page writing the first page.

Index

Note: works cited are by Evelyn Waugh unless otherwise noted.